THE ARTE MILITARY

The Application of 17th Century Military Conflict Archaeology

Warwick Louth

Figure 1: Jacob de Gheyn's drill book for Prince Maurice of Nassau, 1593, depicting an arquebusier charging his priming pan, one of many drills likely to leave an archaeological signature. (de Gheyn, *Wapenhandelinge*, 1607)

'This is the Century of the Soldier', Falvio Testir, Poet, 1641

Helion & Company

Helion & Company Limited
26 Willow Road
Solihull
West Midlands
B91 1UE
England
Tel. 0121 705 3393
Fax 0121 711 4075
Email: info@helion.co.uk
Website: www.helion.co.uk
Twitter: @helionbooks
Visit our blog at http://blog.helion.co.uk/

Published by Helion & Company 2016
Designed and typeset by Farr out Publications, Wokingham, Berkshire
Cover designed by Paul Hewitt, Battlefield Design (www.battlefield-design.co.uk)
Printed by Lightning Source, Milton Keynes, Buckinghamshire

Text © Warwick Louth 2016
Images © as individually credited
Maps © as individually credited

Every reasonable effort has been made to trace copyright holders and to obtain their permission for the use of copyright material. The author and publisher apologize for any errors or omissions in this work, and would be grateful if notified of any corrections that should be incorporated in future reprints or editions of this book.

ISBN 978-1-911096-22-1

British Library Cataloguing-in-Publication Data.
A catalogue record for this book is available from the British Library.

All rights reserved. No part of this publication may be reproduced, stored in a retrieval system, or transmitted, in any form, or by any means, electronic, mechanical, photocopying, recording or otherwise, without the express written consent of Helion & Company Limited.

For details of other military history titles published by Helion & Company Limited, contact the above address, or visit our website: http://www.helion.co.uk

We always welcome receiving book proposals from prospective authors.

Contents

Foreword by Professor Tony Pollard — v
Acknowledgements — vi
Glossary — viii

1	Introduction	11
2	Hypothesis	13
3	Theory and Method	16
4	What is a Military Manual?	19
5	Artefactual Trends	25
6	Irregular Warfare	35
7	Agent-Based Modelling	37
8	Historical Re-enactment and Experimental Archaeology	40
9	Lützen	42
10	Edgehill	47
11	Cheriton	51
12	Naseby	54
13	Original Research	60
14	Tywardreath/Lostwithiel	61
15	Further Heritage Potential	64
16	Defensive Modelling	66
17	Defensive Planning	68
18	Primary Source Material	71
19	Trends	77
20	Destruction	80
21	Theoretical Modelling	82
22	Experimental Archaeology	84
23	Basing House	86
24	Alton	88
25	Conclusion	91

Appendices: Author's Note   92
I   Extracts from *Observations upon military & political affairs written by the Most Honourable George, Duke of Albemarle, &c.* by George Monck, Duke of Albemarle (1608-70) (London: Printed by A.C. for Henry Mortlocke ... and James Collins, 1671).   93
II   Extracts from *The first part of the principles of the art military practiced in the wars of the United Netherlands, under the command of His Highness the Prince of Orange our Captain General, for as much as concerns the duties of a soldier, and the officers of a company of foot, as also of a troupe of horse, and the exercising of them through their several motions: represented by figure, the word of command and demonstration / composed by Captain Henry Hexham, Quartermaster to the Honourable Colonel Goring* by Henry Hexham (1642).   107
III Extracts from *Military discipline: or, the yong artillery man Wherein is discoursed and showne the postures both of musket and pike: the exactest way, &c. Together with the motions which are to be used, in the excercising of a foot-company. With divers and severall formes and figures of battell; with their reducements; very necessary for all such as are studious in the art military* by William Bariffe (1635).   128

Bibliography   143

Foreword

This is not the first time I have had the pleasure of writing a brief foreword for the book of a former student, but it the first time that the book in question has been based on a dissertation which they produced under my supervision. I am sure Warwick will not mind me putting on record that I had long hoped that someone would take a close look at post medieval military manuals and assess their potential application to conflict archaeology. Warwick took up that challenge, first with his dissertation, and now this book, which, free from the constraints of a Masters dissertation, is much expanded from the original work. The result is impressive, taking in the evolution of military tactics, the manuals and treatises through which information spread, and their potential to enhance our understanding of the archaeological residues of battle from the 16th to 18th centuries.

In bringing together such an impressive body of source material, both historical and archaeological, Warwick deploys his experience not only as a practitioner of battlefield archaeology but also as a reenactor and a wargamer. It is fitting that he quotes Wellington, who compared the history of a ball to the history of a battle, not least because I write this from the battlefield of Waterloo, where I am directing an archaeological project. An understanding of deployment and battlefield tactics will be vital when it comes to interpreting the many hundreds of lead projectiles and other artefacts we have now recovered from Hougoumont and its environs, but the same could be said of any number of battlefields subject to archaeological investigation. It is likely therefore that this volume will become a useful tool for anyone engaged in the archaeology of 17th to 18th century battlefields, though in scope it will provide a stepping stone to the interpretation of later sites of conflict, such as Waterloo.

When I first began teaching conflict and battlefield archaeology over a decade ago there were relatively few works dedicated to the topic. That position now seems to be improving on a monthly basis, and I will be pleased to add the present volume to future curse reading lists.

Professor Tony Pollard
Waterloo, July 2016.

Acknowledgements

During the writing of this essay, a number of individuals have contributed in a huge way to the information and analysis throughout this text, none of which would have been possible without them.

First and foremost, to my Dissertation tutors, Dr Tony Pollard and Dr Iain Banks, without whose input on direction, focus and inspiration little of the following work would have been possible. Their encouragement on all matters is hugely appreciated.

Secondly to Andre Schurger, who carried out a mind-boggling archaeological investigation of the battlefield of Lützen, and who provided some much-needed support and pointers as to source material to start looking into when starting writing, which was very much appreciated.

Acting as an inspiring force from an early age, The Sealed Knot Society, in particular Sir Henry Vaughan's Company of Foot, has proved a hugely inspiring force, aesthetically, socially and academically. Housed by a number of learned individuals who know large amounts about their subject area, it has acted as a voice to bounce many ideas off individuals and equally provided a reason for many of the sites mentioned in this work and to experience the landscape and nature of the area for myself, a factor the author is very thankful for. Comrades, colleagues, friends, extended family.

Particular thanks must go to Simon Jarvis and Samantha Jayne Elson. Providing, at the eleventh hour (why the author didn't take these images while he was at university there?), what in effect is a brilliant set of images linked to the surviving 17th century defences in Carmarthen, Ceredigion (the second-best preserved series in the country after Newark), provides a clearly unique selling point, not reproduced in any further publications to the author's knowledge. My heartfelt thanks.

To Phil Steele and the members of the Battlefields Trust, who within the final weeks of completion of this dissertation, while talking over a model of the Battle of Northampton, provided the author with a completely new and unique line of enquiry to pursue. My thanks.

To the staff of The National Library of Scotland, Edinburgh, for being courteous and helpful in sourcing many long out of print texts and documents the author would have found extremely difficult to source otherwise. It has not escaped my notice that the majority of this work was researched and written across the road from Greyfriars Church, a root cause for much of the data within this book. Such coincidences merely make the writing experience all the more enjoyable.

To Charles Singleton, for providing resources and inspirational ideas, a fellow nut on all things 17th century. Asking me to write this book mere hours after graduating as a battlefield archaeologist, it proved a huge morale boost in the insecurity of the post-institutionalised academic world. Words quite literally cannot describe the level of support and information you have given over the past 14 months. It has been a pleasure working with you and I hope this is the first of many such projects.

To the team at Helion and Company Publishing, for making what on the surface looks like a tired, dusty academic tome, into the attractive publication you hold before you. My sincere thanks.

The following for use of images, diagrams and related academic resources, my heartfelt thanks: Dr Glenn Foard, University of Huddersfield; Dr James Bonsall, Institute of Technology, Sligo; Dr

ACKNOWLEDGEMENTS

Xavier Rubio-Campillo, Barcelona Supercomputing Centre; Blake Sporn, Access UAV; John Andrews, Tywardreath/Lostwithiel Battlefield Project; Bettina Stoll-Tucker, Saxony-Anhalt Archaeology; Dr Nick Stoodley, Hampshire Field Club and Archaeology Journal; Dr Vaclav Matousek, Charles University, Prague.

Lastly, but by no means least, my family, as always a huge supporting body. It seems clichéd when you say none of this would have been humanly possible without them, but ultimately, from initial inception of the idea and a standing interest from varying visits to castles, battlefields, museums, constant re-enactments and fuelling that spark of fascination in a little boy, it has ultimately paid off. They have provided and given far more than anyone really should in order that any of this could be written, created or studied.

Obviously a study of this size cannot fully encompass the continually growing body of knowledge that is battlefields and conflict archaeology, and therefore gaps will be represented in the subject area. Any mistakes are entirely the author's own.

Glossary

Artefact Spread – The overall extent and nature of associated discovered artefacts within a particular context.
Bastion – Also known as bulwark, arrow-like projection from earthen rampart, best known example at Carmarthen, provides 180° field of enfilading fire along wall.
Breach – Gap blown by cannon-fire/explosive force through the fabric of a surrounding wall to a fortress. Had to be made practicable/humanly passable before a storming could take place.
Circumvallation – Lines of trenches surrounding the walls of a fortress, preventing movement away from its circle of influence and often aligned at angles parallel to weak points/walls. In turn, in order to prevent besiegers escalating the taking of the siege by surprise, defenders often built their own counter lines of circumvallation.
Counterscarp – Flat angled front and rear of a surrounding ditch, often faced in stone, cut to impede movement of storming parties.
Crowd dynamics – The ability to predict manner in which group of people will act under particular pressures and stresses e.g. football hooliganism, lots of noise, grouping together, creating large profile, with one individual at front before clashing with opposing gang.
Doglock/snaphance – Early flintlock mechanism, given its name through its lack of internal locking mechanism for the lock during loading, thus reliant upon a dogs foot lever holding the serpentine while the weapon is loaded.
Dynamic pattern analysis – Individual analysis of groups of particularly distinct artefacts due to morphology, typology, chemical makeup and discernible deformation, to understand whether they might have been fired or used by the same person and thus provide individual movement and identification within a field of conflict.
Earthworks – Earthen banks and defences, built quickly, started by the Dutch, to absorb the impact of cannon shot.
Experimental archaeology – Using ancient technologies and techniques to recreate items, processes or site formation actions to understand physical, biological and engineering change within said object or item, under replicable circumstances. Often confused with re-enactment, Reynolds (of Butser Farm fame) argued they were completely different in not trying to actively replicate said events or actions, but rather provide analogy and scientific reasoning and interpretation for understanding within the modern era.
Forlorn hope – Often the first and immediate sally by a besieging force before storming the defences. Earned its name from the often suicidal nature of attacking often unpractical and unexplored breaches.
GIS (Geographical Information Systems) – Computer algorithms programme through which historical map information, modern maps, survey charts and reconstructed landscape can be overlaid, compared and overlapped using GPS cross-referencing, for ease of interpretation and analysis.
Glacis – An earthen bank in front of the main gates, often with an H-shaped profile, designed to deflect cannon shot up, rather than forwards.
Graff – Dutch word for enclosing ditch.
Gross pattern analysis – Look at an artefactual assemblage as a whole and through the character and nature of the spacing between finds, area covered and the particular shape it holds, can be linked to associate areas

GLOSSARY

and measurements taken from historical documents, thus associating said artefacts with particular bodies of soldiers.

Half-moon/hornwork – An earthen bank, often built constituent to a line of trenches, acting as firing steps and cover for firing parties/gun crews.

Inherent military probability – Created by Alfred Burne in his 1955 book *The Agincourt War*, arguing the fact that analysis of relevant historiography is unnecessary in highlighting context sites on historic battlefields, but rather focusing upon historic practice and military drill, coupled with limitations within said landscape to highlight where and how the landscape was used, relevant history acting as the limitations upon context. This has largely been disproven in recent years due to the relative free rein/wargaming nature applied to military studies, although these generalisations still theoretically underpin all present battlefield studies today.

KOCOA – Key Terrain Observation and Fields of Fire, Cover and Concealment. Method of tactical command and control exercise increasingly being used by the US military to highlight key features within the landscape for defence, retreat and attack.

Landscape archaeology The analysis of change, development and use of historical landscapes within agriculture, including how it was demarcated.

Map regression – The comparison of modern Ordnance Survey maps with historical estate, tithe, road or even battle maps to understand the level to which the present landscape has been altered, or indeed to what extent the historical map has an underlying alterior motive that might influence our perception of the historical landscape. This is then superimposed upon metal detector and archaeological survey planning to provide context to extant finds.

Metal detecting – Geophysical method derived from invention of the mine sweeper during the Second World War. Has the ability to discover metal objects either of ferrous- (iron-based) or non-ferrous metals below the surface of the ground, often as deep as a metre (dependent upon the strength of the metal detector). Low-lying surface water, like other means of geophysical analysis, is likely to produce varying levels of accuracy. The finds sites are then plotted into a GPS in order to understand the association and nature of accumulated finds.

Pike – A 16–18ft spear, its primary use the protection of musket against cavalry, but equally the engagement of opposing pikemen.

Predictive modelling – By applying trends according to time period, associated bodies of individuals, site formation actions and processes, it is plausible that rules created through analysis can be applied to similar sites within a similar archaeological horizon or period.

Processual analysis – The developmental analysis of how individuals move from one action/process/system of performing a process, to developing a better, more efficient manner of undertaking the same object more easily.

Rampier – A raised mound providing elevation, often to a large siege gun (demi-culverin/12 pdr to cannon/24 pdr).

Ravelin – Triangular outwork, often at an 85° angle, often attached at the corners of a bastion to form a sconce, or alternatively acting as a separate outwork, working very much in a similar manner to a hornwork.

Redoubt – A square-faced earthen outwork, often acting as a separate fortification, allowing relative ease of sallying and counter-battery work to take place.

Salvo (salvee)/caracole – Carried out by musketeers/cavalry, it involves the ability of an organised body to provide continual firepower, and time to reload, onto an opposing enemy. This is achieved through, after one rank firing, reversing said rank to the rear to reload their weapon.

Site formation – The biological, physical and man-made engineering works and actions that contribute to the present survival, enhancement, nature and character of an archaeological horizon/time period within a specific area.

Sconce – Isolated earthen fort combining redoubt with four ravelins.

Stratigraphy – Layers of accumulated soil, detritus, turf, leafmould, chalk etc. that build up as a site is used over time, often like the layering of a Victoria sponge. However, as different man-made actions such as the erection of buildings/earthworks is established, this cuts into lower, earlier contexts. Equally, one material or area might burn faster or separately from the rest of the layer around it, thus forming an isolated context. It is through this that an analysis of site action and development can be made.

Terminus post quem – The discovery of an archaeological small find within an associated soil layer under- or overlaying another archaeological feature. On occasion where a definitive date can be proven, this can then provide a clear point at which we can say a previous feature stood, or was built over the site, providing clear dating parameters.

Tertio – Corps level infantry organisation, working around an army-based organisation model. Derived from Spanish origins, it acted as a self-contained army, combining separate arms of pike, shot and artillery into a conglomerate composite.

Trace Italienne – Developed in Italy during the 15th century, it relied upon firstly stone-cladding all fortifications, for added strength, but equally providing a 109° field of enfilading fire at differing levels of the walls. The reason this was largely abandoned during the mid-17th century was largely due to the slowness of erection compared to Dutch ramparts, although it did receive an enlightenment under Vauban.

Typology – The mapping of style, shape and development of material culture in a discernible diagram, so that the researcher might link engineering and technical development to environmental/socio-political development within said culture.

Use-wear analysis – The microanalytical analysis of worked artefacts (e.g. pottery, musket balls etc.) to understand what processes the object has been subjected to, this being manifest through cut marks, striations and lines, impact ripples, lengths of sprue removed or scrape marks from abrading along a surface e.g. a barrel. Such finds, when highlighted in gross via histogram, provide micromeaning to possible site activity and formation.

Viewshed – Computer algorithm programme, used by the American Battlefield Protection programme. A GIS/GPS package that provides a range of axis and directional measurements from the site of a particular projectile artefact find and, using an analysis of available fields of fire coupled with obvious range/obstacles and terrain layout, is able to highlight likely areas where individuals fired weapons from. Coupled with historiographical interpretation, this provides an axis upon which potential deployments can be situated.

1
Introduction

Historians, re-enactors and wargamers have all made use of drill manuals as a means of showing the organised development of military professionalism through a growth in psychological and technological innovation. Yet their ability to help initiate artefact recovery, predictive modelling and landscape survival has not been understood seriously within academic archaeology and battlefield studies until relatively recently.

The Duke of Wellington, talking about the Battle of Waterloo, described it thus: "One may well try to tell the story of a battle as of a ball."[1] In this sense he might have been talking about the utter chaos and confusion inherent on a battlefield, meaning that one eyewitness would be unable to fully realise every single action and process, but he might have equally been talking about the choreography by which dancers and soldiers alike were able to be deployed and moved according to their leaders' strategy. But while we can marvel at the skill, discipline and finesse of the Brigade of Guards at the Trooping of the Colour, the reality of being able to complete such postures and movements under enemy fire is another matter entirely.

While we can create predictive modelling of fallen artefacts surrounding the uniformity presented through these military manuals, what is to say they represent the reality of military manoeuvre, rather than the ideal? Their enactment on the battlefield merely becomes truncated and simplified according to situation and time constraints. Indeed, the ability to perform the 128 individual movements and orders required in drill-book fashion to load a musket and then engage with the enemy would test even the most hardened veteran. Equally, the movement in perfect unison of 5,000 men at once in a single formation is unlikely to be undertaken with relative ease. Therefore, to highlight the means of tracking and characterising these theories, modelling has to be broken down into two schemes personal and tactical the former consisting of the actions undertaken by the individual, which can be witnessed through evidence of markings identified through use wear analysis; the latter looking at the spatial distribution of artefacts to find common arrangements that mirror the formations likely to have been used. Through this, it is hoped that a means of further tying in heritage boundaries to sites of battle might be established through predictive modelling, prior to large-scale archaeological investigation, in the hope of limiting damage to the surviving archaeological record, while also allowing economic use of heritage resources.

Therefore these questions will be discussed, looking at the interpretative theory and method undertaken for such a project before coming to a clear understanding of what a military manual or battle map actually is. This will be followed by creating a series of rules and trends to which representation of personal and grand tactical archaeological characterisation may be undertaken.

The potential to undertake prospective predictive modelling through agent-based models, experimental archaeology and re-enactment will be briefly highlighted. We will then take three cases

---

1 Barbero, Allessandro, *The Battle: A New History of the Battle of Waterloo* (London: Atlantic Books, 2006) p.v.

studies of sites where comparison between drill book and archaeological reality have taken place at Edgehill, Cheriton and Naseby before looking at Tywardreath, where little cumulative analysis of the archaeological assemblage has been undertaken interpretively (Fig. 26). Finally, we will highlight possible areas to which such an investigation could expand further, both as a means of investigation to further periods of conflict, but equally their integration as a means of implementing widespread landscape and heritage protection. Just as we can apply the same rules to landscapes of war, we can hopefully also apply the same rules to landscape defences.

Through this it is hoped to expose a widespread expansion of the potential of battlefield archaeology to create moving landscapes where we can track particularly important troop bodies and individuals, and thus reinforce a methodology that can be used for similar resource bases to create an ideal learning environment for the general public. What this study intends to be is an exploration of the source material presented through contemporary military manuals and its application within a wider archaeological methodology; to allow for a wider resource base when creating and defining heritage and conflict landscapes, rather than a treatise and exploration of the reality and use of tactical science on the battlefield.

2

Hypothesis

Initial military drill came about through standardised parade ground choreography, allowing a commander to move his troops around a battlefield with ease, combining the skills and manoeuvrability of infantry, cavalry and artillery to meet any particular tactical situation. With the growth of combined arms warfare in the wake of the wars of the Protestant Reformation throughout Europe, individual discipline was paramount in the success of utilising armies' strengths. Whether they formed deep blocks of marching infantry, thinly spread lines of cavalry or indeed a small peppering of independent skirmishers, it is likely that each one of these forms would have lost or dropped items, leaving their mark on the localised archaeological record. This can consist of anything from the humblest hobnail, coin or button lost in general day-to-day campaign life and marching, to items mislaid or destroyed in the chaos of battle such as musket balls and furniture, to individual weapons and armour.

If such a pattern of movements was adhered to at all levels in a uniform fashion, artefact scatters should lead to site formation patterning completely mirroring drills identified in these documents, their characterisation highlighted through correlations of artefacts within metal-detecting surveys in the localised reconstructed landscape, directly associated, or indeed laid out in a pattern suggesting a drill characterisation. Should such a model exist, dependent upon contemporary trends and individuals, it will create boundaries within which a battlefield influence might be applied, based around individual scale of conflict and army composition, dictating the frequency of investigation rationale, both on previously investigated sites and sites waiting to be investigated. McNutt calls this the application of a *modus operandi* whereby troop types are directly chosen to meet the associated terrain they should be fighting through in essence, agent-directing the flow of environment and thus creating a processional system dictating action and creating circuits of influence dependent on weapon system and unit strength and range.[1]

This has the ability to directly truncate the possible area an archaeological team is required to actively survey within the local landscape, utilising and limiting resources to gain the maximum yield, while at the same time eliminating outstanding anomalies just outside the main correlation of the battlefield zone, providing focus for more intensive research elsewhere. If such levels of choreography are visible, higher frequency analysis of the character and materiel of artefact assemblages could discern how much contemporary drill manuals were adhered to and where we can see them enacted, or not as the case may prove. However, in our investigations we have to equally understand that the localised level of preservation is going to vary and differ constantly between sites. What we present here within our research rationale is

---

1   McNutt, Ryan K., Finding Forgotten Fields: A Theoretical and Methodological Framework for Historic Landscape Reconstruction and Predictive Modelling of Battlefield Locations in Scotland 1296-1650. Unpublished PhD Thesis (Glasgow: University of Glasgow, 2014) p.18.

merely a theoretical approach, and the actual historical reality of tactical science enacted within a battle may not necessarily be represented within our study.

Limitations

However, for an investigation of this size to be able to make the best possible yield of this hypothesis, a series of limitations, truncations and omissions have to be addressed. The prime study area addressed shall be the period 1632–1746. At this time, the major artistic, mathematical, philosophical, scientific and technological changes being realised as a result of the Renaissance were being implemented into the widespread contemporary religious wars under the guise of the military revolution.[2] This allowed the implementation of wider gunpowder technology, while integrating mathematical understanding to be implemented into the best use of firepower and hand-to-hand fighting, the effective movement and logistics of armies, harking back to previous military thinkers to allow for a multi-facetted armed force that could bring multiple offensive and defensive capabilities to bear upon each other.[3]

The medieval manner of feudalistic indenture, raiding warfare and localised skirmishing was over. Therefore, this study will exclude the late medieval period, despite the birth of such manuals during this time period; their early realisation often only covered the poetic ideals of the knightly soldier, rather than the reality of campaign life.[4] While we can differentiate tactics enacted at the time, the fact that armaments, training, profile and unit recognition were often identical between forces,[5] means breaking down archaeological investigation beyond merely identifying the main battle zone and events within it are nigh on impossible. Certainly, we can be sure that the tried and tested method of using the three battles model of waging battle was fairly standard throughout the medieval period, although certainly until 1513 tactically sound except where major differences were obvious e.g. the Hundred Years' War.[6] Equally, terminology such as 'the Herce' or plough, alternating bands of men-at-arms with archers (Bradbury, 1985, p.98),[7] is more than likely (although at a lower frequency than later battlefields due to variable preservation and survivability) going to present a similar artefact profile to the later Dutch model demi-hearse, arguing that the move to military professionalism and combined arms started far earlier than previously considered. Making broad generalisations, we can argue that formations such as the schiltrom would likely have a similar profile to the pike block described later, the shield wall providing such little artefact-yield due to the model created for hand-to-hand combat and the massed cavalry charge representing large-scale broken horse furniture and tumbled soil profiles, on a much wider scale than that represented on the 17th century battlefield.

Certainly with something like the Boar's icon discovered at Bosworth, this could act as a perfect signifier for the position of Richard III's retinue, except for the fact that the Duke of Somerset and other members of the York/Neville household also used the same icon, which makes this artefact's positioning and identity convoluted,[8] providing numerous axes of orientation for any potential survey to be based upon.

A common factor, recently pioneered by Marix-Evans, is the theory that initial generalised orientation can be initiated through aerial photography, identifying clear evidence of plough lines and ridge and

---

2 Hale, John Rigby, *The Art of War and Renaissance England* (Washington: The Folger Shakespeare Library, 1961) p.1.
3 Bariffe, William, *Military discipline, or The young artillery-man* (London: Andrew Kembe, 1657) p.127; Knox and Murray (2001) p.12 in Carman (2003) p.148.
4 Allmand, Christopher, 'The Fifteenth-Century English Version of Vegetius' De Re Militari', in Strickland, Matthew (ed.), *Armies, Chivalry and Warfare in Medieval Britain and France: Proceedings of the 1995 Harlaxton Symposium*. Harlaxton Medieval Studies VII (Stamford: Paul Watkins, 1998) pp.30-45.
5 Raymond, James, *Henry VIII's Military Revolution: The Armies of Sixteenth-Century Britain and Europe* (London: Tauris Academic Studies, 2007) pp.7-8, 12.
6 Roberts, Keith, *Matchlock Musketeer 1588-1688* (Oxford, Osprey Publishing, 2002) p.5; Bradbury, Jim, *The Medieval Archer* (New York: St Martin's Press, 1985).
7 Bradbury, Jim, *The Medieval Archer* (New York: St Martin's Press, 1985) p.98.
8 Foard, Glenn, and Morris, Richard, *The Archaeology of English Battlefields: Conflict in the Pre-Industrial Landscape*. CBA Research Report 168 (York: Council for British Archaeology, 2012) p.124; Steele, Phil, 'Plough lines on battlefields' 2014, pers. Comm.

furrow field systems, a factor used increasingly from early modern warfare, to allow the best use of cavalry, without clear-cut tripping hazards, as well as easier movement of artillery vertically rather than laterally.[9] We can merely identify sites of fighting related to a particular battle, without directly identifying context and individual events, thus limiting their study potential.

It is possible on occasion, where significant skeletal and artefactual (such as weapons and armour) evidence do survive, to highlight pathology and use-wear analysis to link back to individual contemporary fight manuals and then relate them to particular units and actions in the battle. Only through a thorough literature analysis coupled with systematic interpretation of metal detecting surveys, as currently being undertaken at Flodden,[10] can the beginnings of a tactical link between early drill books and their manifestation be made.

However, we must remember that a metal detector only has a limited range, and naturally the surrounding geology and land-use may affect the total yield and model created. Such features as ridge and furrow field systems and deep ploughing has the ability to move artefacts, normally so light that they remain on the surface, laterally downwards away from any possible survey signal, while heavy mineralised soils and the increased use of agrochemicals will provide differing signals that interfere or obstruct the artefact signature, or even degrade and replace any metallic content contained.[11] Even features such as use of different equipment, formatting systems, technological boundaries and surveying techniques can often destroy and do more damage to a survey's yield than good, an example being seen in at least two of our later case studies at Edgehill and Naseby, as well as destructively at Marston Moor.[12]

A further expansion of this work into the massed battlefields of the 18th century and Napoleonic periods, will be briefly discussed at the conclusion of this work, although will not feature largely; a lack of large-scale, widespread surveys during this period, mean that currently investigation potential merely complements other study periods. However, battle-maps and plans have been included as they are used for the training of officer cadets at modern staff colleges, their representation of plans in profile, rather than schematically, showing their attempt to show military science in action, a factor that was quickly incorporated and exploited by many 16th and 17th century manuals.

---

9   Fiorato, Veronica, Boylston, Anthea, and Knusel, Christopher (eds), *Blood Red Roses: The Archaeology of a Mass Grave from the Battle of Towton AD 1461* (Oxford: Oxbow Books, 2007) pp.90-102; Thordeman, Bengt, *Armour from the Battle of Wisby, 1361* (Milwaukee: Chivalry Bookshelf, 2001).
10 Burgess, Christopher, 'In to the bog: "silently and in good order. German fashion ... "', in Rotherham, Ian D., and Handley, Christine (eds), *War and Peat: Landscape Archaeology and Ecology*, vol. 10 (Sheffield: Wildtrack Publishing, 2013) p.137.
11 Foard, Glenn, *Naseby: The Decisive Campaign* (Barnsley: Pen and Sword Military, 2004) p.20.
12 ibid.

4

Theory and Method

In order to undertake a clear analysis of the source material presented, we must undertake a study that incorporates historiographical-topographical analysis, in the hope of preventing common assumptions and misdemeanours from being created. Indeed, we should look at tactical action on the field of battle as a very cyclical system, directly influencing, or indeed causing the choosing of appropriate terrain, numbers of certain troops and orders of battle.[1]

While Burne's rule of Inherent Military Probability (IMP) might be tantamount to the investigation we are undertaking, we have to equally account for changes in thought process and localised terrain in order to use it to its full potential. In the past we have relied too heavily upon outdated, subjective source material or looking at a battlefield site at face value, forcing major setbacks within battlefield studies. A key example of this can be seen through Newman's siting of the final position of Newcastle's Whitecoats at the Battle of Marston Moor as being within White Syke Close, based purely on assumption and misreading investigations against primary source material (in itself not necessarily providing a complete view of the battlefield space) without a shred of archaeological, landscape or tactical evidence.[2]

Thus in order to move away from this, Carman believes we are required to break down types of battle and the terrain they are fought over into their component types.[3] Taking an anthropological stance, they highlight the differences and needs of primitive versus true war, ritual versus real war, showing that while one is based far more on the general economy, control of resources and governing body, the other is far more inherent, sporadic and less governed by rationale, thus governing the space, scale and nature of general defence implemented.[4] In order to record the various inputs at play upon landscape, geographical regression is essential in order to fully measure whether our common assumption is true.[5]

But equally this brings into question what we actually mean by battlefield space, whether it incorporates the area where direct military assault occurs, or whether we incorporate the bureaucratic, economic social existence of an army into this space as well.[6] Carman believes it is the space whereby lateral movement by a military force is possible, in some cases overlapping the space where habitation occurs, that allows a model to be created showing the ultimate lack of unified image possible within such a conflict.[7] Thus we are required to take a post-processual approach when looking at a battlefield site, looking at engagement with landscape through human experience and events. By looking at the

---

1 McNutt, Forgotten Fields, p.3
2 Foard, Glenn, Battlefield Archaeology of the English Civil War, BAR British Series 570 (Oxford: Archaeopress, 2012) p.9; Foard, Glenn, 'English Battlefields 991-1685: A Review of Problems and Potentials', in Scott, Douglas, Babits, Lawrence, and Haecker, Charles (eds), Fields of Conflict: Battlefield Archaeology from the Roman Empire to the Korean War (Dulles: Potomac Books, 2009) p.141.
3 Carman, John, and Carman, Patricia, Bloody Meadows: Investigating Landscapes of Battle (Stroud: Sutton Publishing, 2006) p.17.
4 Turney-High (1949) in ibid, p.18.
5 ibid, pp.19-22.
6 Carman, Carman, Bloody Meadows, p.26; Foard and Morris, English Battlefields, p.9.
7 ibid.

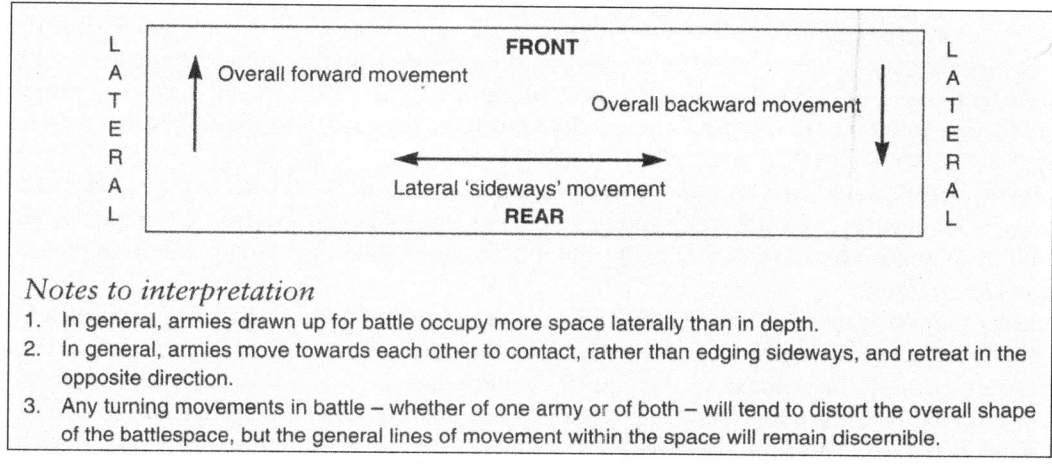

```
                                  FRONT
L    ↑ Overall forward movement                                L
A                                                              A
T                              Overall backward movement       T
E                                          ↓                   E
R                                                              R
A                                                              A
L           ←——— Lateral 'sideways' movement ———→              L
                                  REAR
```

Notes to interpretation
1. In general, armies drawn up for battle occupy more space laterally than in depth.
2. In general, armies move towards each other to contact, rather than edging sideways, and retreat in the opposite direction.
3. Any turning movements in battle – whether of one army or of both – will tend to distort the overall shape of the battlespace, but the general lines of movement within the space will remain discernible.

Figure 2: Bounding the battlefield space. By calculating lateral movement, we create a field of influence that dictates the amount of space relevant to the investigation and thus dictate numbers and manoeuvres necessary to fill and move in designated space. (Carman and Carman, *Bloody Meadows*, Fig. 4.1, p.135)

way people and military organisations work, Barrett agrees that 'for the distinctions [between people] to have operated … it was necessary for people to move between regions; to enter and leave each other's presence, to observe passively or to act, to lead processions or to follow. The practice of social life is thus…performed', in essence making war a game that can be followed easily.[8] However, war defies common action and thus it is only by looking through IMP for dysfunctional behaviour within our normal understanding that allows us to compare and contrast the differences between time periods and the reality of historical military drill.[9]

Thus where little or no archaeological evidence is available, we can apply historical source material and manual evidence to predict the quantity and distribution of archaeological material. However, we have to be aware of technical changes and conditions enacted in drill manuals, often converted from examples created in Spain, Holland or Sweden.[10] We also have to be wary of the sometimes complete lack of secondary analysis to build upon; again the clear ability to create assumptions is visible (Foard, 2012, p.8).[11] Into this we have to mitigate for changes within technological innovation, practice and thought through the spread of industrial, ideological and social Renaissance.[12] In that sense, when looking for general tactical and strategic trends undertaken by the likes of Waller, Hopton, Prince Rupert and others, where first-hand accounts and archaeological data remains elusive, the researcher may fall back on existing knowledge of their previous military conduct, connected with possible innovations picked up during service in the Thirty Years' War. However, in this sense it could make understanding particularly more difficult.

Certainly through the 18th and 19th centuries, common practice was for general drill to follow state-sanctioned regulations, military specialist-produced light infantry drill and, should neither of the above meet the needs, speed and innovation required that commanding officers often instituted their own regulations.[13] These were dependent on unit scale from platoon to brigade, as witnessed by Monro's regulations for the Scots Brigade in Dutch service during the 1680s, meaning that drill manuals were

---

8   Barrett, 1994, p.46, in Carman and Carman, *Bloody Meadows*, p.23.
9   Keeley, 1996, pp.6263, in Carman and Carman, *Bloody Meadows*, pp.23, 26; Foard, *Battlefield Archaeology*, p.9; Scott, Douglas D., Fox, Richard A., Connor, Melissa A., and Harnon, Richard, *Archaeological Perspectives of the Battle of the Little Bighorn* (Oklahoma: University of Oklahoma Press, 1989) pp.146-47.
10 Foard, *Battlefield Archaeology*, p.8.
11 ibid.
12 ibid, p.18.
13 Blake, Andrew, Re-creating the Drill of the 95th Rifles <http://www.95th-rifles.co.uk/research/drill/> (accessed 02/04/2014, 11:24 a.m.).

often never uniformly imposed.[14] Thus in a sense, to create an archaeological character, we must totally integrate historical archaeology, by taking records and knowledge of army composition, order of battle, formation and rules for overall space occupied, filling remaining gaps in our historical knowledge through further resultant archaeological research to create a fully realised three-dimensional regression back to the contemporary day of battle.[15]

By incorporating associated limitations as algorithms within our work such as fatigue and visibility, we can gain an anchor as to why formations, or indeed assemblages, provide the character they do, along with walking surveys in order to understand landscape limitations forcing bounding of areas of archaeological interest.

A clear example of this can be seen through an example like Towton, where the presumed Yorkist battle line is bound by the villages of Towton and Saxton, on a plateau with a ridge to the north, while further being enclosed by a marsh to the east.[16] Therefore, while we can rely upon basic Independent Military Probability linked to assemblage characterisation, the ability to misrepresent the tactical landscape and the way people move through it is quite clear. Only through gradual understanding of the differing facets through which a battlefield space is experienced, both physically and metaphysically through remembrance and historical recording, may a processual, informed use of source material, and in particular military manuals, be used to effectively position the extent and spread of a battle.

---

14 ibid.
15 Foard and Morris, *English Battlefields*, p.21; Foard, 'Problems and Potentials' p.140.
16 Foard and Morris, *English Battlefields*, p.18.

5

What is a Military Manual?

So, theoretical structuring aside, what actually is a military manual? The 'military revolution' of the 16th century required systematic choreography of different troop types within a particular tactical arrangement. This often referred back to the classical works such as Vegetius' *De Re Militari* or *The Tactics of Aelian* by Aelian Aelianus, to memoirs and orations provided by Caesar, Tacitus and Thucydides; using their strategy and philosophy as means of empire-building, their practical use of tactics on the battlefield adapted and changed to suit modern technology. However, in many cases this proved a steep learning curve as tactical innovation was often copied to the letter, evidence of differing ancient Greek styles of counter-march merely confusing the common soldier.[1] Indeed, as early as 1408, manuscript evidence for the siege of Aberystwyth makes references to classical texts teaching Sir Thomas Berkeley the ideal way to take the fortress, a sure sign of the growth of abstract thinking over chivalric ideal.[2]

However, with no localised national conflict or military academies, with many soldiers lacking the level of schooling to understand a classical abstract treatise, it was felt the best way to diffuse military strategy and planning was through adaptation and translation of existing military manuals to accommodate modern fashion. This was achieved through converting archaic weaponry and terms and making them work for the technological limits and needs of musketry (e.g. the 1614 edition of Caesar's *Annals* included an appendix explaining the rudiments of Maurician tactics), along with the widespread publication of new manuals, with drill broken down step by step through pictorial, schematic (Fig.2) and written sources describing and explaining the correct handling and management of an army on campaign.[3]

In Britain in 1640, it was believed only four men knew how to fire a mortar.[4] The creation of military manuals institutionalises and unifies military action; no longer was an individual required to train for years in order to master the longbow, thus saving the commander money, providing him with a cheap asset that would develop and grow according to the level of conflict enacted.[5] With the spate of military manuals available of varying quality, and the duty of any middle- to upper-class gentlemen to be informed of the latest military tradition and technology (10 percent of all men were under arms at the beginning of the war, rising to 20–25 percent by the end, showing the level of diffusion at work), the officer class were far from elite, a factor reflected in a large number of contemporary books and manuals.[6]

---

1 Bornstein, Diane, 'Military Manuals in Fifteenth-Century England', *Medieval Studies*, vol.37 (Toronto: Pontifical Institute of Mediaeval Studies, 1975) p.469; Hale, John Rigby, *Renaissance War Studies* (London: The Hambledon Press, 1983) p.232; Kleinschmidt, H., 'Using the Gun: Manual Drill and the Proliferation of Portable Firearms', *The Journal of Military History* 63:3 (London: The Society of Military History, 1999) p.603; Lawrence, David R, *The Complete Soldier: Military Books and Military Culture in Early Stuart England 1603-45* (Danvers: BRILL, 2009) pp.138, 226.
2 Bornstein, 'Military Manuals', p.469.
3 Lawrence, *The Complete Soldier*, p.119.
4 Blood on Our Hands, (2005), Channel 4, 10 February, 21:00.
5 Kleinschmidt, 'Using the Gun', p.615.
6 Porter, *Destruction*, p.14; Hale, *Renaissance War Studies*, p.233; Raymond, *Military Revolution*, p.9.

THE ARTE MILITAIRE

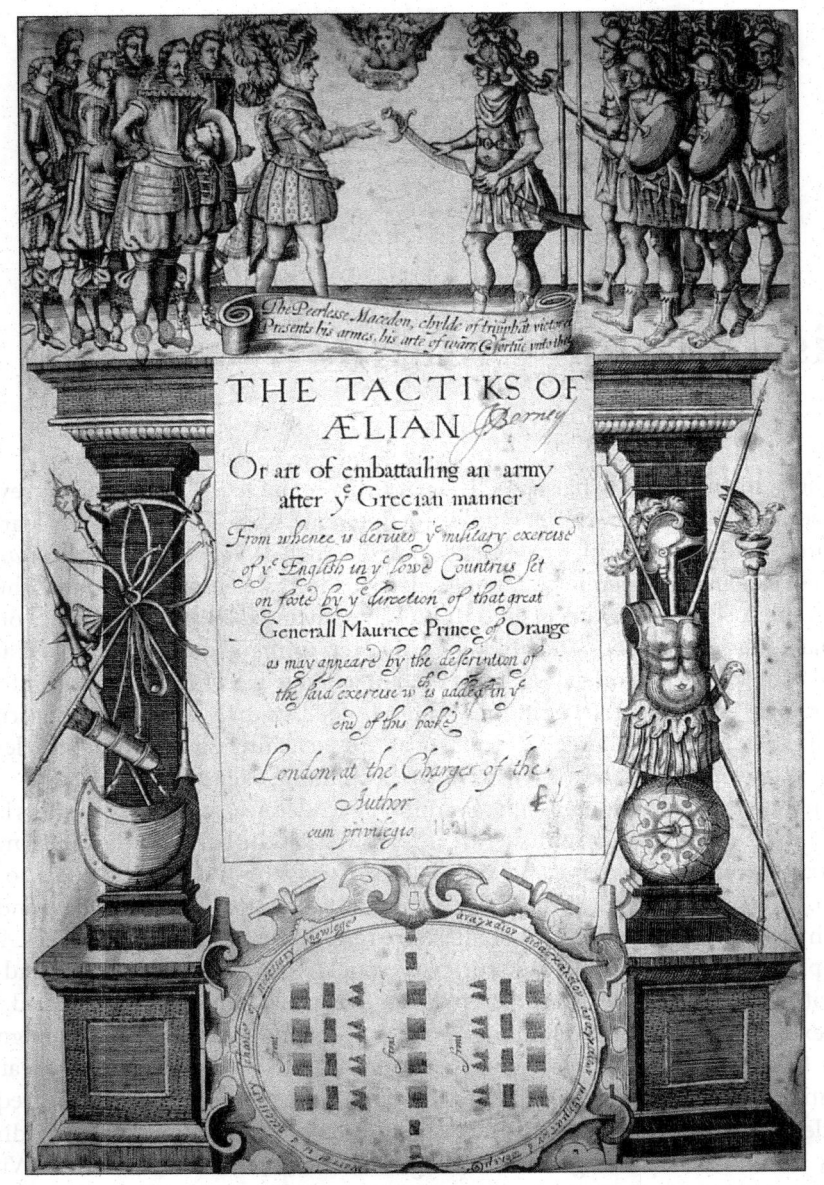

Figure 3: Frontispiece from 1601 reissue of 'The Tactics of Aelian' with representation of similarity between Dutch level deployment and Roman triarii deployment.

These were disseminated by the likes of the Honourable Artillery Companies, veterans and mercenaries returning from wars on the continent, or on some occasions state-sanctioned systematic drill (e.g. Figs. 5–6), although the level to which these were disseminated is not clear due to a wish to leave a modicum of anonymity with a nation's armed forces..[7]

On occasion, particularly effective drill, such as was experienced by the likes of Prince Maurice of Nassau or Gustavus Adolphus, was disseminated and largely felt to be the ideal, as attested through examples like Sir Thomas Audley's *A booke of orders for the warre both by sea and land*, Jacob de Gheyn's engravings or Monro's 1637 *His Expedition With The Worthy Scots Regiment: An Abridgement of Exercise*

---

7   Hale, *Renaissance War Studies*, p.254.

Figure 5: John Cruso's *Militarie Instructions for the Cavall'rie* (1632) illustrating firing from the saddle and marching in line abreast for line harquebusier. The ability to systematically illustrate step-by-step postures of drill allowed such actions to be easily rehearsed into easily manageable drill movements in soldiers' own time, as well as distributed as pamphlets, broadsheets and annotated wall charts at trained band musters.

for the Young Souldier, although this could prove to be merely spreading tactical knowledge to understand enemies' possible weaknesses.[8]

The success of such books must be attested to their ability to being accessible to all ranks of education and soldiery, taking what are essentially abstract theories and movements and breaking them down into individual stages, based upon duties, skills, command structures, signals, postures, methods of training,

---
8 Carlton, Charles, *Going To The Wars: The Experience of the British Civil Wars 1638-51* (London: Routledge, 1992) p.261; Lawrence, *The Complete Soldier*, pp.141, 175, 226.

THE ARTE MILITAIRE

formation movements and tactical situations, all at various scales, from platoon to army-scale tertio, from pike to shot, to individual weapons, thus being applicable from sergeants to generals.[9] It codifies and standardizes the level of learning surrounding basic regimental sciences, allowing mathematical theorem to become common knowledge and be easily undertaken, meaning that square roots allow the optimal movement and use of a military force's numbers and thus create uniformity of impact.[10]

Equally, the ability to impart generalisation and truncation of orders through increased use of images with snippets of text allows maximum knowledge and detail to be imparted to even the lowliest private, as can be increasingly seen with the works of Jacob de Gheyn.[11] This was further compounded through the realisation that ease of transport of these manuals meant that certain military codes and practices were extended into the common knowledge, often through common maxims such as the five vowels of military practice, or oft quoted rhymes, thus breaking down the need for large-scale drill, as realised by the Honourable Artillery Company between 1614–1619, when drill was increasingly published within *broadsheets and pamphlets*.[12]

However, we must remember when looking at pictorial evidence for the running of a military unit that what is presented is an ideal and occasionally (such as Gervase Markham's Wheel, requiring 5,000 men to pivot as if on a parade ground, or equally the mathematical application of wedges, saws and pincer movements that simply cannot be formed in sequence) not workable.[13] Certainly, works like Hexham's *The Principles of the Arte Militarie 1637–42* (32 musket, 33 pike), Fisher's *The Warlike Directions 1633* (48 musket, 65 pike) or indeed Venn's orders for marching "half double your front to the right, the rest pass through to your left and place yourself behind the bringer up" were very quickly abandoned. Bariffe, Cruso and de Gheyn, simple and easy to follow, remained the norm well into the 1680s, with a pikeman becoming reasonably proficient inside six sessions.[14]

Indeed, the situation became so bad that it required the Earl of Essex to issue a decree that the only drill to be adhered to was that sanctioned by the Privy Council.[15] Military innovation often meant such rules were rarely adhered to. Indeed, C.H. Firth believed that we should approach all such manuals with caution, due to the limited scale of resources and conflict between wars on the continent and those fought in Britain, many examples suffused with notions of dramatic romanticism.[16] Equally, Carlton believes that 90 percent of the available literary output of the military revolution is unreliable, the number of books being presented representing the lucrative popularity of such texts rather than a socio-technological emancipation, a factor represented through the general lack of agreement between different texts of the amount of correct drills required to deploy or use a pike or musket.[17] All but the most simplified drill books should be considered thus; everything else would be beyond the comprehension of the typical soldier.[18]

However, that said, it does not assuage the general success and popularity of such texts, a factor represented through 90 manuals being published within Britain in the period 1590–1642.[19] In March 1642, Colonel Edward Harley was willing to spend £2 10s on 11 manuals, representing officers' almost complete reliance on these documents for their education, even as far as to look at an example of Thomas

---

9   Carlton, *Going To The Wars*, pp.71, 255-58.
10 Lawrence, *The Complete Soldier*, p.43.
11 ibid, p.141.
12 Lawrence, *The Complete Soldier*, pp.163, 165, 189-90; Lawrence, David R, 'The Evolution of the English Drill Manual: Soldiers, Printers and Military Culture in Jacobean England', in Langman, Peter (ed.), *Negotiating the Jacobean Printed Book* (Farnham: Ashgate Publishing, 2011) p.119.
13 Hale, *Renaissance War Studies*, p.260.
14 Carlton, *Going To The Wars*, pp.72-73.
15 ibid.
16 Lawrence, *The Complete Soldier*, pp.1, 175.
17 ibid, 9, 152, 162, 165, 224, 249.
18 Callen, Matthew, To what extent did Royalist infantry tactics develop during the First Civil War (1642-1646)? (Unpublished BA dissertation, Bath Spa University 2013) p.33.
19 ibid, 1.

WHAT IS A MILITARY MANUAL?

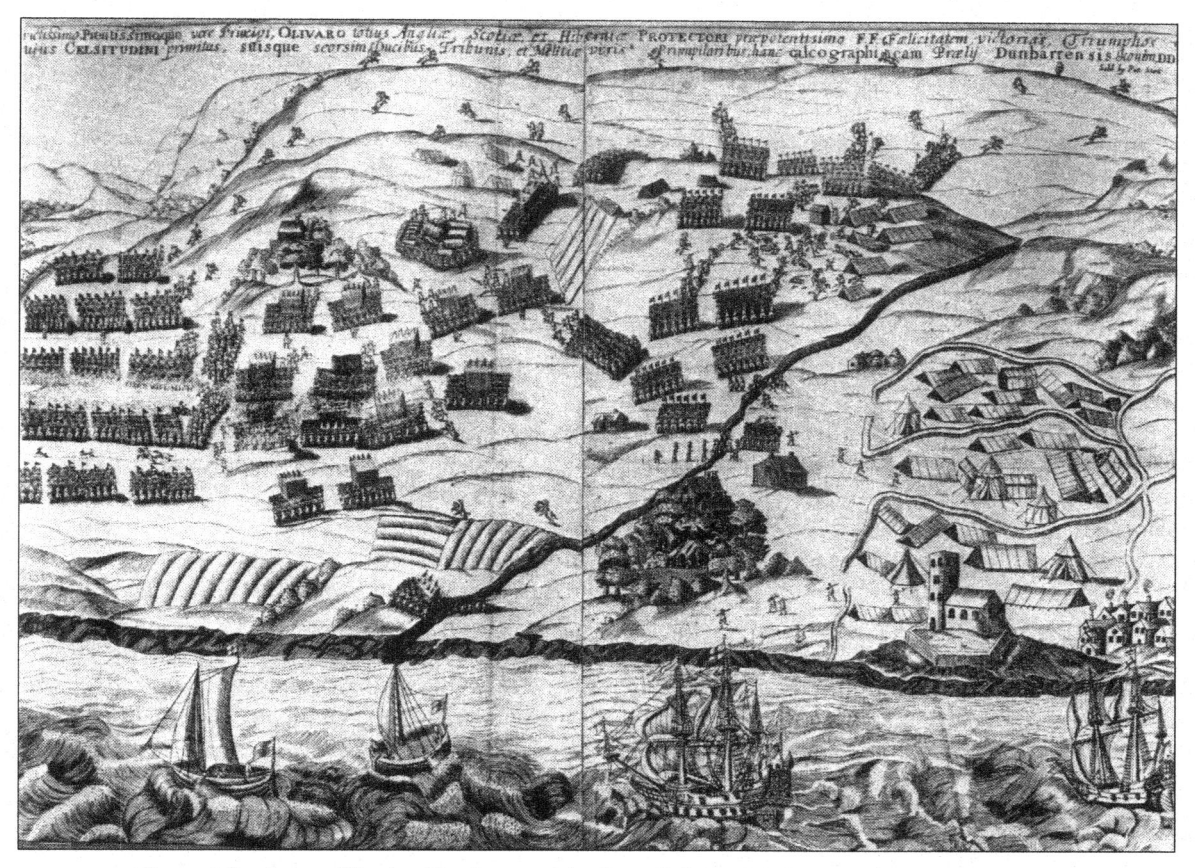

Figure 6: Depiction of Battle of Dunbar, 1650, by Payne Fisher, 1654. Depicted from the east, such a map highlights the issues surrounding limited space on maps the Royalist Army on the far ridge of hills is completely truncated by the Brox Burn on the left. Rather than show the whole battle, it inadvertently recreates a moment in time, creating a fantasy that never occurred.

Styward's *The Pathwaie to Martiall Discipline*, now held in the Bodleian Library, being covered in blood, after its owner, Sir John Gell, was shot, it being in his pocket at the Battle of Hopton Heath, showing their continued application as far as the battlefield.[20] If anything, military manuals represent the physical manifestation of the coming of age of the military revolution, the emancipation of abstract thought, science and mathematics to allow unified force to be brought to bear and be understood at all levels of the military establishment. It provides an archaeological map, should they prove accurate, that provides meaning and movement to a blank landscape.

Yet at the same time as the military manual was coming to fruition, the military map was also being exploited. Often drawn up as the official account of landscape reconstruction and troop movement on the day of battle, the battle map moves from being a profile, almost three-dimensional image of events and drill movements in the 16th and 17th centuries, to a scientifically surveyed schematic in the eighteenth.[21] However, as these maps are often created from the viewpoint of the winning commander, coupled with the limits of space, accurate spacing or indeed covering up/making tactical mistakes for the enemy or assumptions made on the day, mean that a huge level of analysis needs to be undertaken to ascertain the

---
20 Carlton, *Going To The Wars* p.71; Lawrence, *The Complete Soldier* p.196.
21 Woosnam-Savage, Robert C., "'To Gather an Image Whole': Some Early Maps and Plans of the Battle of Culloden", in Pollard, Tony (ed.), *Culloden: The History and Archaeology of the Last Clan Battle* (Barnsley: Pen and Sword Military, 2009) p.164.

THE ARTE MILITAIRE

subjectivity of cartography.

Clear examples of this can be seen indicated on various maps of the battles of Culloden (1746) and Killiecrankie (1689), the former showing Wolfe's Regiment completely covering the Culwhiniac enclosures, dismissing any tactical misgiving causing a threat to the government lines, while in the latter, alteration of the position of General Mackay has the effect of representing him as a more aggressive commander than evidence might represent.[22] However, that said, it provides a working model, integrating contemporary landscape boundaries with working tactical forms, thus creating a blueprint to focus our archaeological study of the modern existence of the battlefield and its environs.[23] Starting with the likes of Pannett's map of the Battle of Pinkie (1547), while the rudimentary features of the military map exist, individual minute representation of unit numbers and types, with an idealistic representation of the surrounding landscape, coupled with English subjectivity, mean that more questions about the subsequent space is created than solved.[24]

Certainly by the time of Lützen (1632) (Fig.11), Naseby (1645) (Fig.24) and Dunbar (1650) (Fig.6), fully represented images of orders of battle, landscapes of tactical significance, firing lines, positions of individuals and tactical movement are fully realised and represented, albeit always subjectively.[25] That said, two main problems stand out. Firstly, all of these maps lack space on paper to fully realise spatial positioning, thus forcing major truncations of forces and landscapes, creating a reality which never truly existed; e.g. the Scots' flank at Dunbar being represented far too close in formation, due to the aesthetic representation of the Scots' camp at Brox Burn (Fig.6).[26]

Equally, a map can merely represent a select point in time, thus creating an existence that was never realised, nor understood on the day of the battle, in essence backing up an ideological fantasy. However, through use of available archaeological resources on a site, linked with regimental identifiers, we can use our current standing knowledge of tactical organisation linked with the image created by the map to create anchor points within the localised landscape to actively pivot and restructure deployment sites to fit the historical reality and limitations with tactical sensibility.

---

22 Woosnam-Savage, '"To Gather an Image Whole"', p.49.
23 Pollard, Tony, 'Mapping Mayhem: Scottish Battle Maps and their Role in Archaeological Research', *Scottish Geographical Journal*, 125:1 (Perth: Royal Scottish Geographical Society, 2009) p.26.
24 ibid, pp.26-30.
25 ibid, pp.30-32.
26 ibid, p.31.

6

Artefactual Trends

So if the reality of tactical innovation is to be represented within the archaeological record, how is this likely to be manifest? Representation needs to take place on two levels; firstly on a personal level, whereby an individual performing drill is likely to deposit a particular artefact and the circumstances under which deposition takes place; secondly, through tactical representation, represented through spatial positioning mirroring the likely form of a tactical body of troops. Through the latter's frequency of investigation, using historical accounts of the battle, linked with localised orientation of associated finds, limited interpretation may be undertaken unique to that space, thus creating a multi-layered landscape that can be unified on a local and national level to create a revisionist perspective of conflict.

Weapons-handling drill varied greatly between type and manual, with the range of 3162 drills for musket, 1565 for pike, 23 for marching and 20 for horseback, although these figures merely represent what should be performed on paper, many of these drills being amalgamated into cycles for ease of movement.[1] In an archaeological sense, six drills leave archaeological remains for musket, two for pike and eight for horse:

Musket[2]

- Place your rest – ability to lose musket furniture (Figs.7.47.5, 8.4).[3]
- Take up your bandolier – ability for cartridge bottle or stopper to fall off (Figs.7.6, 8.2).
- Open your pan possibility of loose or broken powder flask nozzle falling off (Figs.7.3, 8.1).
- Open your charge ability for copper top to cartridge from bandolier falling off.
- Wadding Naked shot Banding from gas expansion, dimpled surface from resting on powder charge. Scratches from gas escaping passed ball.[4]
  ◊ Wad = dimple surface and gas scratch.[5]
  ◊ Wrapped balls cloth leave impression on ball, still spherical.[6]
- Ram home your charge impression of the scouring stick (ramrod) left imbedded in the surface

---

1 Bariffe, William, *Military discipline, or The young artillery-man* (London: Andrew Kembe, 1657) p.2; Cruso, John, *Militarie Instructions For The Cavall'rie* (Cambridge: University of Cambridge, 1632) pp.39-41; de Gheyn, Jacob, and Blackmore, David J. (ed.), *The Renaissance Drill Book* (London: Greenhill Books); Matthew, Christopher (ed.), *The Tactics of Aelian or On the Military Arrangements of the Greeks: A New Translation of the Manual that Influenced Warfare for Fifteen Centuries* (Barnsley: Pen & Sword Military, 2012); Ward, Robert, *Animadversions of warre; or, A militarie magazine of the truest rules, and ablest instructions, for the managing of warre* (London: John Dawson, 1639); Wright, Simon, *Militarie Disciplines For The Royalist Army of the Sealed Knot* (Southampton: The Sealed Knot, 2003).
2 de Gheyn and Blackmore, *The Renaissance Drill Book*, pp.111, 127, 130, 141, 149.
3 Bariffe, *Military discipline*, p.2.
4 Harding, David F., *Lead Shot of the English Civil Wars: A Radical Study* (Oxford: Oxbow Books, 2012) p.67.
5 ibid.
6 ibid.

THE ARTE MILITAIRE

- of musket ball, number of faces associated with a number of taps.[7] Normal for metalled weapon, so firelock. (Figs. 7.1, 8.3).
- Evidence of gnawing associated with musket balls equally may represent issues with commissariat, resulting in balls provided of the wrong calibre.[8] Also belief that draws saliva and gunpowder into wound e.g. Goring's order, Colchester, 1648/Garrison, Hopton Castle however disproven.[9]
- Cock your match an insecurely fastened serpentine (hammer) to the musket lock springing off (Fig.9.1).
- Evidence of sprue left on the bullet evidence for paper cartridge, possibly linked to doglock weapons.[10]
- Double shotting surfaces touching each other in barrel flattened 90°. Same for triple shotting, although middle ball has two surfaces flattened, also gas release scratches.[11]

Pike

- Charge your pike represented through pike heads discovered in isolation.[12] Battles between forces using lances against pikes require further analysis of possible heads to differentiate between the two.[13] Accumulations of small finds represent fallen wounded (Figs.7.2, 9.2).[14]
- Push of pike taking soil samples to understand the level of compaction at a stratigraphic horizon to identify trampling (Fig.13).

Horse

- Order your hammer serpentine springing off.
- Bend your cock losing priming pan on lock.
- Load with bullet pistol balls with scouring stick impression, evidence of extensive sprue might represent loading through waxed paper cartouche.
- Gage your flask loss of priming flask nozzle.
- Draw your Rammer possible tinned scouring stick.
- Span your Pistol brass pistol butt, wheel lock spanner for lock.
- Present and give fire fragments of iron pyrite (wheel lock) and lost gun flints (flint/doglock).
- Any evidence of loading and firing from horseback should be proficiently represented, due to the difficulty therein.
- Close-quarter fighting/engaging with the enemy any evidence of pierced or damaged armour due to inaccuracy of contemporary weapons. Also look for weapons impact inflicted upon armour for links to particular manuals and drill.
- Equally, the mere representation of horseshoes and nails, fittings for tack (bit, girth buckle, stirrup, spur etc.), fragments of armour broken off by insecure attach/horse bolting or dying, particularly from visor and articulated attachments to the shoulders, arms and upper legs, are possible signs of a force of cavalry, quantifying the levels of artefacts gauging their level of

---

7 Harding, Lead Shot, p.47; Sivilich, D.M., 'What the Musket Ball Can Tell: Monmouth Battlefield State Park, New Jersey', in Scott, Douglas, Babits, Lawrence, and Haecker, Charles (eds), *Fields of Conflict: Battlefield Archaeology from the Roman Empire to the Korean War: Searching for War in the Ancient and Early Modern World* vol. 1 (Westport: Praeger Security International, 2007) p.47.
8 Sivilich, 'Musket Ball', p.89.
9 Harding, *Lead Shot*, p.78.
10 ibid, p.45.
11 ibid, p.85.
12 de Gheyn and Blackmore, *The Renaissance Drill Book*, p.211; Wright, Sealed Knot, pp.14-15.
13 Cruso, Militarie Instructions, p.34.
14 Wright, *Sealed Knot*, p.15.

ARTEFACTUAL TRENDS

Figures 7.1 and 7.2: Many of the items commonly associated with drill all found at Edgehill. Original and experimentally fired musket balls, showing the effects of lack of wadding, allowing gases to expand around the bullet, the low melting point causing the projectile to expand and score the sides of the barrel. This is also typologically highlighted through the pitted texture to the lower hemisphere of the projectile, due to the bullet resting on the black powder charge. (Foard and Morris, *British Battlefields*, Fig.4.15, p.77)

Figure 7.3: Musket ball impacted against a hard surface, thus forming this mushroom typology. This is likely to be a pebble or stone, as experimental firing undertaken at The Centre for Battlefield Archaeology has proven that unless hitting bone, lead projectiles retain their morphology even after passing through a body. This is likely to represent raw troops firing too low. A similar morphology is created when double-shotting a musket. (ibid, Fig.4.16)

Figure 7.4: Slug bullet good for expanding power against armour (Foard, 2008, p.286). While it has previously been argued that typology is based purely due to ease of manufacture, experimental firing and corroboration of this type of shot in low frequency areas, assumed to be where push of pike has taken place, corroborates its role. (Foard and Morris, *British Battlefields*, Fig.4.17, p.77)

THE ARTE MILITAIRE

Figure 7.5: Powder flask nozzle. Often these are good indicators of individual firing positions, due to the difficulties inherent in loading from horseback. Clearly identified in quantities highlighting Sulby Hedges at Naseby, a clear progression for associating firing positions would be to eliminate hedgelines from OS readouts and focus metal-detecting comparatively to see whether loading in isolation is deposited behind cover. (ibid, Fig.7.19, p.124)

importance.[15] Equally, sites where levels of horse-related paraphernalia is discovered might also be soil-tested for a horizon of compression, although this might equally be caused through pike/artillery positions.[16]

By being able to identify artefactually sub-spaces within the wider battlefield area through use-wear analysis linked to particular processes, the ability to orientate individuals within the wider armies and therefore groups they were associated with becomes apparent. However, only through looking at the spatial orientation and layout of these particular finds, is any meaning, facing and direction offered to contain battlefield events.

Military drill on the battlefield of the 17th century was extremely formalised, with particular models being instituted according to nation and school of thought. In this sense, by quantifying the available spatial schematic information from contemporary battle-plans, accounts, drill and known influences, our knowledge of individual generals can be modelled within a database, so that when investigating one of the battlefields they fought over, we can model over the current landscape the expected deployment and manoeuvres associated with them. Thus, here we shall quickly cover the three main deployment models associated with the 17th century through the Dutch, Swedish and English models.

Instituted by Maurice of Nassau in 1593, the basic Dutch regimental deployment of infantry at the time was a pike block flanked by sleeves of musket, with cavalry flanking these units, the position of honour being in the vanguard on the right of the line, due to the necessities of deploying an army from march to order of battle.[17] This was based around the Roman triarii system of three lines, the last two acting in reserve to fill holes within the depleted front ranks. This is represented through a checkerboard profile, with the alignment of differing lines staggered to feed troops into the tactical situation (Fig.11).[18]

Firing was carried out by salvo (salve) or caracole, the front rank firing before retiring to the rear to reload, thus allowing rear ranks to advance and continue the hail of fire.[19]

Thus, archaeologically this should be represented at high frequency through alternating blocks of high density musket ball scatters, with areas of little ordinance-based evidence. Equally, these scatters should represent parallel roughly linear associations of multiples of 6–32 ranks and 3–16 files, representing the contemporary depth of units, 38–100 artefacts representing an identifiable associated unit scatter.[20] It is

---

15 Cruso, *Militarie Instructions*, p.35.
16 ibid, pp.39-42.
17 de Gheyn, and Blackmore, *The Renaissance Drill Book*, p.9; Roberts, Keith, and Tincey, John, *Edgehill 1642: First Battle of the English Civil War*, Campaign 82 (Oxford: Osprey Publishing, 2001) p.24; Roberts, Keith, *Pike and Shot Tactics 1590-1660* (Oxford: Osprey Publishing, 2010).
18 Matthew, *The Tactics of Aelian*, p.45; Roberts, *Pike and Shot Tactics*.
19 Roberts, *Pike and Shot Tactics*.
20 Bariffe, *Military discipline*, pp.5, 7, 9; de Gheyn and Blackmore, *The Renaissance Drill Book*, p.9; Matthew, *The Tactics of Aelian*, pp.194-5; Ward, *Animadversions of warre*, pp.226-31; Wright, *Sealed Knot*, pp.4-5.

Figure 8: Typical postures resulting in archaeological remains. (de Gheyn, 1607, figs.129, 141, 149, 167)

THE ARTE MILITAIRE

Figure 9: Typical postures resulting in archaeological remains. (de Gheyn, 1607, figs.177, 211)

Figure 10: Cavalry postures resulting in archaeological remains; (.1) Return your hammer, (.2) Pull down your cock. From John Cruso, *Militarie Instructions for the Cavall'rie*. (Cambridge: University of Cambridge, 1632)

ARTEFACTUAL TRENDS

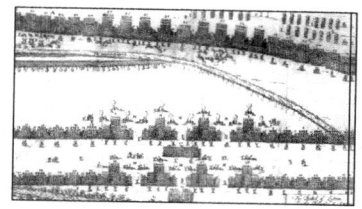

Figure 11: Image from *The Swedish Intelligencer* (1632) showing the Battle of Lützen. Swedish troops in the foreground showing typical Swedish model deployment, compared with Imperialist troops at the top of the picture representing typical Dutch deployment model.

clear that when engaging with the enemy, as the majority of battlefield scatters are likely to represent, an artefact mean frequency of 1.5–3.3ft (0.91m) [5ftx10ft {1.52mx3.04m} for cavalry] should be represented between artefacts, showing likely ordered and close-order spacing within a unit.[21]

However, while it is clear that we have allocated spacing for musketeers, it is likely this was subject to change by more unwieldy pikemen with different needs and formations on the battlefield.[22] By measuring the frequency of shot, we can understand the orientation and deposition conditions undertaken contemporary to a battle. Thus, if the frequency extends above the listed range, the possibility of that particular unit being caught while standing or on the march is greatly increased.[23]

Equally, Bariffe and Hexham show firing systems as firing by block and then retiring to the sides, represented by fired balls identifying parallel linear block profiles, either massed as in the Swedish method, or sporadic groupings across the field, like the Dutch, unfired balls representing smaller blocks further back from the firing line, made up of raw troops.[24] These unfired balls are equally important in identifying the possible localised fire position. Through the use of a quantifiable histogram, we can look for correlations in differing calibre of ball, identifying differing weapons systems used by either side.[25]

Establishing the possible site of a unit, we can then work out the accuracy of surviving battle-maps and accounts as well as the modern position of contemporary actions through taking approximate unit distributions and appointments into account. Thus we can place measurements of 300m between divisions, weapons divisions 4–150m and individual companies 20–100m, between lines consisting of about 20–70m, the rear line being the shortest at 700m.[26]

Breaking this rule down even further, we can look at individual regimental spaces and the areas they take up. Therefore, a regiment's total frontage consists of 700x300ft, with calibrated frontages for every single division and line equally 7,392m$_2$.[27] By looking at the frequency and spatial form to which an assemblage takes place, we can equally narrow down the tactical situation or event being reacted to.

Thus, if there is a high percentage of cavalry in the nearby vicinity, the assemblage will appear to be a tightly compacted correlation, identified through a circular grouping of mixed artefacts and a ring of musket balls, represented if we are following Bariffe's model in a series of alternating bands in multiples of four.[28]

Where these horizontal bands of musket balls are represented in association, we must also look for evidence of deformation regarding tactical firing at differing ranges. A raw regiment or indeed a regiment

---

21   Bariffe, *Military discipline*, p.10; Cruso, *Militarie Instructions*, p.45; Foard, *Battlefield Archaeology*, p.125; Matthew, *The Tactics of Aelian*, p.25; Wright, *Sealed Knot*, p.5; Schurger, Andre, 'Die Schlacht von Lützen – Stumme Zeugen einer blütigen Schlacht', *Archäologie in Deutschland* vol. 1, (Stuttgart: Konrad Theiss Verlag, 2009) p.136.
22   Callen, Royalist infantry tactics, pp.29-30.
23   The Sealed Knot Society, 'Handy hints from the Infantrie Garden by Seed-drill No.5 – Keeping Your Distance', *Orders of the Day*, December/January (Nottingham, 2002).
24   Roberts, *Pike and Shot Tactics*; Wright, *Sealed Knot*, p.18.
25   Sivilich, 'Musket Ball', p.87.
26   Cruso, *Militarie*, pp.60-61; Ward, *Anima'dversions of warre*, pp.99, 316; Wright, *Sealed Knot*, p.12; Schurger, 'Lützen', pp.22-25.
27   Cruso, *Militarie Instructions*, p.38; Ward, *Anima'dversions of warre*, p.70.
28   Bariffe, *Military discipline*, p.127; Wright, *Sealed Knot*, p.18; Sealed Knot, 'Keeping Distance' (2001).

in dire straits would likely fire at long ranges, according to Bariffe and backed up by recent experimental firing as being at 100–1,500yds from the target, and thus represented as a band within the assumed enemy assemblage of differing sized musket balls, their morphology largely intact due to their spent nature.[29] Likewise, at effective to optimal ranges of 110–500yds, this representing two trained units engaging, the representation is likely to be the same but with a hypothetical 70:30 ratio of malformed balls, this ratio remaining the same for point-blank range, although likely to be mirrored by a larger level of similar diameter balls being found in that group's firing position, representing fumbling at close quarters.[30]

A middle point between the two forces should be represented through evidence of broken weaponry, but largely devoid of ordinance-based evidence, identifying evidence of both sides engaging in hand-to-hand combat, the reality of damaged weaponry such as dented trigger guards, buckles, weapons and pieces of armour highlighting them from the rest of the battlefield space.[31] Such assemblages should consist of a wider frontage of coverage than other assemblages, due to the tactical need for a larger number of fighting men when engaging with the enemy, normally providing coverage of about 12ft of doubled front.[32]

However, we need to look within these often blank areas for evidence of isolated musket balls, representing sporadic firing by forlorn hopes, either advancing through files of multiples of eight or acting as a general skirmish line, either directed on the armies' flanks or generally in front, often anchored on hedge/wall lines/field boundaries for cover, in bodies spreading around 22m.[33] These would be identified through limited linear groupings, one end of the assemblage proving denser than the other, representing rapid advance and retiring according to the advance of the enemy. Flanking cavalry action should be represented by small-scale linear correlations of small-calibre pistol and carbine shot, or a mixed assemblage with no association, representing firearms used during the melee of two bodies of horse.

However, defensive positions taken by infantry cannot be clarified, often through the huge range of differentiation between calibre of bore discovered in particular areas, to alternating infantry and horse-based furniture confusing interpretation.

Nor should we look at infantry forming into squares, or indeed hedgehogs, as being particularly common. Bariffe clearly highlights the fact that pikes are so immobile and muskets are diminished by space and circumstance. On the other hand, horse are fast and can fire with pistols from afar, so that their use against infantry is hugely diminished and treated as a weapons system limitation when employing troops in the field; its preponderance within continued interpretation of the period is merely a later horse and musket Napoleonic preconception.[34] Indeed, Reid highlights clearly individualism within and differentiation between manuals through using Elton's example of Tillier doubling and reversing his ranks to provide a wall of ported pikes, thus making best use of both arms of service, confusing existing trends further by vertical horizontal lines of shot being represented.[35]

Although it has been proved that lead bullets do not deform on moving through bodies, a number of these balls may prove misshapen, owing to the common practice propagated by Vernon of shooting at the ground, allowing for a ricochet.[36] The possibility of small-scale soil analysis in the above might be undertaken to understand compaction and inclusions representing a small-scale horizon of large-scale trampling as a result of a push of pike or cavalry charge (Fig.10).

---

29 Bariffe, *Military discipline*, p.127; Harding, *Lead Shot*, p.8.
30 Harding, *Lead Shot*, p.8.
31 Pollard, Tony (ed.), 'Capturing the Moment: The Archaeology of Culloden Battlefield', in *Culloden: The History and Archaeology of the Last Clan Battle* (Barnsley: Pen and Sword Military, 2009) pp.130-62; Wright, *Sealed Knot*, p.26.
32 Bariffe, *Military discipline*, p.10.
33 Bariffe, *Military discipline*, p.87; Ward, *Animadversions of warre*, p.68.
34 Bariffe, *Military discipline*, p.147.
35 Elton, Richard, 'Complete Body of the Arte Military vol. II', in Reid, Stuart, *All the King's Armies: A Military History of the English Civil War 1642-1651* (Stroud: Spellmount, 2nd ed. 2007) p.7.
36 Harding, *Lead Shot*, p.10.

ARTEFACTUAL TRENDS

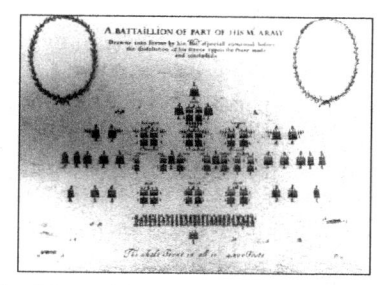

Figure 12: Tertio showing hybrid English model, combining the composite nature of Swedish with the linear combined arms Dutch model, a factor to grow increasingly after the Battle of Edgehill, as the need for fluidity of tactical movement reinforced recommendations from veterans of the Thirty Years' War. (Hollar, Wenceslas: *Portrait of King Charles I with diagrams showing the formation of his troops during the Bishops' War, 1639*)

However, this system might be complicated through the adoption of Gustavus Adolphus' Swedish deployment model, revolving around the demi-hearse. Sleeves of musket would advance and connect to form a firing line. Their volley fired and they again disconnected, allowing the pike to advance. Thus our model would be presented by a series of linear large-scale musket ball assemblages, accompanied by a large gap before they pick up again. Swedish-style deployment took an arrowhead form, blocks of pike forming a composite centre, composite bodies of musket flanking them and also forming a reserve between lines, thus creating a composite sandwich (Fig.8). However, using KOCOA, we must remember the brittle, intersupporting nature of such bodies, which were required to work in tandem with each other to create a series of interlocking fields of influence, in order not to present an open flank to massed cavalry, limiting their role on the battlefield to vertical manoeuvring.[37] McNutt comes to the conclusion that we can often predict a likely tactical standpoint simply by giving a cursory glance to the topography of a battlefield; if it is intersected by lots of hedges, field boundaries (key to understanding likely firing positions) etc., units are likely to adopt compact deep formations (e.g. Newbury/Naseby), but if the landscape is relatively open, a wider fronted Dutch-style is more easily managed (e.g. Edgehill, Lansdown Hill).[38]

When advancing, the musket would advance as two bodies and combine in front of the pike to form a firing line and thus antagonise the enemy, unforming and retiring when both forces decided to engage in hand-to-hand combat, the pike being allowed to advance.[39] Thus, as we can tell that a Swedish unit was supposed to hold 1,204 files, at a spacing of 50cm–1m$_2$ the likely space it incorporated was 1,000–2,000m$_2$, the distance between the horn battle [a 17th century term to describe a two-pronged attack, in that the pikemen were flanked by two musketeers. The muskeeters advance, give fire and then retire – allowing the pikemen to advance and engage with the enemy] and the main body being 10–20m.[40] The equal increasing use by Gustavus Adolphus of swine feathers sharpened stakes used as a deterrent against cavalry might lead towards the identifying of musket firing positions and better characterisation of drill manuals and artefact assemblages through highlighting stratigraphic evidence of pits. Such methods of defence were commonly incorporated by veterans of the continental wars and act as a major indicator of patterns of where particular individuals were situated on the battlefield, such as Sergeant Major General Henry Tillier or Sir William Waller's Triple Firing System (pike flanked by shot, shot advancing, retiring, followed by pike advancing).[41]

All of this is likely to be represented at an archaeological level through large-scale musket ball assemblages being situated on the peripheries of the field, the centre dominated by merely broken

---

37 McNutt, *Forgotten Fields*, p.343.
38 ibid, p.353.
39 Roberts, *Pike and Shot Tactics*.
40 Matthew, *The Tactics of Aelian*, pp.27–35.
41 Bariffe, *Military discipline*, p.127; Sealed Knot, 'Keeping Distance' (2001).

weaponry, representing pike blocks.

However, within Britain and Germany, with the conclusion of the Thirty Years' War and the beginning of the English Civil War, officers found these formation styles too static and thus adapted the two systems. These were composed of Swedish formations organised on a Tertio level, using the alternating Dutch method. Thus, alternating linear bands of musket ball assemblages, with large gaps between, would be represented archaeologically. Certainly, with the rush of technological innovation spreading out from the War of the Three Kingdoms, it is clear that in a British context, from July 1643 and the widespread dislike of carbines engendered by Cromwell after his victory at Gainsborough, it is likely their representation on the battlefield would more likely highlight dragoon and commanded shot units.[42]

How much of an honour-based organisation there was around horse and pike requires continued investigation, particularly where there is uncommon positioning of these troop types on the right (the perceived position of honour on the battlefield) or discrepancies with musket-pike ratios.[43]

Using localised Viewshed analysis and Landscape regression, the ability to presume firing orientation and direction, providing an anchor profile upon which to start orientating surviving battle accounts and plans and thus possibly identifying units engaged, we can positively identify to history the approximate position of groups of soldiers and historical personalities with a higher than average level of accuracy.

---

[42] Harding, *Lead Shot*, p.10.
[43] Callen, Royalist infantry tactics, pp.29-30.

7

Irregular Warfare

But while we can create models surrounding these military hierarchies, conflicts and forces incorporating clan, militia or ethnic groups such as encountered with Montrose's forces during the War of the Three Kingdoms, the Jacobite Rebellions or rebel forces during the Monmouth rebellion, purely because their system of irregular warfare is based far more upon ideological allegiance, rather than sound, scientifically tested tactical knowledge, often incorporate 'backwards', archaic methods that do not sit well within the borders of military science.

However, to discredit their role and possible representation within conflict archaeology would be to create a major flaw within the project remit. Rather than looking at the irregular soldier, such as highland troops, native tribes or indeed irregular troops within regular armies as the noble savage, with backward weapon systems and systems of command, we should actually be looking at formations which were just as in-tune with the latest in weapons development as everyone else, merely being unable to financially afford the levels to which they would leave a clear mark or impact on the battlefield. However, McNutt presents an alternative to this perceived view, arguing instead that a predominance and common association with sword and shield (targe) fighting amongst 17th century Scots armies is equally due to a diffusion of continental, particularly Spanish, fight school and methods of swordfighting being adopted by Irish and indeed Scottish mercenary companies fighting in the same theatres.[1] He supports this by referring to a similar observation by Garret Barry, who wrote *A Discourse of Military Discipline* (1634) while serving in the Spanish army, associated to MacColla's Irish Brigade and thus inadvertently filtered down to Scottish clan fighting (also supporting the lack of basket-hilted broadswords represented in the 1638 Blair Atholl census, due to exclusive training and them being rank-associated).[2] Equally, McNutt highlights Montrose's *modus operandi*: working with few cavalry, he has the tendency to place what cavalry he has on his right flank, balancing this with the Irish Brigades on his left, its object being to use typical cavalry tactics unhorsed in the manner of a full cavalry charge to balance his equine inequality by instilling in them cavalry drill that could be diffused throughout his army.[3]

Certainly, it cannot be denied, before even doing an effective metal detector survey, that applying a basic topographical survey is important for understanding particular features tied into the strategic analysis of the battle or that particular formations may well have anchored upon. Such analysis has recently been completed by McNutt on the battlefields of Kilsyth. Montrose needed a position with clear observation and cover from Baillie's Covenanter army, while equally also being able to cut any link from their reinforcements under Lord Lanark. Rather than sitting astride the main Stirling to Glasgow road

---

1   McNutt, Forgotten Fields, p.345.
2   McNutt, Forgotten Fields, p.345; Singleton, Charles, *'Famous by My Sword': The Army of Montrose and the Military Revolution*, Century of the Soldier 1618-1721 1 (Solihull: Helion and Company, 2014) p.23.
3   McNutt, Forgotten Fields, p.352.

and thus deny their ability to react effectively to such situations, it is more likely Montrose' camp and deployment position was situated on the high meadow, just above the present road, providing commanding views across the glen, as well as effectively blocking the line of advance to Baillie along Hollinbush and Bonny Road, the approach from Edinburgh.[4] Just as likely was it for Baillie to advance along the old road adjacent to Banton Burn, rather than any of Montrose's assumed positions, as it provided a completely covered means to deploy, although the hilly terrain clearly presents reasoning for the gradual separation of Home from Baillie's command.[5] The extant remains of the Berryhill enclosures and dykes, with their natural closeness to contemporary buildings at Auchinrivock, provides an anchor upon which to the site the initial clash between Hume and Montrose's outer pickets, supported by localised metal detecting identifying a scatter of impacted musket balls to the west of Auchinrivock, along the near contemporary line of localised field boundaries, corroborated in the 1859 Ordinance Survey map.[6]

It is always going to be difficult to highlight an ephemeral irregular system, so what we really need to be looking at is discrepancies, oddities and what is missing from government profile assemblages, in order to build up a characterisation of artefact site formation. Arguably, if we know particular troop types were trying to come to hand-to-hand combat, we firstly need to look at projectile morphology around the site. Certainly, with the obvious accuracy discrepancies individual muskets hold, officers were more likely to hold off fire until relatively close range, in the 2050 yard barrier. This should be represented by a wider range of small-scale linear deformation in relation to established deployment position, undeformed balls representing firing low at legs, a possible curve representing differing time between platoon volleys, as represented at the Leanach enclosure, Culloden and also Killiecrankie.[7] This should equally be mirrored by quantities of grape and case shot.[8] If the government forces were aware of this, then it is equally likely Jacobite forces were as well and therefore amongst this assemblage a similar representation of smaller calibre bullets will be represented.[9]

By the time both sides engage in hand-to-hand combat, we need to be looking for material artefacts of a non-military nature, such as buttons, buckles, hobnails and other ephemera likely to be cut, torn or simply lost in this aggressive push; on occasions, such as at Killiecrankie, these might be vital as they might display early clan crests such as Clan Atholl.[10] In such scraps, individuals are likely to use any object that they have to hand as a weapon, with muskets turned to clubs, as is quite clearly represented at the Leanach Enclosure at Culloden, where a range of musket furniture has been discovered, bearing telltale signs of being lost either from close-range musket fire or from the downward cut of a broadsword.[11]

While these come from a battlefield where military professionalism was well and truly clearly identified, similar ephemeral signatures can likely be transferred to the battlefields of a century beforehand, a mere change of equipment to more efficient models being the only real difference. By breaking down the background clutter that makes up the majority of metal detector surveys and looking for similar isolated occurrences, could we possibly create a highlight for such irregular warfare? Only continued adaptation, review and building upon previous lessons for spatial interpretation of metal detector surveys will reveal the extent to which this mode of warfare can be pursued.

---

4   ibid, p.374.
5   ibid.
6   ibid, p.381.
7   Pollard, 'Capturing the Moment, p.155; Pollard, Tony, and Oliver, Neil, *Two Men in a Trench II: Uncovering the Secrets of British Battlefields* (London: Penguin, 2003) pp.233-34.
8   ibid.
9   Pollard, 'Capturing the Moment', p.145; Pollard and Oliver, *Two Men in a Trench II*, p.232; Pollard, Tony, and Banks, Iain, Culloden Battlefield: Report on the Archaeological Investigation Project 1981 (Glasgow: GUARD, 2006) p.28.
10 Pollard, 'Capturing the Moment', p.151; Pollard, and Oliver, Two Men in a Trench II, p.231.
11 Pollard, 'Capturing the Moment', pp.143, 149.

8

Agent-Based Modelling

If we can create such a series of certainties about the drills and movements enacted within the battlefield space, a number of generalisations can start to be modelled according to landscape type, conditions of deposition and possibly subsequent landscape and agricultural procedures representing the battle's archaeological character. This should leave a system of gross patterning that should be roughly similar over different battlefields of a similar type.

To undertake this, we have to perform a range of speculative area modelling, by taking into account groups and numbers of troops likely to be incorporated within such a body and the distance they took up and likely distances between units, when building a battlefield landscape model; but equally also building crowd dynamic algorithms that can model fluid movement, action and practice throughout the battlefield area, using particle dynamics and psychological/sociological constraints gained from historical research to identify under particular stresses and situations, the current mathematical and technological-based resources being able to run at too low a frequency to manage the huge numbers involved in such conflict.[1]

During the 1980s investigation of the Battle of the Little Bighorn, such spatial analysis was first considered. In order for individual actions to be defined within mass battlefield assemblages, individual actions at various levels from regimental to platoon must be identified as individual archaeological contexts. The former uses gross pattern analysis, while dynamic pattern analysis is used to show typological development and movement of archaeological behaviour across the space investigated, using common firearm identification and forensic analysis of projectiles to identify characteristic faults in particular firearms.[2] Thus clusters, distributions mirroring tactical innovation and common patterns, have the ability to link to our historical knowledge of the vagaries of particular units and link our site interpretation with particular alignments.[3]

Equally, we should also be looking for anomalies such as isolated pistol balls and human remains, possibly related to individual actions and events unrecorded in common knowledge.[4] By using dynamic theory, it provides three-dimensional movements to the landscape and provides chronology of movement, allowing theoretical alignments to be established.[5] Thus a site with similar characteristic musket balls might represent the target site of one individual's particular firing position, although localised soil sciences need to be provided to calibrate these approximate results.[6]

---

1 Clements, Richard R., and Hughes, Roger L., 'Mathematical modelling of a mediaeval battle: The Battle of Agincourt, 1415', in *Mathematics and Computers in Simulation* (Elsevier, 64, 2004) pp.259-69.
2 Scott, Fox, Connor and Harnon, *Little Bighorn*, p.146.
3 ibid, p.147.
4 ibid.
5 ibid, p.148.
6 Nolan, T.J., 'Geographic Informations Science as a Method of Integrating History and Archaeology For Battlefield Investigation, *Journal of Conflict Archaeology*, vol.5 (Glasgow: Centre for Battlefield Archaeology, 2009) p.94; Scott, Fox, Connor and Harnon, *Little Bighorn*, p.148.

Thus there are a number of ways such patterns and rules can be established and applied to these sites. Through a combination of GIS (Geographic Informations Science) and Viewshed technology, we have the ability to spatially identify individual units and individuals in the battle-space by placing the approximate sites of units, as described in written accounts, within a reconstructed landscape and then recreating approximate drill and lines of march around the battlefield. However, rather than leaving such bodies and organisations within cloud isolation, such drill systems need to be placed within topographical context using the US Battlefield Preservation Service KOCOA system, originated as a military training exercise to use effective terrain, cover, observation and method of approach.[7] Overlaid onto a high-frequency metal detector survey, the ability to find correlations of undistorted musket balls, representing possible fumbling during the loading process, can identify the only possible evidence for a firing position we are likely to find.[8]

But how do proper bodies work, particular when investigating the use of pike during the period, when very little information about their use en masse can be gleaned? While certainly not contemporary to the battle, recent mathematical analyses of the battlefield at Azincourt, renowned for its often overlooked use by the French, of massed bodies of knights and troops, has the ability within the crush of the battleline to reproduce something of the particle physics likely still being enacted 230 years later. Clements and Hughes argue that in order to gain an advantage over their enemy, while adhering to chivalric norms of the periods, blocks of men-at-arms are likely to have imparted the same frontage area and thus enacted the same level of force when fighting against each other.[9] As such, this exerted force needs to be released somehow: obviously pressure placed upon the ground that they trample during hand-to-hand fighting will be imparted as a isolated strata context, but equally, as momentum overtakes the force exerted laterally against the opposing group, the body of men is likely to flare out to engage in one-to-one fighting. In this case, metal detector surveys based around individual unit actions can be interpreted as starting with a lateral linear alignment, flaring out as the coherency of the body of troops is lost, the winning side identified through a shallower, less coherent assemblage of finds.

With continual battlefield metal detector surveys being undertaken, the available information, coupled with experimental historic firearms data and computer-aided modelling, can start providing predictive models for archaeological yield on investigated battlefields. Such systems take account of the total number of soldiers taking part, their tactical make-up, orientation, range of weapons, morale and surrounding obstacles and choreography, and we can start to group behavioural characteristics and distribution according to possible archaeological work, thus acting as a further means of corroborating existing or non-existent orders of battle within the historical record.[10]

This therefore provides a clear window into site formation, allowing the archaeologist to understand subjective influences on possible investigation rationale. With a time lapse of one second, such an artificial intelligence model can show the reality of particular drills and their cohesion under differing pressures, such as reloading, proximity to the enemy, success etc. (Fig.9).[11]

However, as this acts as a mere crowd dynamics programme at the moment, the morale-boost provided by officers and events surrounding a unit cannot be modelled and thus this merely mirrors what a group should do, rather than what it does do. As a unit fires, the fall of shots velocity and height are recorded at a continuous loss to record distribution, while hitting another cell mirrors wounding a soldier, although this does not mirror the angle of the musket, thus largely missing the point of predictive modelling, only

---

7   McNutt, Forgotten Fields, p.22.
8   Nolan, 'Geographic Informations Science', pp.81-104.
9   Clements, Richard R., and Hughes, Roger L., 'Mathematical modelling of a mediaeval battle', *Mathematics and Computers in Simulation* (Elsevier, 64, 2004) pp.259-69.
10 Rubio-Campillo, Xavier, Cela, Jose Maria and Cardona, Francesc Xavier Hernandez, 'Simulating archaeologists? Using agent based modelling to improve battlefield excavations' (*Journal of Archaeological Science*) vol. 39, (Elsevier, 2012) pp.349-50.
11 Rubio-Campillo, Cela and Cardona, Simulating archaeologists? pp.349-50; Rubio-Campillo, Xavier, Cela, Jose Maria and Cardona, Francesc Xavier Hernandez, 'The development of new infantry tactics during the early eighteenth century: a computer simulation approach to modern military history' (*Journal of Simulation*) no.7, (2013) pp.174-5.

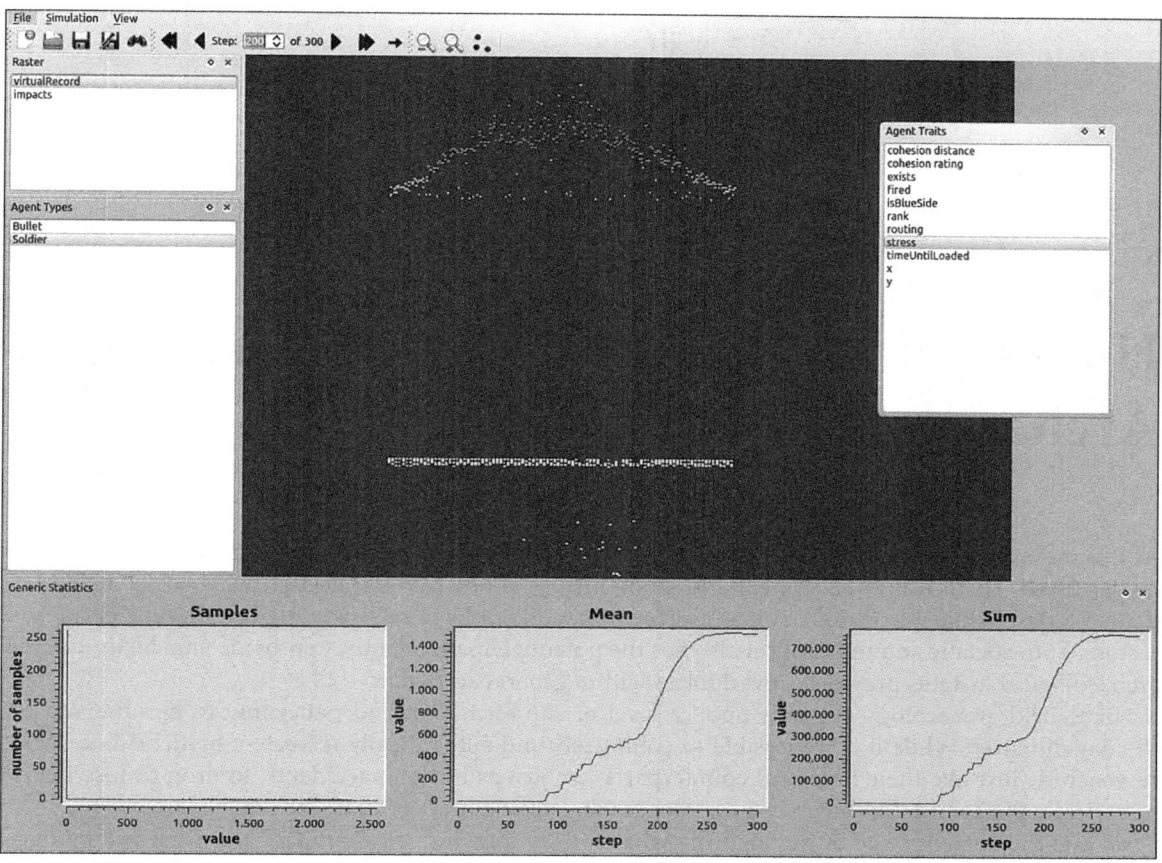

Figure 13: Computer readout showing the level of technological modelling now achievable, inputting various levels of skill, stress and outside influence upon the cohesion of tactical units to start to understand quantitative and spatial patterning of archaeological assemblages. (Campillo et al., 2013, Fig.2/195)

providing a partially complete range from which musket balls may be collected, within a 4.55m radius.[12]

This merely records artefact loss and distribution at a constant rate and fails to model differing times for loading between veteran and green troops, error margins or simple loss due to casualty positioning.[13] If anything, while the progress of such programmes is welcomed, to move such studies away from the parameters of video games, a higher level of command and control, coupled with individual influence, needs to be incorporated into any study. It is not enough to merely argue that algorithms and parameters can be created to model individual sites and how they should be presented in the archaeological record without looking at site-specific chemistry and impacts. Only through creating a historiographical-archaeological methodology may these models be implemented without purely relying upon them.

---

12   Clements, Richard R., and Hughes, Roger L., 'Mathematical modelling of a mediaeval battle', *Mathematics and Computers in Simulation* (Elsevier, 64, 2004), p.352.
13   Rubio-Campillo, Cela and Cardona, 'New infantry tactics', pp.176-7.

9

Historical Re-enactment and Experimental Archaeology

At this moment, it would be apt to note that there is indeed a third area of source material that needs to be discussed. Historical re-enactment and living history is one of the fastest-growing social activity in Britain today. While we can look at it as an eccentric, odd hobby to be recreating certain time periods in history, both socially and militarily, it also has the potential, inadvertently, to provide vital historical and archaeological insights previously overlooked within general academia.

Battlefield archaeology depends upon a level of site formation and patterning to be observed on the day of battle. While it is impossible to completely and authentically recreate a battlefield scenario, re-enactors, just like their historical counterparts, are just as liable to accidents, to drop or lose items/historical replicas and thus form a new context of archaeological potential (Fig.10).

While the current issue of highlighting what is a genuine historical artefact and what is a modern replica is creating ripples within the battlefield studies subject area, the equal ability to ask the perpetrator what particular activities or drill allowed the artefact to be dropped in the first case is being realised through this pastime. From belt ends and buckles to knives, sword fittings, hobnails and even down to an incorrectly tensioned serpentine on a musket, this provides the ability to positively identify individual artefacts within an archaeological assemblage, and through comparative use-wear analysis, highlight the action responding to the deposition. Even the author is guilty, having lost a reproduction coat button recently on the west flank of the Naseby battlefield.

Equally, but inadvertently, by placing a group of individuals into, for all intents and purposes, a historic world for a weekend, values, actions and attitudes start to mirror their historic counterparts. Indeed, at a recent event the author was privileged to attend, while both reconstructed armies attempted to deploy, the constant words on the participants' mouths were that there was a genuine lack of room for an effective deployment and movement, a factor mirrored when we try to align assumed battlefield actions with the surrounding reconstructed landscape, showing that such issues have not changed within 400 years (Fig.14).

Also, as the vagaries of stress and tiredness, coupled with veteran participants' confidence, grows and wanes, many postures represented within a drill manual will become truncated or summarised to make loading and moving procedures easier, thus already compounding the fact that the written manual merely represents the ideal and never the true reality on the battlefield.[1] Thus, as co-operation between the archaeological heritage and re-enactment communities becomes realised, the ability to further the frequency and scale of archaeological artefact investigation will become apparent, providing meaning to items without an identity.

---
1   Carlton, *Going To The Wars*, p.73.

Figure 14: Seventeenth century War of the Three Kingdoms-recreated Royalist army, showing the potential in numbers to recreate, understand the effectiveness, use and limitations such formations might undertake. (http://accessuav.co.uk/wp-content/uploads/2013/09/war_1_1000x543-220x170.jpg, DOI: 13:20 05/03/2014)

10

Lützen

Our first case study will look at the extensive investigation undertaken by Andre Schurger of Sachsen-Anhalt Archaeology on the Lützen 1632 battlefield site in Saxony. The crowning glory of Gustavus Adolphus' military career and the highest pinnacle of Swedish dominance in the Thirty Years' War, it provides the largest survey within this theoretical investigation at a total area of 600ha, growing as the author continues and publishes the finished investigation.[1] The main focus of the investigation currently covers a 17ha stretch of the proposed position of the Imperial left wing, where a particularly large accumulation of 1,880 musket balls have been recovered along a north-west alignment to the Floßgraben line. This has previously been identified by Brzenzski as a site of possible interest due to comparative similarities between Bianchi and Swedish battle maps depicting both wings of the Swedish army inclined at a 45o angle due to constriction from the burning of Lützen, the Floßgraben and Via Regia road to Leipzig, creating a focal point for engagement between both forces.[2]

Using the rules created earlier regarding military spacing with the associated tactical and landscape-based contemporary limitations, we can assume that the frontage extent for this cavalry wing is 2,150m.[3] In order to further locate our position within the battlefield, we need to refer to orders of battle and battleplans in order to draw interpretation and meaning from meaningless metal detector surveys. Therefore, on the furthest line of the Swedish deployment was Stalhandske's Finnish cavalry reiters in eight squadrons of 250 troopers each, intermixed by Colonel Eberstein's five companies of 200 commanded shot, creating an overall deployment frontage of 75x115m, thus presenting a firing profile of a mixed shot, cavalry melee, being only lightly represented as isolated associations.[4] Opposing them to the north were four regiments of Imperial Croat light cavalry, Isolani's and Revay's numbering 250, Beygott's only 100, with a proposed 113m frontage and appearing to deploy at the confluence of the Floßgraben and Via Regia in a skirmishing role 500m advanced from the main line, thus likely to be clearly identifiable through associated finds and not linked to further Imperial deployment.[5] This isolated engagement came about through a belief that this light cavalry was covering and presaging the initial movement of heavier troops along the Imperial line in an attempt to outflank the Swedes.[6]

Although initially having success in pushing back this light cavalry, Fleetwood's account argues this met with little success, turning into stalemate with reinforcement of commanded shot forcing the

---

1 Brzezinski, Richard, *Lützen 1632: Climax of the Thirty Years War*, Campaign 68 (Oxford: Osprey Publishing, 2001); Meller, H., Friederich, S., Schürger, Andre, Alt, Kurt W., and Nicklisch, Nicole, 'Lützen Ein Ort der Erinnerung', *Archäologie in Deutschland* vol. 4 (Stuttgart: Konrad Theiss Verlag, 2013) p.13.
2 Brzezinski, *Lützen 1632*; Meller, Friederich, Schürger, Alt and Nicklisch, 'Lützen', p.13; Schurger, 'Lützen', pp.22-24.
3 Meller, Friederich, Schürger, Alt and Nicklisch, 'Lützen', pp.6-8; Schurger, 'Lützen', p.26.
4 Meller, Friederich, Schürger, Alt and Nicklisch, 'Lützen', pp.6-7.
5 Schurger, 'Lützen', p.5; Meller, Friederich, Schürger, Alt and Nicklisch, 'Lützen', pp.8-10.
6 Brzezinski, *Lützen 1632*, p.53.

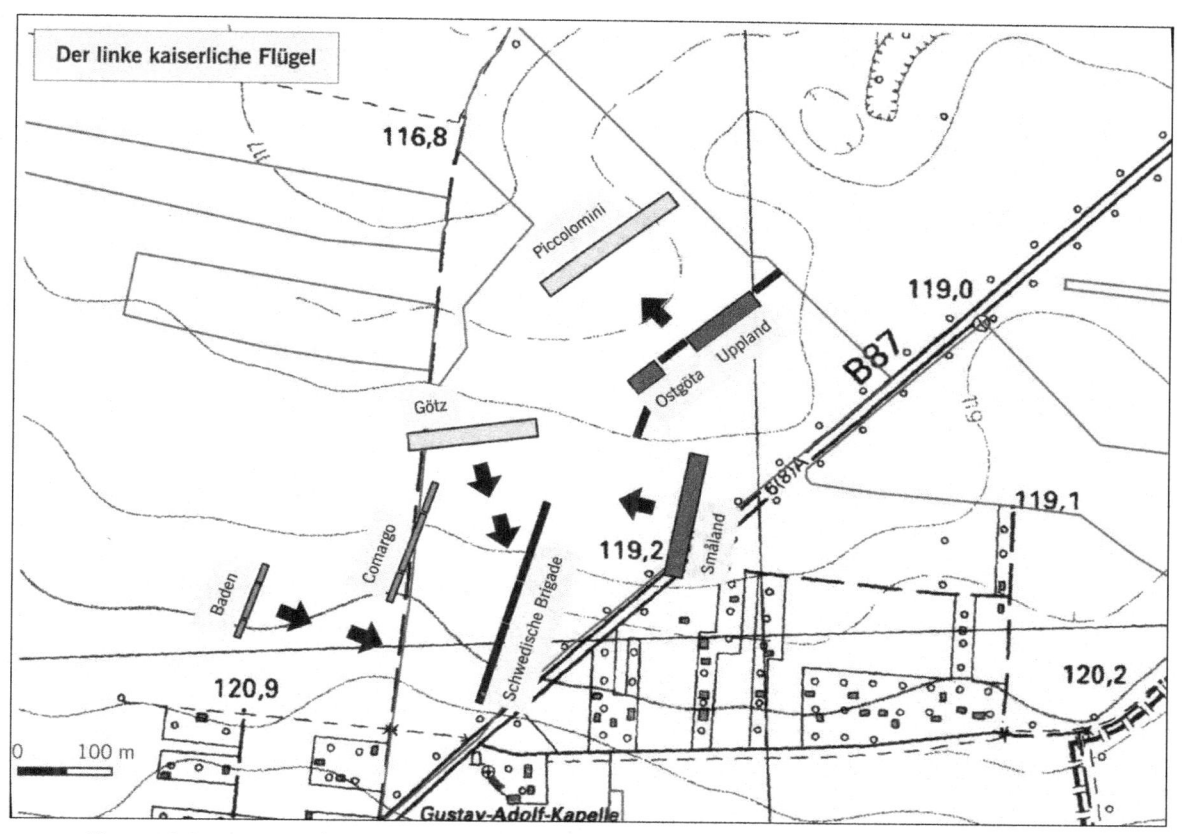

Figure 16: Approximate deployment of cavalry and mounted shot on the Imperialist left wing anchored on the Floßgraben, overlaid onto modern topography and landscape. (Schurger, 'Lützen' 2009, Fig.8, p.143)

Swedes back to their initial positions in consolidation after Gustavus Adolphus' death.[7] Ultimately, this has been characterised within the limited metal detector surveys as three isolated assemblages, with a gap of 150m between them, representing compounded individual actions profiled on top of each other throughout the course of the battle.[8] In order to break down the individual actions, we need to lower the frequency of survey and look for typological similarity of ball morphology, diameter and weight. Due to the continued arms races apparent throughout the period, it is not possible to categorically identify armament specifically used by either side, but we can highlight density of engagement and link to severity of fighting at various points during the battle, while cataloguing and quantifying projectile types to agree with associated orders of battle.[9] Therefore, we can highlight approximate positions of individual troops within the contemporary battle. Thus, upon the Imperial side of the field, the ratio of musket to carbine to pistol is 50:10:40, on the Swedish side 80:10:10, concurrent with current practice to include commanded shot for flexibility of manoeuvring and fire.[10]

However, we are required to place limitations upon particular assemblages, as obvious firing variables mean that a model grouping of shots is unlikely to represent the clear nature of a contemporary unit. Firstly, we need to understand that a unit in close order has a 180o template of fire of 50–100m, creating a fried-egg profile to its fore.[11] However, general melee is likely to present a less ordered, irregular profile,

---
7 Brzezinski, *Lützen 1632*, p.54; Schurger, 'Lützen', p.5.
8 Schurger, 'Lützen', pp.5-10.
9 ibid.
10 Schurger, 'Lützen', p.9; Meller, Friederich, Schürger, Alt and Nicklisch, 'Lützen', pp.12-13.
11 Schurger, 'Lützen', p.4.

THE ARTE MILITAIRE

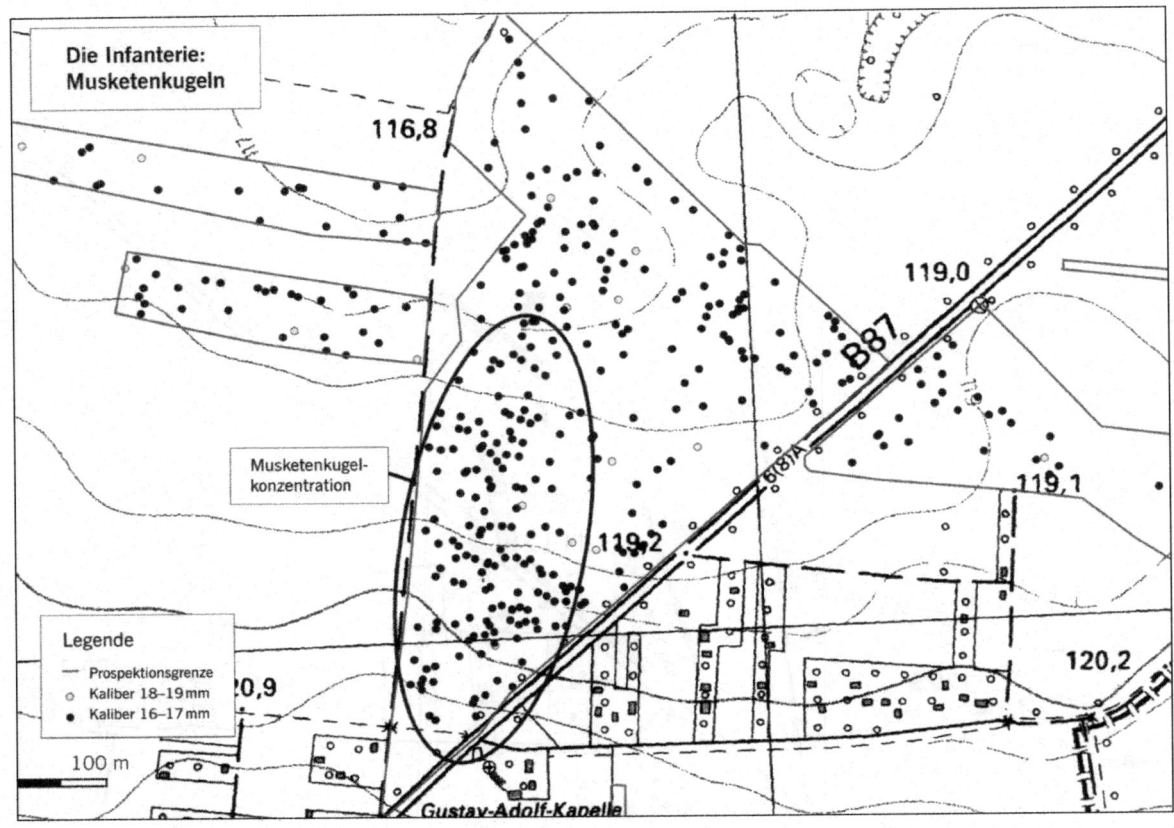

Figure 17: Initial metal detector survey, currently unrefined, but creating immediate assumptions through gathering a collection of larger calibre shot into one area of survey, providing a possible mirror for profiling similar-scale firefights. (Schurger, 'Lützen', 2009, Fig.9, p.143)

reliant upon the discovery of individual limited troop equipment providing the key to identifying the type of engagement engendered (ibid). Nor can we purely take the viewpoint that assemblages merely represent one engagement; certainly with cavalry melee, these are likely to swarm around areas where other engagements have occurred during the day. Thus, certainly with the centre assemblage represented in the Lützen survey, an average range of 25–75 balls per hectare represents an area of heavy fighting, individual actions being highlighted merely through collating projectile ratio and significant gaps within the profile to represent the ebb and flow of certain units.[12] There are too many carbine balls represented and therefore they cannot represent initial skirmishing from Croat light cavalry, and due to the lack of direction or source conclusiveness, we can merely assume such an assemblage represents an inconclusive withdrawal.[13] The left-hand assemblage, however, presents a profile for a mixed unit action due to the ratio of finds containing 76 percent gun furniture, conducive with large-scale cavalry charges upon a fixed infantry position.[14] The ratio of 14 balls per hectare is concurrent with the presence of a single unit possibly strung out in line. Associated cavalry material forms an eastwest oblong along the Via Regia, possibly representing an Imperial column of charge, dips and growths in density of material possibly marking a way by which we can measure the progress of the conflict.[15] By taking unit numbers

---

12 Meller, Friederich, Schürger, Alt and Nicklisch, 'Lützen', p.15.
13 Schurger, 'Lützen', p.4.
14 Meller, Friederich, Schürger, Alt and Nicklisch, 'Lützen', p.13.
15 ibid, p.14.

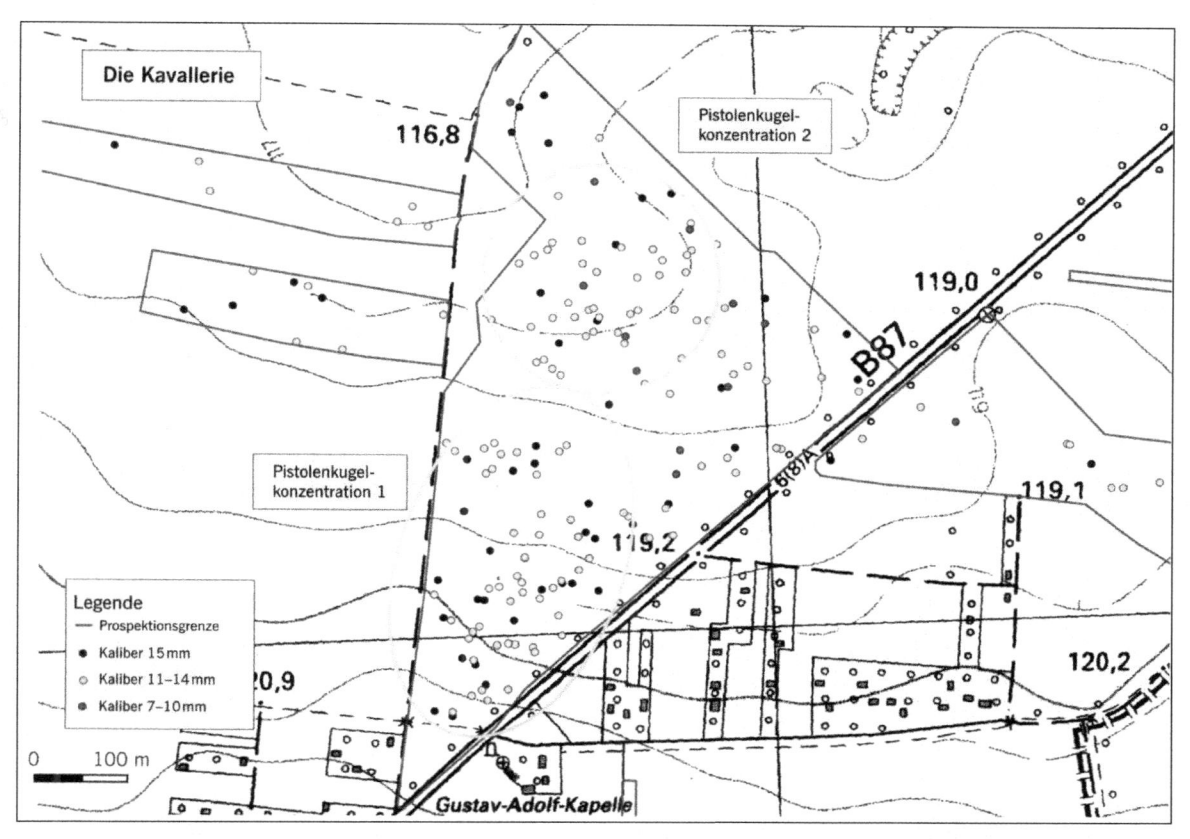

Figure 18: Further analysis of collection survey has further highlighted two more spheres of influence, in this case associated with initial gains by the Swedish cavalry, before being swept from their positions. Such analysis is an important lesson in artefact analysis as it is all too easy to see an artefact assemblage and assume that they were laid down at the same time, rather than contemporary continual movement across the site leaving varying overlaid deposits. (Schurger, 'Lützen', 2009, Fig.10, p.144)

and associated frontages, we can take the diameter of the assemblage (45m) and compare this to the understood localised order of battle; in this instance only one unit, that of Beygott, could fit into the space provided, providing a precedent for identifying possible unit formations within further archaeological studies, including recent work undertaken at Naseby.[16]

Finally, moving onto the right-hand assemblage, this has a far lower density than the previous two assemblages at 3.2 balls per hectare, suggesting a possible short rearguard action along a tube-like 185m long area.[17] Distribution is too low to uniquely identify troop movements, although a slight spike of Imperial carbine ball diameters is represented to the west of the assemblage, suggesting a possible Imperial counterattack late in the afternoon.[18]

Ultimately, Lützen remains the high water mark under which all subsequent 17th century battlefield studies must measure themselves, both theoretically and archaeologically. It takes away the idea that battlefield assemblages may merely be used to understand the starting positions of individual armies, and through effective interpretation provides a way by which the fighting in the course of a battle might be measured. Indeed, few if any battlefield studies have pushed their understanding of such assemblages

---

16   ibid.
17   Schurger, 'Lützen', pp.2-3; Meller, Friederich, Schürger, Alt and Nicklisch, 'Lützen', pp.16-17.
18   Meller, Friederich, Schürger, Alt and Nicklisch, 'Lützen', p.17.

THE ARTE MILITAIRE

to such a level of innovation, and it is hoped that the models and themes raised will continue to be built and propagated as further study continues.

11

Edgehill

Edgehill in Warwickshire was the site of the initial major battle of the War of the Three Kingdoms. A tactically distinct battle, with either side deploying in tactically clear-cut formations of Parliamentarian Dutch versus Royalist Swedish pattern models, allows us to create three distinctive spheres of influence, based on societal norms of precedence, around two sleeves of cavalry with a composite infantry centre.[1] Therefore, using De Gomme's battle map completed for Prince Rupert, corroborated with various written accounts, we can take an initial view that the area of Royalist deployment was on top of the Edgehill scarp, the extent of deployment restricted and therefore anchored by a pre-enclosure series of hedges.[2]

Using this estimated location, we can apply Ward's law of frontages to understand the approximate area to which archaeological activity provides potential. Therefore, an average ratio for the Royalist army of 14,000, with 10,000 foot covering a collective space of 2.4 miles, 2,500 cavalry 2.6 miles and 800–1,000 dragoons 300 yards, provides an average 5-mile stretch over which the Royalist army was deployed, the Parliamentarian army with similar numbers occupying a similar sphere of influence at the foot of the hill, all these measurements extending slightly further due to gaps between units.[3] Using these distances and figures provided by the historical order of battle, taking an assemblage of 300 shot over 800m on the Parliamentarian cavalry left, should by body create a distribution of 38 shot per 100m. This is represented through the fact that cavalry were likely to only fire one round before engaging or falling back. For a compact infantry centre with 530 bullets found within 100m, the proximity within 1m of approximately 41 musket balls, shows the propensity for drawn-out volley firefights, rather than protracted skirmishing.[4]

By undertaking small-scale landscape regression, using a combination of Pannett's 1970s landscape survey and Beighton's 1726 map depicting the events of the battle, we see the main action aligned along a northsouth tangent, the gap between the forces depicted as 1,000m, accounted for by the weapons of the period's short range, low rate of fire and inaccuracy, as well as the initial psychological hesitation among either force to engage.[5] However, both surveys' calculated frontages do not fit well within a partially enclosed landscape, merely truncating and making either force into a single linear grouping, thus misappropriating contemporary tactical innovation.[66] Indeed, using this model of deployment, the Parliamentarian cavalry has been forced forward, further than is deemed necessary, on a steep inclined knoll, where it will have little influence on the passage of battle. It also obstructs and overlaps the successful movement of any neighbouring unit and truncates the Parliamentarian right to the point where

---

1 Foard, *Battlefield*, p.123.
2 ibid, p.124.
3 ibid, p.125.
4 ibid, p.170.
5 ibid, pp.135, 137.
6 ibid.

THE ARTE MILITAIRE

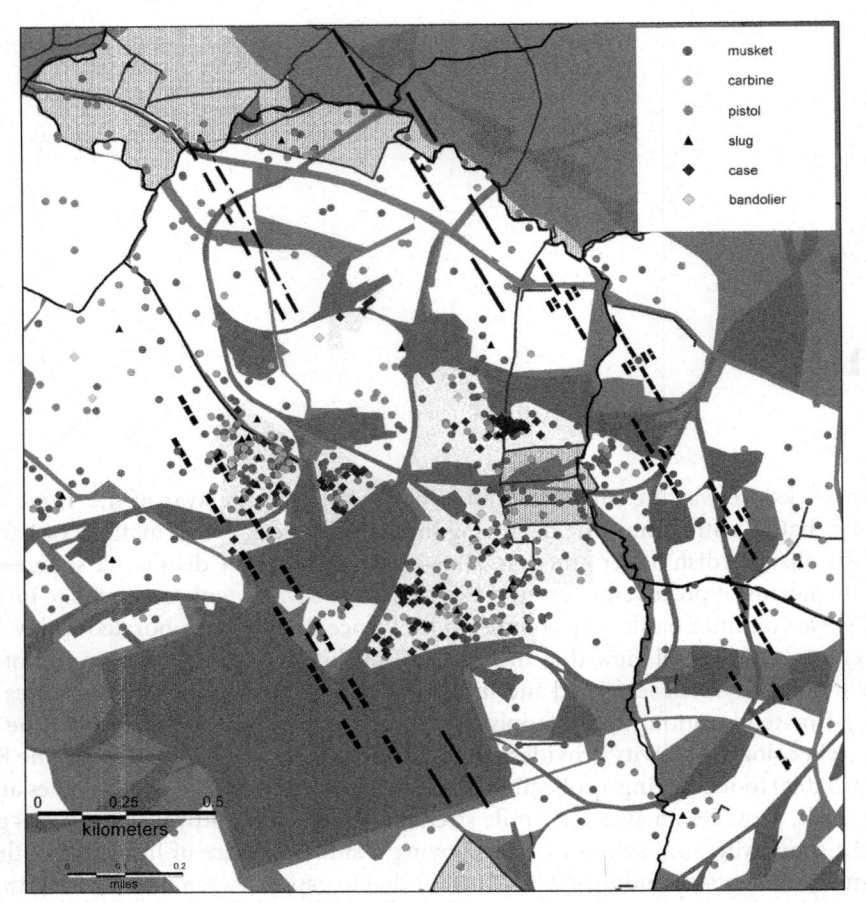

Figure 19: Refined deployment model from Young, Roberts and Tincey, showing assumed frontages (3ftx7ft, 300yds infantry; horse, 5ftx10ft, 10yds) and unit depths (eight ranks). This shows obvious Dutch vs Swedish tactics before tactical innovation could come to play during the early Wars of the Three Kingdoms. Reconstructed landscape and associated metal detector finds are overlaid, showing high-scale correlations being used as anchor points for varying troop types within the landscape. (Foard, 2012, Fig.7.22, p.125)

it is tactically unsound.[7] Foard, however, has dismissed these shortfalls, arguing that disparagement and anomalies within contemporary drill manuals means that the contemporary order of battle and therefore calculated frontage are not accurate; the lack of topographic evidence presented within written accounts of the battle, even accounting for tactical inexperience within the officer corps of the Parliamentarian army prior to initial conflict, might be used to explain this apparent anomaly.[8]

Moving onto the actual artefactual assemblage represented, clear differentiation between either side's firing lines can be discerned through the proliferation of 28.5 bore Parliamentarian and 12.5 bore Royalist shot. This suggests rather than the proliferation of similar calibre weapons by either side for easier logistical use, a number of foreign or indeed older pattern firearms were in circulation to place as many soldiers in the firing line as possible.[9] However, the similarities between the calibre of a number of carbine and musket balls means that often it is spatial analysis according to surviving accounts and plans that provides weight to archaeological interpretation. A contested assemblage in this instance represents

---

7   ibid.
8   ibid, pp.125-35.
9   ibid, p.156.

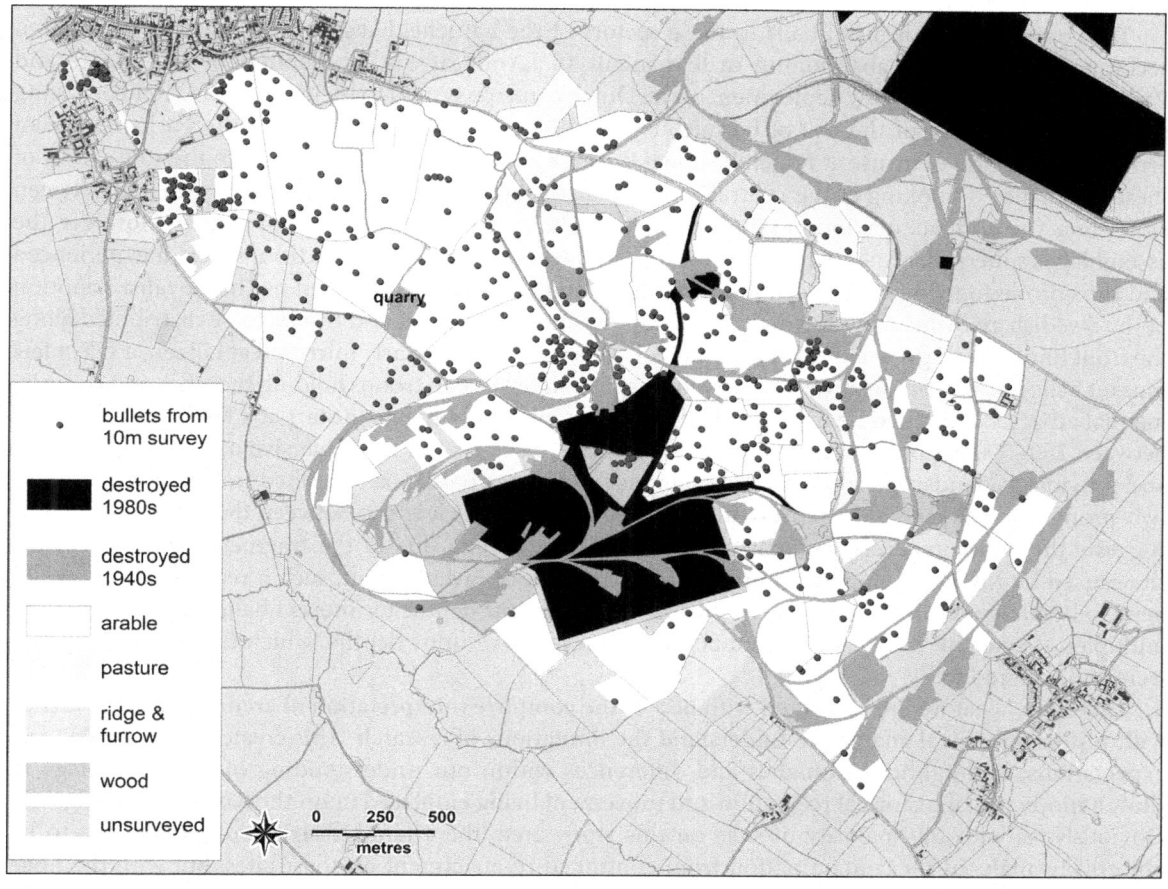

Figure 20: Associate metal detector survey, superimposed against reconstructed landscape and field boundaries. Red symbols=bullet finds; other symbols=other finds. Blacked out areas represent modern RLC/MOD depot. (Foard, 2012, Fig.7.14, p.122)

the Parliamentarian baggage guard, due to the risk of a stray spark from other firearms.[10] Equally, the high proportion of non-regulation slug bullets, represented within low density areas possibly identifying the position of pike blocks, suggests a widespread break from manual tradition, experience forcing musketeers fighting against armoured troops to use such a projectile for its stopping and expansive force, like a modern dum-dum bullet.[11]

However, while we can differentiate troop types on a part of the battlefield according to weapon type, the low frequency of survey merely provides a profile characterisation of the intensity of fighting, rather than highlighting individual units; their movements and events, musket volley scatters being equally mixed with hail shot.[12] Looking at such an assemblage, it is clear that either side of the central accumulation there are distinctive gaps, possibly representing sleeves of cavalry. Metal detector survey supports the drill book Swedish deployment, landscape analysis of existing pre-enclosure boundaries showing the extent to which such a unit spread, although the presence of a number of hedgerows rather than a clear plain supports de Gomme's view of integration of supporting dragoons.[13]

---
10   ibid, p.157.
11   ibid, pp.162, 165.
12   ibid, pp.156-57.
13   ibid, p.162.

THE ARTE MILITAIRE

The complete lack of pistol balls in these sectors of the battlefield suggests accuracy of the written account, Prince Rupert abandoning drill manuals in favour of the momentum of the charge and Parliament retaining the slow deployment of the Dutch caracole system to their detriment (Reid believing due to literal reading of the use of harquebusier by the original officer corps of the Parliamentarian army), a suggestion of its use at Edgehill shown through a series of linear groupings to the south-west of these anomalies.[14] Looking at the central main infantry battle line, we can see a 300-yard gap between either line, the ultimate maximum range to which a soldier was likely to hit his opponent. However, the assemblage's spherical, rather than deformed, profile suggests that many of the troops were inexperienced and thus prone to firing high and not hitting their target (a factor propagated by the Royalist adoption of the Swedish arrowhead deployment, requiring experienced officers and troops to be distributed along the front line, negating any experience available). This pattern is similarly mirrored at Lützen, a select few musket balls mushrooming at 100yds, possibly as a result of veteran troops holding their fire and going by manual advice.[15] However, clearly identified Royalist calibre shot seems to start at a far wider interval of between 250–500m, continuously holding its uniformity, suggesting the expansive use of firing by salvo and providing a landscape area to which manoeuvre by horn battle [as described in Chapter 6, this is a two-pronged attack] might be represented archaeologically.[16] A clear gap between the two lines possibly suggests the widespread engagement of push of pike, although due to the fragmentary nature of the site caused by MOD development and lack of correlation of investigation, such a representation would need to be further examined. However, by and large, frontage depths for musket balls are represented in multiples of six-eight, mirroring contemporary calculations of units depths, which this early in the war were still adhered to.[17]

Therefore, what we are presented with here is the complete interpretation of archaeological evidence with historiographical analysis to understand the limitations of research. This creates a set of rules and expectations, highlighting anomalies and differences within our understanding of the assemblage to show a modicum of historical recreation and movement being emplaced upon the battlefield at Edgehill. Obviously, as with the majority of sites on this study area, the artefact distribution always has to be objectively analysed for contamination from continued re-enactment on these sites, but with the huge yield of ordinance-based evidence available, a number of clear-cut conclusions can be made. Very rarely are the tactical systems used by either army so polarised and distinctive from one another, a major contributory factor to this investigation, so Edgehill provides a solid benchmark of how archaeology drill manual analyses can be applied to one another.

---

14 Foard, *Battlefield*, p.162; Reid, *All the King's Armies*, p.11.
15 Foard, *Battlefield Archaeology*, pp.161, 165; Schurger, "Lützen, p.24; Reid, *All the King's Armies*, p.21.
16 Foard, *Battlefield Archaeology*, p.170.
17 ibid.

12

Cheriton

The second battlefield we shall look at is Cheriton, in Hampshire, the site of Sir William Waller's crowning victories in April 1644, forcing the War of the Three Kingdoms to centre upon the Home Counties. Although not easily accessible at the time of writing, small-scale ongoing investigation of other Waller battlefields at Lansdown Hill and Roundway Down might be compared to see genuine model and artefact correlations associated with particular tactical styles.

As with Edgehill, Cheriton proves that Marix-Evans' belief about effective use of cavalry through alignment along existing plough lines to provide battlefield orientation seems to equally bode true here.[1] Based on a south-westnorth-east orientation, essential artefact differentiation between musket and pistol balls was essentially achieved. With topographic map regression, this has allowed the demarcation of five isolated bodies of troops linked to field boundaries for cover.[2]

Focus was therefore based around large-scale correlations, allowing a higher frequency of understanding to the individual soldier's zone of influence and understanding of the surrounding battlefield.[3] This can be understood through the psychological manifestation of particular boundaries and markers as a means by which soldiers may keep in formation and in focus within the chaos of battle, as well as a morale-booster, being used as a barricade to provide defensive enfilading fire against offensive cavalry, as can be suggested through associated horse pendants and pauldron (shoulder) armour plates.[4]

Thus we can provide effective, logical movement, which can be linked to first-hand accounts of the battle and further broken down into tactical models.[5] Therefore, in the metal detector survey we can see the Parliamentarian line, situated to the north, start an advance along a south-west incline, the vertical wide spread of musket shot possibly representing the Royalist fighting retreat towards the plateau and cover of Cheriton Wood, between zones I–III.[6] A clear defined gap between the Royalist firing line represented through the linear block in zones II–III and that of Parliament in zones IV–V possibly shows the site where re-evaluation may reveal more evidence for hand-to-hand fighting and push of pike.[7] An individual possible loading position of a musket block caught in a crossfire can be identified; its purpose identified through isolated cartridge and powder flask nozzle recoveries.[8]

---

1 Foard, *Battlefield Archaeology*, p.337; Battlefields Trust/English Heritage/National Monuments Record, *Cheriton* <http://www.battlefieldstrust.com/media/578.jpg> <http://www.battlefieldstrust.com/media/579.jpg> <http://www.battlefieldstrust.com/media/580.jpg> (accessed 24/07/2014, 14:55 p.m.); Steele, (2013), 'Ploughlines and orientation'.
2 Bonsall, James, 'The Study of Small Finds at the 1644 Battle of Cheriton', *Journal of Conflict Archaeology* vol.3, no.4 (Glasgow: Centre for Battlefield Archaeology, 2007) p.35.
3 ibid, p.37.
4 ibid, p.35.
5 ibid, p.45.
6 ibid, p.46.
7 ibid.
8 ibid, p.38.

THE ARTE MILITAIRE

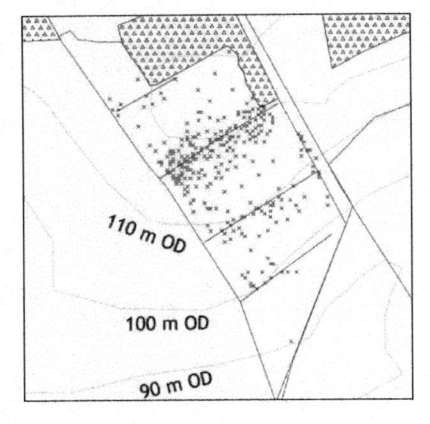

Figure 21: Metal detector survey of a section of Cheriton battlefield. At this frequency and with little interpretation, the spatial results mean little. Only through further investigation highlighting correlations and spheres of influence may an explanation for this artefact patterning start to be realised, as here showing the breakdown into five phases. (Bonsall, 2007, Fig.3/37)

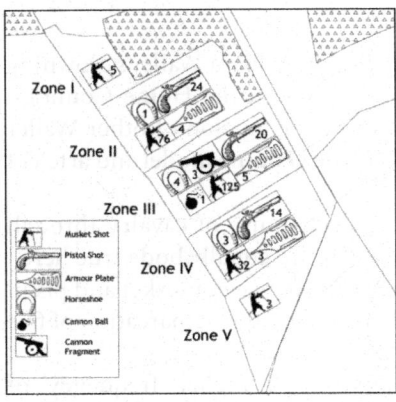

Figure 22: By further breaking down these correlations into their component types and uses, we can start to dictate the possible position of troop types and associated individuals upon the battlefield, as well as tactical trends, here represented through an English model Dutch deployment pattern. (Bonsall, 2007, Fig.4/39)

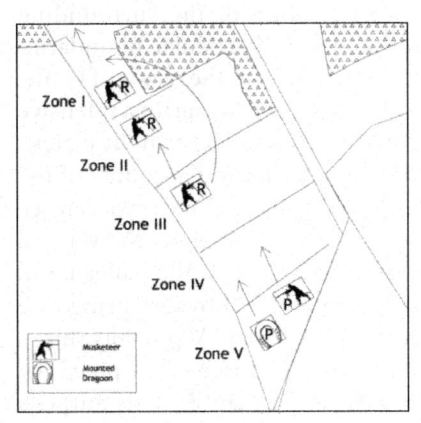

Figure 23: By further examining the artefact assemblage for characteristic abnormalities, forensically identifying individual weapon systems, we can start to track the movement of troops across the battlefield, as well as positively identify the historical events contributing to the archaeological record. (Bonsall, 2007, Fig.6/45)

While the survey is too low-frequency to positively identify individual groups of troops, looking at identified associated groupings of musket balls, particularly those associated with zones III–IV, many of the depths of these associations occur in multiples of six, proving that tactical mathematics was often adhered to. Isolated groupings within this gap may relate to the breaking of Bard's regiment in square by Hazelrige's cuirassier cavalry, as identified through a number of localised impacted musket balls possibly bouncing off armour. This is highlighted by three pieces of pauldron armour being discovered, the localised presence of cavalry being confirmed through the identification through the Gloucester 1644 keyhole typology of eight contemporary horseshoes.[9] Such evidence of heavy resistance may well have resulted in the support of Hazelrige's attack by a forlorn hope of dragoons, represented by a linear band of 58 small-calibre musket shot (carbine), to finally break up Bard's formation between zones IIV, forcing the Royalist line further back.[10]

While it is difficult with such a low frequency to break down individual fighting units and their formations, the metal detector survey and style that Bonsall has produced does provide the ability to quantify spatially the distribution of finds to an easily understandable standard. From this we may make the generalisation that both armies were roughly forming an English model deployment, formed of individual Swedish composite bodies within a checkerboard pattern for flexibility of strategy. Equally, the differentiation of the possibility of broadly identifying two individual units involved Bard's and Hazelrige's provides a further potential for anchoring the boundaries of the battlefield. However, we must remember that this merely constitutes a small strip of the entire battlefield; such an investigation provides the means to possibly predict archaeological potential throughout the rest of the site, while also providing a case study for archaeological movement to be measured against on other sites.

---

9   Bonsall, 'Battle of Cheriton', pp.41, 46; Adair, John, *Roundhead General: The Campaigns of Sir William Waller* (Stroud: Sutton Publishing, 1997).
10 Bonsall, 'Battle of Cheriton', pp.39, 46.

13

Naseby

Finally, we shall look at the battlefield of Naseby, the decisive battle of the Wars of the Three Kingdoms and the site that forced a turnaround in battlefield and historic landscape protection in Britain. Depictions of Naseby really border the change between military cartography in two individual maps created after the battle. Firstly we have de Gomme's depiction created for Prince Rupert many years after the battle, using the typical 18th century way of depicting battlefields as schematics, with units depicted as blocks and with little evidence of movement or indeed terrain obstacles, merely represented through arrows.[1]

However, the more famous depiction is Robert Streeter's map from Sprigge's history of the New Model Army, *Anglia Rediviva,* published in 1647. This represents both armies in profile, with stylistic representation of the surrounding landscapes taken from notes and forms of battle applied at the time by Sergeant-Major-General Phillip Skippon on 11 June 1645 and corresponding memoranda from his Royalist counterpart, Sir Jacob Astley.[2]

However with little to no representation of the actual terrain on the ground, idealised formations, erratic scale and little detail provided to the Royalist army, it is clear that such a source needs a reinterpretation, rather than be taken at face value.[3] We can tell that the choice of ground might have been prompted by lessons learnt at Marston Moor the previous summer; fought on open landscape with little cover, it meant Parliament was able to turn the flanks of the Royalist positions.[4] Indeed, Streeter and Victorian antiquary Carlyle (who performed small-scale excavations on the battlefield) believed that there was no evidence for the New Model Army forming on the tactical high ground of Closter Hill with its slopes covered by the Sulby Hedges this position intersects the main road, with streams dividing any climb but rather at the bottom of the slope, in the valley bottom, which allows a further advance of dragoon forlorn hopes along the hedges to the Royalist positions, despite poor drainage, high agricultural land and a series of rabbit warrens breaking up any considerable advance from the Parliamentarian right.[5] What might be clearer is that a combination of the two systems were employed, the Parliamentarian line placed on an incline, the left moved forward to allow the maximum range of fire to be employed by Okey's Dragoons, the Parliament right remaining on the hill top, for ease of movement and bolstering of weak points within the line.[6] This forced a Royalist withdrawal to the rear of the hill, Streeter depicting their left as squashed against the outer limits of Clipston village. This is not due to poor deployment, but merely because Streeter has tried to place every unit within the limited space of the page, thus truncating the accurate scale available, while heightening the prestige of the New Model Army by depicting their right

---

1 Foard, *Naseby*, p.17.
2 ibid.
3 ibid.
4 ibid, p.21.
5 ibid, pp.21, 224, 229.
6 ibid.

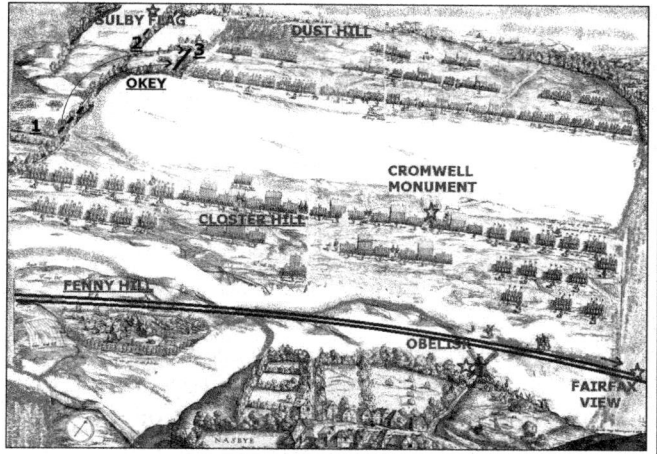

Figure 24: Robert Streeter, *Anglia Rediviva*, 1647, depiction of the Battle of Naseby, with a large Parliamentarian subjectivity, with major modern landmarks and focal points of fighting superimposed upon the image. (Steele, 2009, http://ecwbattles.files.wordpress.com/2009/07/streeters-naseby-adjusted.jpg, DOI: http://ecwbattles.files.wordpress.com/2009/07/streeters-naseby-adjusted.jpg, accessed 20/08/14, 14:06)

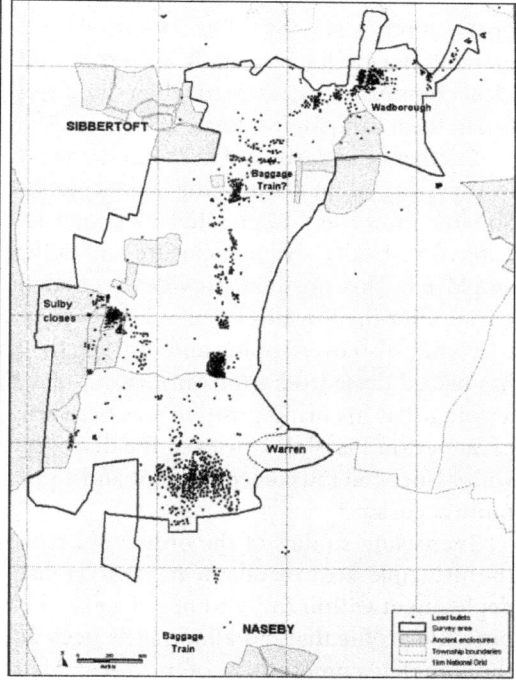

Figure 25: Metal detector survey of the Naseby battlefield, superimposed upon historic landscape, the elongated nature of the survey showing the fighting withdrawal and eventual collapse of discipline within the Royalist army. (Foard, 1995, amended Marix-Evans et al., 2002, in Foard, 2008, Fig.7/284)

flank as overextending that of the Royalists to make up for this cartographical flaw.[7]

However this does not mean there was ample space on the battlefield, as the musket ball assemblage from the valley bottom shows that there is a clear 2,000ft linear collection, rather than the calculated 2,850ft frontage suggested by recorded orders of battle, showing units combining together due to truncation from the bad landscape features on the right of the field, forcing the typical 36ft spacing between troops to be abandoned.[8] Other explanations for the abandonment of this drill book manoeuvre have included desertion and disease rates increasing after the siege of Leicester, the New Model Army's previous muster numbering 7,000 infantry, falling by 1,700 to 5,300 men.[9] Distinctive gaps with sparse representation of ordinance either side of this grouping may suggest the relative position of cavalry, although directly relatable identifiers are not discernible.[10] However, small-calibre musket balls, presumably identified as being fired from carbines, have been found along a 2,000ft stretch left of the Sulby Hedges at the valley bottom. This suggests, as 20ft was the recommended distance between divisions, that any likely cavalry evidence would be found 20ft in front of this grouping.[11] For the right wing, the optimal frontage for the other half of calculated cavalry would be 4,000ft, although a 700ft gap between associated pistol ball scatters and a rabbit warren limits our current knowledge of Parliamentarian cavalry numbers and

---
7 ibid, p.232.
8 ibid, p.241.
9 ibid.
10 ibid.
11 ibid.

distribution at Naseby.[12] Differing frontages throughout the Parliamentarian lines clearly suggest that manuals may well have simply been regarded as guidelines to which military formations would adhere in ideal circumstances, adapted when the surrounding terrain was inadequate, their use merely as the basis for an ideal campaign system.[13]

Further quandaries are raised as to the positioning of Okey's Dragoons during the battle, the majority of surviving accounts limiting their position to a simple skirmish line barriered by the Sulby Hedges. Streeter, however, despite his inadequacies, places Okey's Dragoons crossing the barrier between Lankyford Hedge sheep enclosure and Sulby Hedges, even to the extent of further dragoon units being employed. This position provides a good firing position across Broadmoor and the assumed line of advance for the Royalist cavalry. However, tactically it is too near to the Parliamentarian line to be of any use, while also overlapping and limiting the use of Parliamentarian cavalry, thus suggesting that Streeter has placed these troops too far forward, due to lack of space.[14] This is further confused by Okey himself, arguing that his firing position was between Coate Green Pasture and Archwrong Close, on the border of Sibbertoft Parish.[15] However, the discovery of 80 musket balls directly between the two hedge system, with associated musket equipment and eight pewter bandolier tops, suggests Streeter's positioning is the more accurate.[16]

Increasing studies of the orders of battle for the New Model Army have led to the re-evaluation of the principle area of deployment previously investigated to understand the ability to allow effective deployment within the confines of a pre-enclosed landscape. This is an area providing a mathematically provable profile that has all too little been addressed within conflict archaeology, its realisation proving the complete enmeshment of historical archaeology. Evidence gained from recent re-enactments on the site has suggested mean evidence of spacing 2ft8in for pike and 3ft4in for musket agreeing fully with Ward's rule for spacing (page 29). This, coupled with the research of David Blackmore, using army pay records, has created an alternative breakdown of the makeup of the New Model Army:

Regiment	Pre-Naseby	Regiment	Pre-Naseby
Fairfax's	1,397	Skippon's	1,533
Waller's	560	Hammond's	788
Pride's	1,151	Montagu's	1,025
Pickering's	1,126	Rainsboro's	888
Lloyd's	93	Ingoldsby's	63

Singleton (2014) believes such numbers relay the presence of multiple battalions in the field on the day of battle. Such a tactical movement would provide a wider front upon which the Royalists were forced to engage. Marix-Evans thus provides the following:[17]

---

12 ibid.
13 ibid, p.242.
14 ibid, p.246.
15 ibid.
16 ibid, p.247.
17 Marix-Evans, Martin (2013), 'New Model Army Lists', email, 31 August 2013; Blackmore, David, 'Counting the New Model Army', *Civil War Times*, No. 58, (Leigh-on-Sea: Partizan Press, 2003) p.3 <http://djblackmore.wordpress.com/articles-2/counting-the-new-model-army-2/> (accessed 28/08/14, 23:45 p.m.).

Regiment	Pike (men)	Shot (men)	Frontage Pike (metres)	Frontage Shot (metres)	Regt. Frontage (metres)
Skippon's	508	1,030	69	170	239
Waller's	185	375	25	62	87
Pickering's	372	754	50	125	175
Montagu's	338	687	46	113	159
Fairfax's	461	936	62	155	217
Front Row totals	1,863	3,783	252	625	877
Pride's	380	771	51	127	179
Lloyd's	31	62	4	10	14
Hammond's	260	528	35	87	122
Rainsboro's	293	595	40	98	138
Ingoldsby's	21	42	3	7	10

What is clear from looking at the metal detector survey undertaken by Foard of the battlefield area (Fig.25), is the site where he indicates the majority of fighting being undertaken would be hard-pressed to contain the first-line frontage of the New Model Army. Differing explanations have been given for this reasoning. On the one hand, Marix-Evans believes that such a small frontage could be achieved through combining these multiple bodies into a single body, removing the gaps for ease of movement and thus forming a composite hedgehog, supporting the composition of high-density metal detector findings found at the foot of Broadmoor (Fig.25).[18] We know that the New Model Army had only been engaged as a fighting body in siege warfare prior to Naseby; thus an ideal campaign deployment decided upon by the commanding officer would not be realised, accounting for the initial general withdrawal and tactical inexperience compared to norms of the time. Equally, could, as we see with spread of shot not correlating with associated numbers at Edgehill, there be the possibility of lack of space possibly allowing the movement of troops forward, as the line became truncated and made best use of the amount of space available, or indeed spreading outwards beyond the spread of the initial survey as this formation gradually broke up to accommodate the strategic situation?[19]

Indeed, the records presented here do not even represent the spread of cavalry or artillery on the battlefield, arguing that with manual science becoming further understood and applied, our understanding of the landscape of Naseby is simply too small to encapsulate the numbers involved in such a battle, thus arguing the need for continued historiographical-landscape archaeological integration to revolutionise interpretation on this site. Investigations such as these argue the continued need for document analysis within such battlefield studies. It equally supports the role experimental archaeology and re-enactment can support academic battlefield studies.

Furthermore, the mysterious second body is identified by an isolated accumulation of 16 musket balls directly to the right of Okey's main position, suggesting Fairfax was pushing harder on the Royalist right than has previously been suggested.[20] Initial skirmishes and clashes between either side can be identified by looking at sites near the field's edge connecting to original road lines. In this case, the road leading up the west of the Broadmoor ridgeline, along Gibbs Hill, has an isolated grouping of several musket balls,

---

18 Marix-Evans, 'New Model Army Lists'.
19 Marix-Evans, Martin, *Naseby 1645: The Triumph of the New Model Army*, Campaign 185 (Oxford: Osprey Publishing, 2007) pp.38-42.
20 Foard, *Naseby*, p.247.

providing us with the image that the Royalist deployment was not enacted in an easy peaceable action, their tactical stance continually harried in a running battle.[21]

Looking towards the infantry centre, a scatter of 40 musket balls across Broadmoor Slope suggests further running engagements pushing towards the Royalist centre as the New Model Army advanced from skirmishing forlorn hopes, although the low frequency of investigation means it is difficult to tell whether this was achieved in tandem or piecemeal.[22] The summit of Broadmoor Hill, however, completely lacks any archaeological material, suggesting that both lines engaged in hand-to-hand combat before the Royalist line pulled back 300ft to its second stop line, represented through a dense scatter along the hill top.[23]

Investigation frequency is too low to identify individual unit spacing. But by breaking down directly related accumulations of musket balls, the ability to identify the space and extent occupied on a brigade-divisional level, and thus a generalised banding, whereupon the broad position of a regiment was placed, allows the beginnings of direct predictive modelling with historiographical analysis using Streeter's distribution and Skippon's order of battle to provide absolute interpretation.[24] Thus we must look to accounts to understand the varying positioning of particular troops at different times in the battle, as well as what troops still survived. Thus a gap, just before the brow of the hill and the site of the Royalist baggage train, roughly similar in dimension to those represented previously, might identify the position of Langdale's troop of horse covering the Royalist retreat. Equally, a closely compact assemblage of musket balls on the rear slope of Broadmoor between Chapel Close and Pierce's Quick Close might show the position of the Royalist baggage guards.[25]

A further way of identifying possible sites of regimental engagements and indeed last stands, such as witnessed by Rupert's Bluecoat regiment, can be through correlations of identified, both traditionally and archaeologically, sites of mass graves. Thus, on the assumed position of the Parliamentarian left flank, where Skippon's Brigades are supposed to have been sited, Fitzgerald discovered in the 1850s the site of a small massed grave, a factor that should be keyed into surrounding scatters of musket balls, associated frontage and numbers of troops.[26] A linear gap within this assemblage possibly relates to cavalry among these units, showing the final moments of organisation within the Royalist army, before routing northwards towards Sibbertoft.[27] A series of gradually diminishing linear correlations of musket balls running towards the summit of Broadmoor Hill (a factor more clearly seen in the following study of the Battle of Lostwithiel), these accumulations start radiating towards period hedge lines and sunken lanes, disordered troops routing towards the areas of the greatest cover.[28] Certainly by the time we reach the north-west side of Clipston Parrish and Wadborough Hill, an assemblage of over 130 musket balls, with no clear alignment, delineation or order just mixed in together shows the final stand of the Royalist army, the possible resting place of Rupert's own regiment and the total collapse of drill book etiquette and military science.[29] A further study would do good to take such examples to build a characterisation and model upon crowd dynamics and representation of the battlefield route within the archaeological record, a subject matter that is likely to produce more artefactual material and less historic material than most current battlefield studies.

Naseby does not present a coherently accurate representation of the archaeological yield and nature of finds, due to varying survey techniques. However, it does clearly show a battle late in the war that ultimately does away with the vagaries of uniform drill, in favour of a hybrid, more effective

---
21 ibid, p.226.
22 ibid, p.251.
23 ibid, p.263.
24 ibid, p.229.
25 ibid, p.278.
26 ibid, p.263.
27 ibid, p.275.
28 ibid.
29 ibid, p.279.

characterisation according to the contemporary tactical limits, a subject deserving of its own research and modelling. While we can obviously make informed generalisations according to particular accumulations that mirror our supposed understanding of tactical formations according to distances and profile, our modelling system prepares us in no way for the unchoreographed level of movement associated with an army routing from the field. In this sense, with such a high level of artefacts and low-level survey, there is little spatial analysis we can provide. However, at a lower level is this made any easier?

14

Original Research

Due to the often continuing nature of, or indeed lack of, information retained or recorded by systematic mandatory archaeological surveys ahead of alteration to public amenities, the availability of survey information is often lacking, where it has merely focused upon conservation concerns rather than the site as a centre for conflict. Thus, while there is a plethora of information on sites such as Braddock Down, Lansdown Hill, Roundway Down, Nantwich or indeed sites pre- and post-dating our time range, there is often not an interest or funding base to make this material available to the public and provide a profit, hence why they have not largely been included here.

Therefore, original analysis within this work shall focus briefly upon an independent survey. We shall focus on Tywardreath, situated on the western flank of the Lostwithiel battlefield in Cornwall, the site of a further repression of the Parliamentarian army of the Earl of Essex from taking the West Country in 1644, fought as a running battle. The site suffers from the issue that due to differing, limited and on occasion unprofessional survey methods, any material lacks clarity within spatial organisation of artefacts through the exclusion of necessary grid references and scales. A wider database with said diagrammatical spatial information is owned by the researcher, although the inability for further research and access from outside means that any survey schematics provide very little information, other than showing the scale of the survey data in general. On the one hand, it is understandable that a number of this series of data is excluded from these documents purely for a wish to limit the impact of possible illegal metal detecting, thus acting as an active conservation concern, which should be commended, but the above statements merely act as minor limitations upon further advancing this data set.

15

Tywardreath/Lostwithiel

So firstly let us look at Tywardreath. The Earl of Essex's 1644 Lostwithiel campaign was not fought as a single engagement, but rather as a running set of dwindling skirmishes, Royalist ascendancy assured in Cornwall due to a lack of support and supplies by local Parliamentarians.[1] Retreating to the west of the main Lostwithiel battlefields, Tywardreath to Golant acted as a stop line for Essex's withdrawing army, his position reinforced by the earthworks of Castle Dore against a possible rearguard action enacted by 500 of the King's Lifeguard of Horse.[2]

The sector which this survey covers was assaulted by the forces of Grenville, Bassett, Northampton and Appleyard against Parliamentarians Robarte, Reynolds and Essex's regiments of foot.[3] The initial engagement occurred when, at 4:00 p.m. on 31 August 1644, Essex ordered a counter-attack with 200 of Leighton's Plymouth horse, 100 commanded shot and Essex's own regiment, forcing a wedge through the Royalist left, although this was countered by the King's Lifeguard.[4] With Goring supporting the Royalist position with a further 2,000 horse, Essex fainted towards Castle Dore, but was stalled by Northampton, forcing his further forces into a general rout to the waiting boats and to withdraw.[5] There is a clear correlation between historical and archaeological source material in that this was a very unusual battle for the 17th century, relying more upon the best use of cover and fast movement, highlighting possible evidence still to be recovered of large-scale hand-to-hand fighting, the centre of these field enclosures further highlighting the ferocity and chaos of this kind of warfare.[6] With such a heavily enclosed landscape, therefore, ease of movement depended upon possession of roads, a factor that needs further analysis to find correlations at such sites as we have seen with Okey's Dragoons at Naseby with the Sulby Hedges, and also the small-scale evidence for Cheriton, all located along similar confluences of landscape features.[7] Therefore, we can surmise the possibility of bodies of dismounted dragoons and commanded shot being present, highlighted through long linear accumulations of multiples of three, made up of musket furniture, buckles, the possibility of broken weaponry, buttons and limited horse-related artefacts. Even shattered or lost gunflints are represented, with the growth and spread of snaphance/doglock/flintlock weaponry, showing the move towards linear and small-scale uniform warfare. Thus we need to be looking to the open landscape of local agricultural fields for accumulations of finds associated with large formed bodies of troops, allowing easier access of movement towards the sea; current metal

---

1 Ede-Borrett, Stephen, *Lostwithiel 1644: The Campaign and the Battles* (Farnham: The Pike and Shot Society, 2004) p.41.
2 ibid.
3 ibid, p.46.
4 ibid, p.43.
5 ibid.
6 Ferguson, Natasha, 'CSI Cornwall: Investigating a battlefield', *The Searcher*, October 2009 (Greenlight Press, 2009) p.28.
7 Ferguson, Natasha, Tywardreath Artefact & Distribution Analysis Report <http://archive.today/FDyB5> (accessed 21/05/2014, 13:01 p.m.).

THE ARTE MILITAIRE

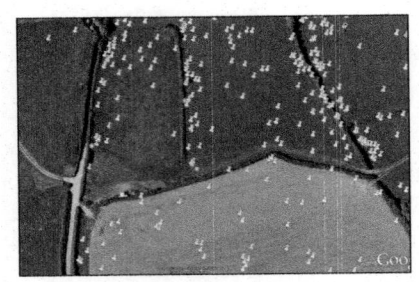

Figure 26: Metal detector survey of Tywardreath battlefield. The low frequency of survey, coupled with lack of clear referencing features, while being for archaeological security of the site, creates difficulty in outside study and understanding. However, series of correlated lines adhering to hedge lines show the increasing tactical use of the landscape. (Ferguson, 2010, Fig.5)

detector survey results orientate on a north-westsouth-east orientation.[8]

Certainly round the Castle Dore area, an erratic correlation can be seen orientated westwards, with a more composite accumulation positioned to the east, presumably representing Royalist forces funnelling Parliamentarian troops towards the sea, an indentation in this correlation around St Austell Hill possibly representing a flanking counter-attack.[9] Such variables of constriction, coupled with morale and assumed time of battle, linked with the number of volleys fired, could certainly be modelled using Campillo's system, to see what variables allow for such a distribution. Looking at the width and depth of the assumed Royalist assemblage, eight deep by twelve wide, is very much concurrent with Bariffe's model for unit deployment. This argues the point that the basis for military organisation was retained, mere preference and adaptation to wider adoption of firearms being used.[10] Equally, there is a clear gap midway across the assemblage, presenting the possibility of push of pike occurring here, further surveying possibly revealing evidence of broken weaponry concurrent with such activities. Looking at the evidence itself, an assemblage of 485 provenanced finds were identified, including 392 musket balls (81 percent), 46 pistol balls (9 percent), 36 carbine balls (7 percent) and two slugs (0.7 percent), roughly reflecting a rise in the ratio of musket to pike and also supporting extensive commanded shot units.[11] Bore standardisation throughout the assemblage is not reflected, with individual ball weight ranging 0.11.5oz, a factor that is clearly identified by the extensive evidence of tooth marks, the musketeer being forced to chew the ball in order for it to fit down the barrel.[12]

However, this could just as easily be a means of truncating suggested loading procedures in the majority of contemporary drill manuals by holding the bullet in the mouth before loading, showing the growth of learning and innovation amongst veteran soldiers.[13] Further drill development can be seen through a number of musket balls retaining their moulding sprue, allowing a waxed paper wadding cartridge to be wrapped around the bullet, thus increasing the speed of loading and uncomplicating the postures needed to undertake it.[14] Ferguson believes that as this only occurs in one part of the field, along with the rate of movement associated with this battle, that this may represent the presence of at least one body of cavalry.[15] However, with the largely enclosed nature of the surrounding landscape, coupled with the majority of the battle occurring across the plough line, the ability for cavalry to be put to good use is highly lacking.[16]

---

8 ibid.
9 Ferguson, Natasha, "CSI Cornwall: Investigating a battlefield" *The Searcher* October 2009 (Greenlight Press, 2009) p.28
10 Bariffe, *Military discipline*, pp.12-15.
11 Ferguson, *Metal detecting*, p.165.
12 ibid, p.165; Ferguson, 'CSI Cornwall', p.28; Sivilich, 'Musket Ball', p.89.
13 Ferguson, 'CSI Cornwall', p.28.
14 Ferguson, *Metal detecting*, p.168.
15 ibid, pp.165, 168.
16 Steele, 'Ploughlines and orientation'.

Therefore, what we are presented with at Tywardreath is a site that, rather than presenting nothing at all due to mixed collection rationale and general spread, through small artefact analysis, landscape understanding and close inspection of minor groupings within the main survey, can reveal a lot previously unknown about the battle, enough to provide a modicum of protection. As we shall further see, looking at this site in a wider survey and context has the ability to connect and create a landscape of conflict not previously experienced in the Early Modern Age.

16

Further Heritage Potential

So how could such a study further itself and provide heritage potential? Ultimately, looking at military manuals in such a way leads our understanding to ask how differing armaments, fortresses within the landscape and movements of troops might be manifest within the archaeological record and whether our historical understanding of these subjects necessarily reflects the reality. Certainly, the potential is there to go back to medieval battlefields and ask the same questions as have been asked here, using much deeper reading of tactical treaties and verse to gain a wider understanding.

Equally, we could apply the same questions to the later Age of Enlightenment and the wars of Napoleon to see how this was manifest, the only reason it was not addressed here merely due to lack of time and limited source material to work from. Cavalry combat will have certainly changed little in this time period, the main difference being represented through more thorough, denser, longer linear characterisation of bullet assemblages parallel to each other.

A gap might be identified between these two assemblages, representing the rare occurrence of bayonet charges or limited skirmishing, the former if occurring more frequently than thought, showing the use of the bayonet is more than presented within historical documentation.[1] Equally, representation of a square or the limited associations of artefacts may suggest a revision of the success of infantry square. Further investigation may be made outside of this study into subject areas such as the modelling and characterisation of skirmishing troops, the route or indeed the increasing of survey rationale and frequency to allow an absolute, positive identification of troop positions.[2]

On a wider tangent, by using theories used then just as now, such as the theory of Tranter's rule of marching distances, coupled with those suggested as common practice throughout major military manuals, we can expand military tactical thought as a choreographic model beyond the battlefield.[3] Soldiers, in order to reach the battlefield, are required to approach it by the route that provides the quickest, yet most strategically sound effect to their campaign. Coupling together our knowledge of the fatigue and nature of soldiers, the conditions they faced, plus their associated gains for the military campaign facing them, with recommended contemporary marching distances brought to an average through Tranter's variations along with established military maps such as Roy's survey of the Highlands or the Ordinance Survey maps, we could extend the sphere of influence of the battlefield. The battle zone defines the moving reality of investigation, with the wider context of troop movements within the surrounding landscape, allowing a historio-archaeological watching brief to be considered in further development along major military road systems and landscapes (*Naismith's Rule of Walking*, 2008).[4] Further integration through

---

1   Griffith, Paddy, *Forward into battle: fighting tactics from Waterloo to the near future* (California: Presidio, 1990) pp.27-28.
2   ibid, p.51.
3   Naismith's Rule of Walking <http://www.bbc.co.uk/dna/place-london/plain/A29848558> (accessed 25/08/2014, 08:15 a.m.).
4   ibid.

designation of marching camps and possible small-scale defences being discovered has the ability to connect and share across a broad knowledge base and thus connect investigation through a common methodology with similar conflict studies into one over-branching knowledge base and landscape context. Ultimately, the study base, to which the study of the reality of military manuals is endless, has many facets that need to be continually explored.

17

Defensive Modelling

When studying defensive landscapes, we have to understand their positioning and character according to the tactical needs of the locality and the overall grand strategy dictating this site is defended. Of course a defensive site will very rarely be ideal; the military engineer on the ground making best use of what is available to them. He is forced to compromise and supplement the landscape with manufactured terrain features in the form of ramparts, ditches, firing positions, isolated fortlets and defensive architecture designed to deflect incoming fire and provide the safest existence and resource yield possible under trying circumstances.

When looking at the predictive modelling of defensive works, our job becomes equally difficult, as there has to be a clear match between the topographical landscape and the presentation within the manual. While we would all like to have an extensive, inclusive set of fortifications to rival those of Newark, the continuing expansion of urban sprawl means that such a study will continually diminish as evidence is lost.

The archaeology of sieges is a relatively new focus of conflict archaeology. During the Wars of the Three Kingdoms, Britain was subjected to 242 individual sieges, 223 during the first war and 19 during the second, which we can reduce to 189 due to consecutive besieging of a number of these sites.[1] Barratt provides the statistics that sieges were responsible for at least 21,000 confirmed casualties during the war, making up 21 percent of the total Royalist casualties and 31 percent of Parliamentarian (possibly representing the relative inexperience compared to the Royalist officer corps at the beginning of the war), with sieges dictated far more by tactical progress than field battles.[2]

In that case, we should be providing just as much in regard to the topographical profile within conflict archaeology and understanding of the Wars of the Three Kingdoms, if indeed it proved such a contributory factor, which is certainly mirrored in books by Ward and Elton. We do have to provide some limitations, however; such a study can only really understand the extent of defensive planning, rather than individual actions within a siege. Just like our previously mentioned cavalry actions, sieges were often small areas of land continuously fought over until a practicable breach could be appropriated. As such, while major weaknesses, focal points and breaches may be identified through widespread analysis of shot-spread and fall, it is likely to represent a composite association, rather than an individual action, and therefore would provide a subjective survey result. As a result, this work will merely focus upon the often ephemeral defensive earthworks such archaeological sites might retain, whether overtly, as in a standing earthwork, or covertly, such as remnants of previous earthworks being retained in street patterns, frequency of modern buildings and street frontages.

---

1 Foard, Morris, *English Battlefields*, p.127.
2 Barratt, John, *Sieges of the English Civil Wars* (Barnsley: Pen and Sword Military, 2009) p.1.

DEFENSIVE MODELLING

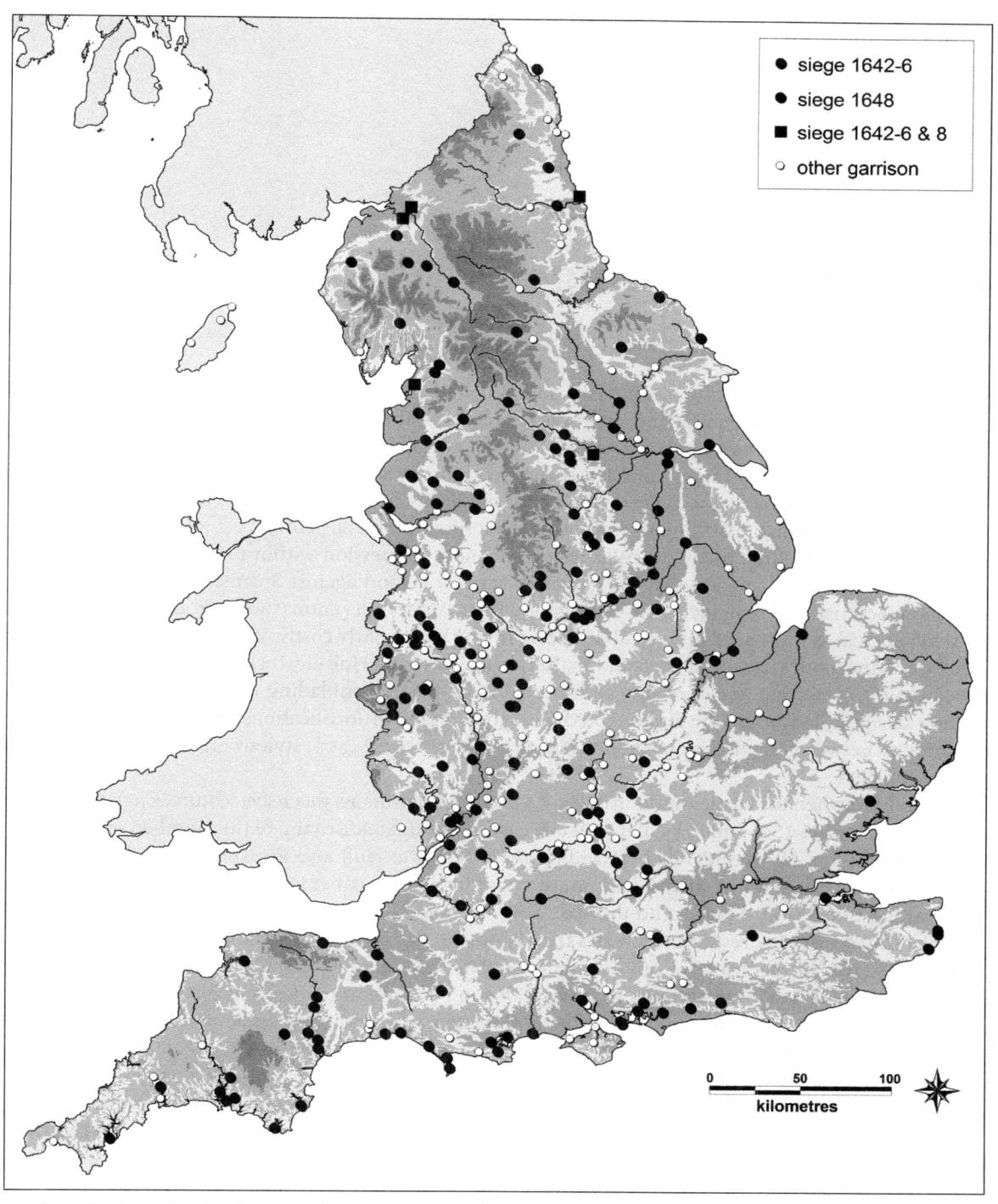

Figure 27: Map of scale of sieges in Britain during the War of the Three Kingdoms. (Foard et al., 2012, Fig.7.23, p.127)

18

Defensive Planning

What actually is the point of defence? Hill and Wileman characterise it as being broken down into three stages: economic, personal and interpersonal control of the relative local area dictating physical and psychological barriers against large-scale movement of troops within a strategic model. Indeed, it is this they believe that forces complex society within times of conflict to production, supply and defence, imparting hierarchy, social and ideological significance to particular areas (e.g. London, Oxford, Newark); its networking providing the means for nationhood to be sustained.[1]

A century of fractured ideology, coupled with economic recession within Britain prior to the Wars of the Three Kingdoms, meant that the ability to actively defend against Spanish, French, Dutch and, internally, Scottish and Irish incursion during the early to mid-17th century was seriously compromised, with ideological as well as technological division proving particularly costly. While the increasingly used Trace Italienne model, as seen at Portsmouth, Berwick, Plymouth, Hull etc. (using stone-clad fortification based upon intersecting angles of fire, with mutually supporting enfilading fire based on a low-profile bastion design), had briefly been attempted with the Henrician fortifications on the South coast, the turnaround between fortified innovation meant that many of these castle styles were obsolete before they were completed.[2]

In a period when the castle was increasingly a home, rather than a defensive feature, England quickly fell behind; Leland's 1543 Itinerary lists 500–600 castles throughout Britain; of this number, only 91 were in good condition, 30 were derelict (including the arsenals at Hull and Portsmouth) and 137 ruined. There was a broad trend of inland and South coast fortifications being in bad condition due to the diminishing threat from France, and those on the West and North coast in better condition due to the Catholic threat from the rest of Britain and the Continent.[3] By combining Leland with Camden's (1605) and Speed's (1611) itineraries, we can see that town defences were just as much in dire straits, requiring less than adequate 'make do and mend' applications to be made to the walls of Nottingham, Beverley, Shrewsbury, Leicester, Arundel and Pontefract.[4] A century of economic recession within Britain meant that a patched-up repair method was often the reality. Small updates to earlier lines of defence, such as at Leicester, Pembroke, Coventry, Hereford, Worcester and Northampton etc., provide a good starting place for defensive evolution within an urban sprawl environment.[5] While we consistently take the view that the increase in gunpowder weaponry mirrors the growth in size and elaboration of defensive works, their need within relatively poor countries such as Sweden and England mean that something man-made,

---

1 Hill, Paul, and Wileman, Julie, *Landscapes of War: The Archaeology of Aggression and Defence* (Oxford: Tempus, 2002) pp.51-52; Harrington, Peter, *English Civil War Archaeology* (London: B.T. Batsford, 2004) p.13.
2 Porter, *Destruction in the English Civil Wars*, pp.24; Harrington, *Archaeology*, p.38; Lawrence, *The Complete Soldier*, p.316.
3 Barratt, *Sieges*, p.2.
4 Harrington, *Archaeology*, pp.13-14, 38.
5 ibid, p.15.

DEFENSIVE PLANNING

Figure 28: Arguably the second best preserved set of 17th century town defences in Britain, behind Newark, the defences of Carmarthen designed by Captain Richard Steele extending a quarter mile further into the town, incorporating the castle and remains of Greyfriars Monastery, are a lesson in point regarding the often textbook nature of defences of this period. Arguably comparable to those outworks seen at Bristol, Gloucester, Worcester and across the Western Association, its redoubt retains its 90° angle of fire to the town walls, with a clear magazine depression in its centre. As for the remaining bulwarks, although largely cut away during the creation of the police station, local shops and amenities, the remnants of a ravelin and nature of the encircling ditch can still be discerned. (Jarvis and Elson, 2016)

easily constructed and taken down afterwards, primitive but effective, was the order of the day.[6]

While Britain might have been relatively sheltered from the religious wars of the Continent, the diffusion of military ideas and writings certainly weren't, as evidenced by the use of foreign and archaic terms for these defensive systems, alien to the English language.[7] Thus the wide adoption of Dutch model fortifications in the form of sconces, bastions and redoubts, ravelins, glacis, rampier and earthern ramparts.[8]

The likes of Whitehorne (1560), Digges (1588), Ive (1589) and Papillon (1645) created models around which effective siegework could be enacted, which can be applied to contemporary works of the period.[9] Add to this the idea that a large number of the officer corps fighting within Britain at the time of the Wars of the Three Kingdoms had blooded their swords in the wars of the Continent (e.g. Waller, Skippon, Hopton, Gage, de Gomme) and it argues the point that a number of widely publicised sieges and their defences of the period (Breda, Hertogenbosch, Maastricht and Ostend) were simply transplanted to Britain and thus can be seen replicated at sites such as Basing House, Oxford and London.[10]

Therefore, in order to understand how much we can rely upon manuals as a means of retracing

---

6 Courtney, Paul, 'The Archaeology of the early-modern siege', in Freeman, Peter W.M., and Pollard, Tony, *Fields of Conflict: Progress and Prospect in Battlefield Archaeology*, BAR International Series 958 (Oxford: Archaeopress, 2001) p.105; Foard, Glenn, 'The Archaeology of attack: battles and sieges of the English Civil War', in Freeman and Pollard, *Fields of Conflict*, p.98.
7 Lawrence, *The Complete Soldier*, p.314.
8 ibid, pp.320-27.
9 ibid, pp.327-34.
10 Lawrence, *The Complete Soldier*, pp.334, 362; Harrington, Peter, *English Civil War Fortifications 1642-51* (Oxford: Osprey Publishing, 2003) pp.8, 17; Wiggins, Kenneth, *Anatomy of A Siege: King John's Castle Limerick, 1642* (Martlesham: The Boydell Press, 2001) p.57.

THE ARTE MILITAIRE

Figure 29: 'The Siege of Ostend', John Blaeu, 1641, showing the intricacy and nature of out and earthworks erected around the city.

defensive circuits, we have to equally rely upon a comparative analysis of the survival of Continental defences to British ones, as much as upon contemporary manuals.

Landscape

Rather than simply relying upon drill manuals and maps as a means of recovering potentially lost defensive structures, in this instance we have to actually use the landscape and built remains as a starting point and fixed position to fit the often generalised plans provided by military writers. This can prove problematic and ephemeral, but by focusing on a range of themes and trends, we can create a fixed position within the landscape upon which we can model contemporary defences. This can be achieved through using building surveys, original schematics overlaid onto original street patterns for enfilading angles to fields of fire, evidence of reuse of masonry previously intended for other purposes, evidence of repair or deliberate destruction, or indeed simply field walking and identifying period lumps and bumps which aerially can be interpreted as original features. Equally, through comparative analysis to similar properties, buildings and structures, particular regions of influence, inspiration and style can be highlighted and mapped.

20

Primary Source Material

Defensive planning in the outset requires a huge amount of administration, development, design collaboration and analysis to be undertaken before it can take on the built form. Therefore, the form of documentation, diary entries, maps, accounts and occasionally military manuals prove extremely important in focusing our initial studies. Certainly at a site such as Basing House, with its plethora of individuals such as Inigo Jones and Wenceslaus Hollar being members of the garrison and likely designing a range of defences, it is more than likely by looking at further illustrations and designs undertaken subsequently to the siege, that a number of similarities would be apparent.[1]

Diary entries from the likes of Hugh Peters, revealing that the original width of the ditches surrounding the house were 1m wide, and Nehemiah Wharton, describing the extensive bulwarks to the north-east of Fort Royal sconce at Worcester, provide initial interpretations to what the individual is likely to find represented upon excavation, in this case a series of rubble and chalk cores, with limited tip lines from settling, reinforced with timber revetting and turf binding.[2]

They also often link non-surviving features to surrounding names and landmarks, important for orientating and highlighting approximate positioning on surviving maps, a factor that is being increasingly realised through analysis of the likes of Dalbier, De Gomme and Johann Roswurm's engineering maps for the varying sides.[3] These towns, such as Bristol, have often outgrown their original civic boundaries, thus forcing us to truncate our original research area; using de Gomme's schematics, we can lower the area to the following: walls 3-5ft high; ditch 67ft, depth 45ft; prior hill 45ft ditch 4ft deep and 18ft across, highest point 12ft, curtain 10ft, Brandon hill 412ft, while also providing Viewpoint data highlighting the approximate positioning of potential batteries and bombardment targets within future GIS models.[4]

Of course many of these engineers earned their knowledge serving in the religious wars on the Continent and thus diffused their knowledge further through drill books and manuals. Arguably, we could use the same means of recording drill manoeuvre on battlefields/camps as identifying siege actions. However, creating a complete unorganised model for assault, without mistakenly overlapping consecutive actions within one survey, within current analysis technique is extremely problematic. Occasional forlorn hope and garrison sally models could be created through similar finds scatters found in isolation, with local landmark/written evidence supporting their interpretation. Equally, the ability to be able to identify firing positions for the garrison, through tallying available weapon ranges (within a variable range of 350m, wider for round shot) and size of volleys fired from walls/loopholes, is possible through isolated

---

1   Allen, David, and Anderson, Sue, *Basing House Excavations 1978-1991*, Hampshire Field Club Monograph 10 (Bristol: Hampshire Field Club and Archaeology Society, 1999) p.23.
2   Allen and Anderson, *Basing House*, p.7; Atkin, Malcolm, *Cromwell's Crowning Mercy: The Battle of Worcester 1651* (Stroud: Sutton Publishing, 1998) p.42.
3   Barratt, *Sieges*, p.93.
4   Harrington, *Fortifications 1642-51*, p.17.

THE ARTE MILITAIRE

Figure 30: 'The Siege of Bazinge Hoyse', engraving by Wenceslaus Hollar, 1644-45. Although often described as fantastical and not matching our understanding of the structure of the original building, it does match many of the structures still standing, such as the brick bastion tower marked C. Wenceslaus Hollar, who with Inigo Jones and fellow engraver Robert Peake were part of the garrison and helped design the defences, gives a clear insight into the integrity and nature of defence in the closing days of the siege, referencing earthen redan and embankments enclosing The Old House.

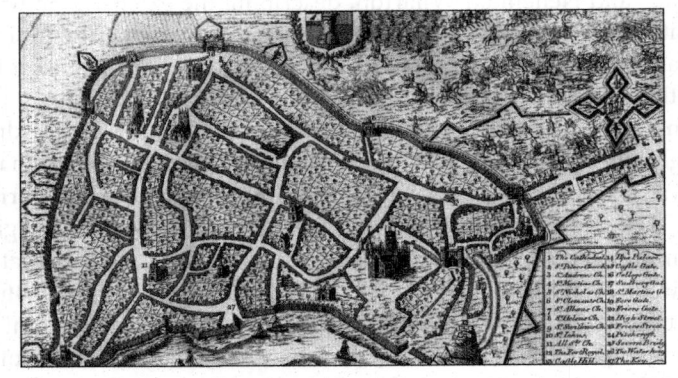

Figure 31: 'An exact ground plot of the City of Worcester as it stood fortifyd 3 Sept 1651', Dr Threadway Nash's Collections in the History of Worcestershire (1781). Clear differentiation of ravelin defence on the western defences, comparative to redans on the eastern side, possibly suggest the work of two separate engineers working on a two-layered defence. Fort Royal to the north-east, clearly taking the four-winged sconce form, is largely undetectable today, only remnants of its south-west bastion remaining.

mushrooming musket balls' cone-shaped scatters, a change in possible calibre equally representing firing positions for besiegers.[5]

However, as we have discovered previously investigating Lützen, these areas of ground were progressively fought over for a prolonged period of time; many identified isolated engagements might actually be two different fire fights at completely different times, their archaeological profile merely mixing together to appear like a single engagement.[6] A means of possibly differentiating between the two might

---
5 Barratt, *Sieges*, p.5; Foard and Morris, *English Battlefields*, p.135.
6 Foard and Morris, *English Battlefields*, p.135.

PRIMARY SOURCE MATERIAL

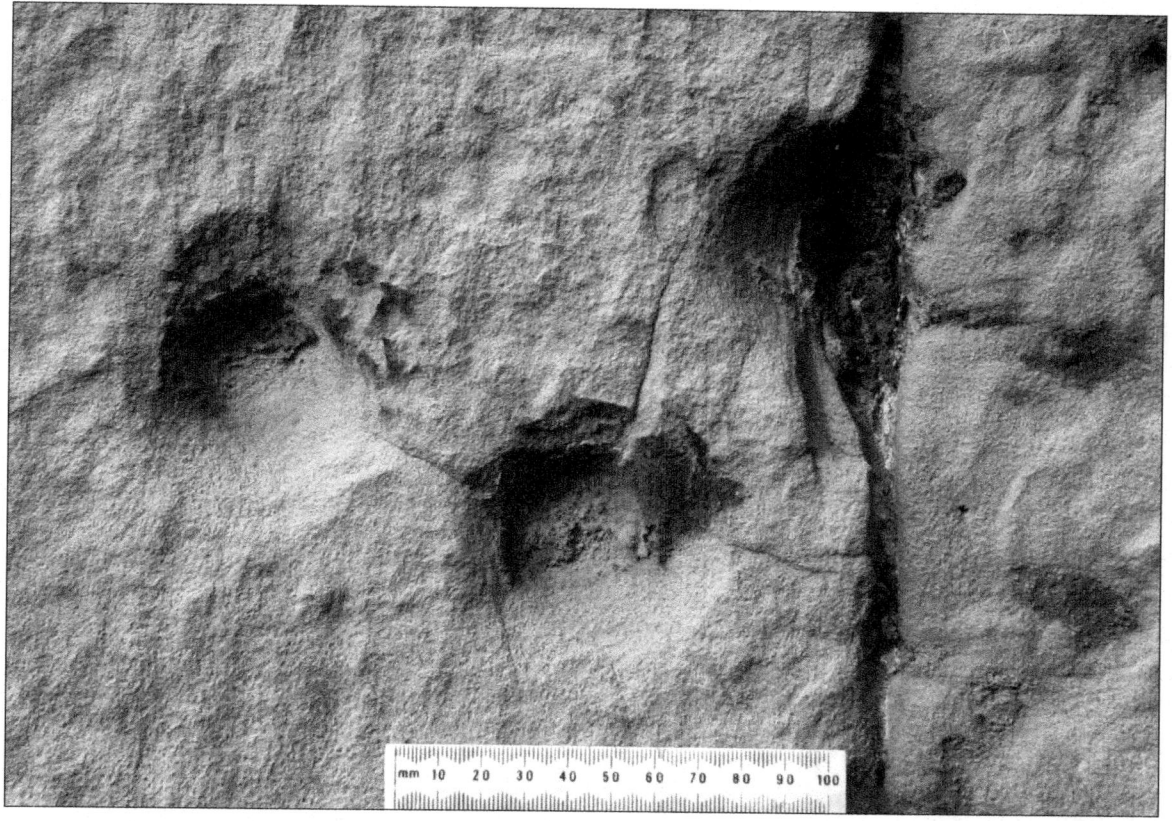

Figure 32: Bullet impact strikes on sandstone, Ashby-de-la-Zouche Castle, displaying a clear cup-shape typology, the surrounding cracking in the stone due to the proximity to the edge. (Foard et al., 2012, Fig.7.24, p.128)

be simply to focus upon a generalised view, that an army in the field has certain standards and manners to adhere to in the fair waging of warfare, represented through easily identifiable rules, formations and profiles a body of troops adheres to, and thus will be represented likewise in the archaeological profile. But within a siege action, priority is placed upon the preservation of life and the fast neutralisation of a defended position.[7] As a result, archaeological metal detector scatters are likely to have a higher density of finds, but they are unlikely to be interpreted in as coherent a manner as for battlefields. In essence, the best laid plans never survive first contact with the enemy.

Looking at the officer corps involved in the building and development of many of these defensive systems, the similarities to contemporary Continental examples is uncanny. In 1627, there were two English translations of Hugo's popular history of the Siege of Breda.[8] There is further diffusion of the ravages and means by which a complete encirclement of a town often got blown out of proportion through popular newssheets, such as the sack of Magdeburg and Monro's regiments taking part in the siege of Frankfurt 1631, both of which are often likened to the sack of Leicester.[9] As such, these images are likely to have imprinted themselves on the national psyche as Britain came nearer to plunging into the complexity of a European religious war *per se*. After all, Rupert had served at the siege of Linz and Rheinbund, and de Gomme at Breda and Ostend with similarities to the defences of Bristol Gage had been at the siege of Antwerp and was subsequently responsible for the defences at Basing House, and

---

7   Barratt, *Sieges*, p.40.
8   Porter, *Destruction*, p.8.
9   ibid, pp.9-11.

THE ARTE MILITAIRE

Figure 33: The Sack of Magdeburg. (Matthäus Merian)

Skippon at Maastrict, Breda and Hertogenbosch, again possibly comparative to London's fortifications.[10]

As for authors of military thought, the list almost acts as a who's who of governors of English garrisons: Hexham had been at Nieuport; Nathaniel Nye, the author of the *Art of Gunnery* (1670) was the governor of Worcester; William Prynne had helped design the outworks for Bristol, Hereford, Exeter, Taunton, Lincoln, York and Colchester; and lastly Papillon, the author of *A Practical Abstract of the Arts of Fortification*, published in London in 1645, which was to become the manual upon which further contemporary military architectural models originated from by simplifying and breaking down basic angles, divisions and basic mathematics, was also the military designer for Gloucester poignant when his book shows the identical design for the defences of Leicester and Northampton.[11]

This places an important precedent upon the officer corps of the Wars of the Three Kingdoms as to whether defensive systems can be directly compared to Continental examples. Indeed, we can already see this being enacted through looking at Clampe's 1646 map of the King's Sconce at Newark, depicted as the size of its sister, the Queen's Sconce, and being directly drawn from Paul Ive's 'The Practise of Fortification' (1589).[12] Therefore, in order to see to what extent diffusion of these trends occurred, comparative analysis of the area, size and nature of defensive structures needs to be considered. Rather than focusing purely

---

10 Harrington, *Archaeology*, p.8; Lawrence, *The Complete Soldier*, pp.334, 362.
11 Porter, *Destruction*, p.49; Lawrence, *The Complete Soldier*, p.364.
12 Warner, Tim, *Newark: Civil War and Siegeworks* (Nottingham: Nottinghamshire County Council Leisure Services, 1992) p.23.

PRIMARY SOURCE MATERIAL

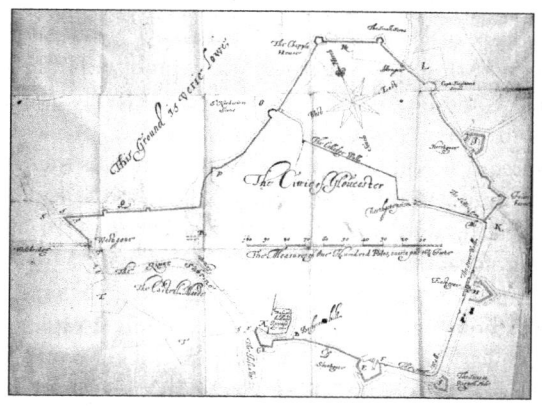

Figure 34: Defences of Gloucester circa 1646. Application of clear equilateral systems of defence, coupled with systematic survey and scale, has the ability to greatly increase the ability to model and discern within the modern landscape the remains and extent of defence.

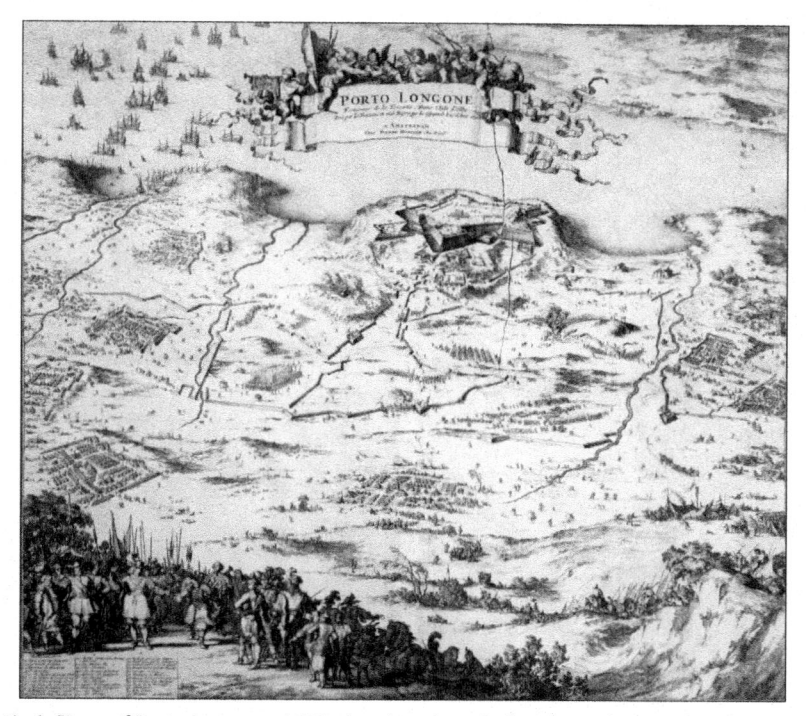

Figure 35: Mortier's Siege of Porto Longone 1650, showing clear similarities with Newark siegeworks, 1646, as well as those erected by Papillon at Gloucester, showing a clear diffusion and reference to those clearly illustrated and described in Ive's 1589 "The Practice of Fortification". (Mortier, Pierre, Nouveau Theatre de l'Italie, Amsterdam, 1704-5)

upon the comparative nature and planning between British and Continental examples, the often differing nature, means and object of defence, coupled with often grandiose power bases next to minor logistics bases, may mean that survey technique would be increasingly subjective in trying to find a means by which both fortresses were comparative.

It is all too easy to compare Breda to Oxford and say that both have the same number of bastions, therefore they are direct descendants, only to then admit that only part of Oxford is enclosed, the rest being divided by the Cherwell/Isis, whereas Breda has a continuous ring of fortlets; and that neither

THE ARTE MILITAIRE

site shares the same footprint, Oxford being far more expansive, whereas Breda has a more networked defensive ring.[13] If you were to take this view, the researcher would find little of use other than highlighting differences in structure. What would be more productive is to actually undertake a comparative analysis of British fortification types in order to build stylistic categories that can be attributed to particular theatres of Continental warfare. This will focus upon features such as the length of walls, size of ditches, direction of breaching gaps, mines, number of bastions, length of siege, number of outworks, angles of fire etc., in the hope of creating and identifying logical spheres of influence refining to particular practices and individuals. Therefore, we could argue that towns with a 36ft rampart width represent the works of Bernard de Gomme and his adherants, as noticed at Worcester, Bristol, Exeter, Lathom House and presumably Oxford, Portsmouth and Carmarthen etc., while a rapid need to refortify en masse at sites such as Gloucester and Newark relies increasingly upon thicker banks which can absorb shot rather than bring to bear the widest fire.[14] By looking at the precise diameters and profiles of ditch construction, we see two clear groupings emerging at 4m depth x 1012m width, as highlighted at Gloucester, Basing, Liverpool and Plymouth through earlier features palisaded, and Exeter, Shelford Manor near Newark and Derry with clear preference for artificial characterisation and reworking previous defensive works through extensive palisade soil retention and incorporation of earlier structures into their make-up.[15]

---

13 Barratt, John, *Cavalier Capital: Oxford in the English Civil War 1642-6*, Century of the Soldier 1618-1721 No.3 (Solihull: Helion and Company Limited, 2015).
14 Barratt, *Sieges*, p.98; Harrington, *Fortifications 1642-51*, pp.17, 50-53; Humphries, Julian, *Enemies at the Gate: English Castles under siege from the 12th century to the Civil War* (Swindon: English Heritage, 2007) p.83.
15 Allen, and Anderson, *Basing House*, p.20; Atkin, Malcolm, and Howes, Russell, 'The use of archaeology and documentary sources in identifying the Civil War defences of Gloucester', *Post-Medieval Archaeology*, issue 27 (The Society for Post-Medieval Archaeology, 1993) p.24; Harrington, *Fortifications 1642-51*, pp.28, 51; Harrington, *Archaeology*, pp.18, 21, 26, 67.

21

Trends

A comparative model as to where besiegers and defenders were likely to place defensive earthen outworks merely raises the possible variables according to strengths, weaknesses, existing architecture, local soil chemistry and available ordinance, confusing and complicating any possible model available. At sites such as Lathom House, Newcastle and Bristol, these kinds of extramural positions correlate at sites of extended observation over major rivers, roads, supply sources, bridges or indeed in opposing manor sites of antiquated defence, marshland or presumed gaps in architectural defence. The ability to actively plot the possible areas such fortifications occupied remains elusive, although using models such as Lathom House, Basing, Plymouth, Raglan Castle and Lichfield, we can assume that said batteries occur at multiples of roughly 50m.[1] By actively referring to presumed angular alignment of presumed lines of circumvallation, it is further possible to highlight likely, although not proven, sites of investigation.

Nor can it be assured of what particular material said defences are likely to be made from. While we can look at sites at Carmarthen's bulwarks and Basing's series of sconces and make the generalisations that all period defences were earthen, occasionally practicality and need for defence argues for reuse of siege rubble and material, predetermining indeterminate use, as seen at Carr's Battery on Croft Street and Plummer Tower at Newcastle upon Tyne, as well as Fort Royal at Bristol.[2] While we can only provide speculative analysis at present, certainly by looking at the Royalist strongholds at Carmarthen, Isle of Man and Colchester, these all seem to take up an area approximately 300m$_2$, a likely starting point for placing multiples and variables upon slighted landscapes and trying to associate original fortifications with their present remains, banks conforming to the de Gomme speculative model represented above.[3] Of course, however, this is not to completely omit the majesty of the best surviving set of defences currently remaining in Britain, the sconces at Newark, with particular referral to the Queen's Sconce.

Strategically important as holding the crossing point between the Fosse Way and the Trent, although the only enclosed part of the town remains the castle precinct, the level of defence surrounding Newark expands far wider. The defences consist of counter-circumvallation through bastion, earth and clay cushioning and revetting, graffs, horns, half-moons, counter-scarps, redoubts, pitfalls, turf palisades, stockades as well as the 'ring of iron' defended villages at the likes of Muskham Bridge, Crankley Lane and Shelford Manor, all of which meant that Newark could quite rightly be considered impregnable.[4] While again it is ultimately clear there are far too many variables to actively model an ever-changing morphology to Newark's defences, by looking at Clampe's 1646 map, the identical representation of both the Queen's and King's Sconce, encompassing an area 3 acres$_2$ measuring 7m/23ftx21m/69ftx3.25-

---

[1] Harrington, *Fortifications 1642-51*, pp.32-33, 47, 53; Harrington, *Archaeology*, p.93; Porter, *Destruction*, p.53.
[2] Atkin, *Worcester 1651*, p.42; Harrington, *Archaeology*, pp.21, 27, 29; Foard and Morris, *English Battlefields*, p.129.
[3] Foard, *Naseby*, p.135; Harrington, *Archaeology*, pp.93, 100; Porter, *Destruction*, p.19.
[4] Warner, *Newark*; Harrington, *Fortifications 1642-51*, p.23; Harrington, *Archaeology*, p.29; Pollard, Tony, and Oliver, Neil, *Two Men in a Trench: Battlefield Archaeology the key to unlocking the past* (London: Penguin, 2002) p.223.

THE ARTE MILITAIRE

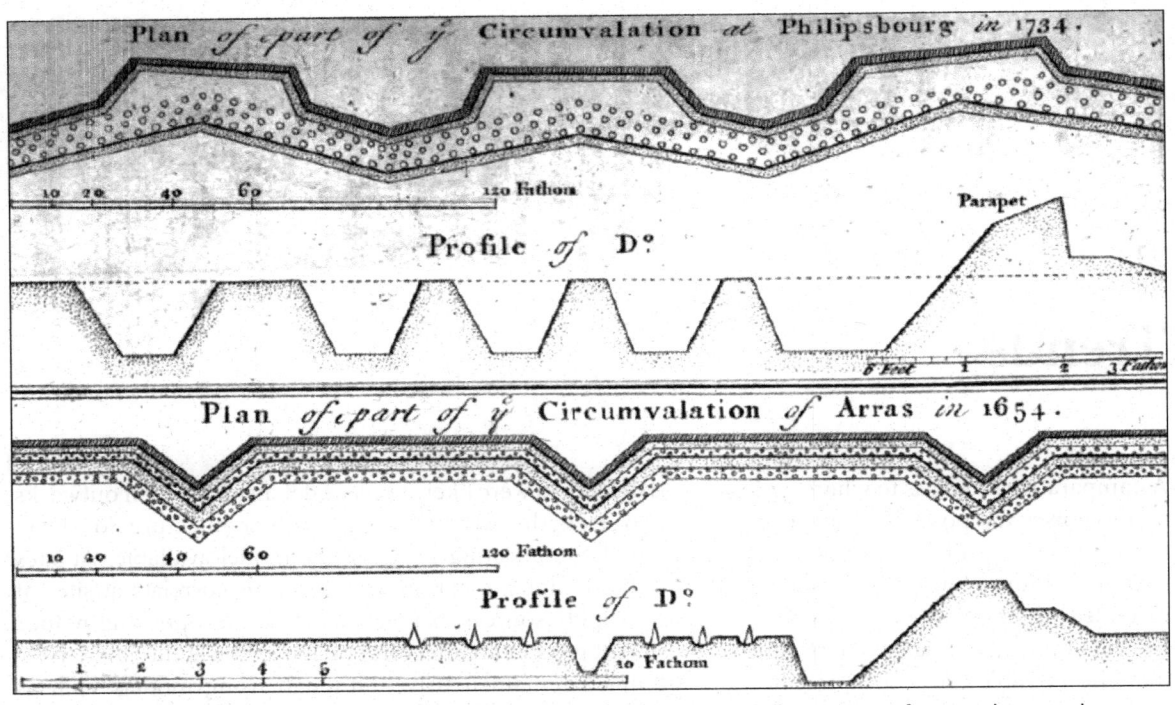

Figure 36: Lines of circumvallation as described in Vauban, showing the uniform nature of saps and approaches to walls, making them an ideal starting point for uniform landscape regression and remodelling.

4m/11.75-13ft, and directly identical to those represented in Paul Ive's 1589 'The Practise of Fortification', begs the question that should such features be represented so identically barely a few miles apart, they must equally be representative throughout the country. This could be further highlighted by cataloguing particular units and individuals, and their eventual destinations, who passed through Newark between 1643–46, thus providing a narrower field for further defensive classes to be modelled within.[5]

However, the validity of such an object can be directly brought into question by looking at extant remains of Colonel Gray's Sconce, occupying a 7 acre$_2$ area, with a 5.5ft rampart, which lacks any of the complexity of its sister fortifications. It ultimately looks very much like a last-ditch attempt at providing enfilading fire along the Trent and preventing gunships from bringing their guns under the defences of the town.[6] If this is the case, then this equally brings into full question how much we can ultimately rely upon Clampe's map. It is undeniable that the surviving Queen's Sconce is a textbook model upon which all modern perception of 17th century defence in depth is based, but the map was drawn in 1646 during the closing days of the siege, when many of the defences, for lack of resources to be manned, would have been destroyed and sacked, a feature that is all too clear through the complete invisibility of Meldrum's Redoubt in the ruins of Spittal Mansion. Thus the identical representation of the King's Sconces is merely applying for aesthetic appeal a text book model to Newark.[7]

Certainly in the few cases where we do have the remains on an approximated site of a defended campsite, as can be seen on the 400ft$_2$ Island at Newark, known as 'Little Edinburgh' due to its inhabitation by the Scots Covenanter Army, can be easily compared with its compatriot camp at Duns Law on the Scottish borders, measuring 60mx30m/197ftx98ft. This takes a rhomboidal redoubt form, protected on each flank by a demi-bastion, but largely left undefended, due often to being out of range or threat

---

5 ibid.
6 Warner, *Newark*, pp.46-48.
7 ibid, p.22.

Figure 37: Paul Ive's 1689 'The Practise of Fortification', showing almost identical typology to Newark's defences, suggesting the application of this treatise by the commander and his engineers during the defence of the town.

from sallies by opposing garrisons (there is the possibility of identifying unidentified examples through localised phosphates analysis to isolate latrine positions linked to large groups of men).[8]

Arguably, therefore, if we are to model siegeworks, we need to be focusing upon features unlikely to change, in this sense besieging batteries and earthworks, or indeed sites that can be directly relatable to associate or training manuals, rather than simply taking extant and often unrelatable measurements of defensive works and trying to fit them into a modelable research agenda. Each area is going to adhere to different military architectural norms, but these do not necessarily, with the ravages of slighting and archaeological degradation, add up to a credible, demonstrable model. If anything, where these examples do not exist anymore, we should be looking at a lower, more ephemeral level at the investigation area strata and contemporary section development, to understand the varying processes occurring during this short timespan equating to shortlived defences. This should be characterised by large linear, aligned compressed deposits and dips in present-day topography, representing the outfill and spoil heaps from speculative fortifications. Within unique contexts within a trench narrative, it may be possible to identify the possible positioning of gabions, either represented through circular differing deposits of compression or soil material. Measurable and identifiable postholes would be represented at regular intervals, representing soil revetting and retention. Differing layers of turf with compressed soil should be represented in stratigraphic profile (representing reinforcement of these banks by allowing root growth) and the continual slumping of said banks left open (represented by a sealed context containing large levels of gravel inclusions, consequently representing tip lines). The equal inclusion of levels of burning, stamped chalk surfaces or indeed extant root growth could equally represent the gradual clearing or planting of hedges to prohibit or clear the field of fire.

---

8   Harrington, *Archaeology* p.100; Pollard and Oliver, *Two Men in a Trench:* p.232; Warner, *Newark* pp.40, 42.

22

Destruction

One of our more defining images of the Wars of the Three Kingdoms within Britain is the abject destruction of stately homes and castles, defying Royalist forces of defensible fortifications to rely upon, leaving behind a romantic ruinous landscape that limits the level to which further archaeological analysis of these defensive structures can be undertaken. Slighting and breaching itself can hardly tell us about the modelable defensive qualities of a series of fortifications, again due to the issue of variance, but it does provide a means of linking and observing further remains of earthworks. Presuming the range of most siege guns is up to 1,000yds, by providing a relative 90° field of fire in front of said breach, relevance and connection is made between possible earthworks and the town. Equally, the ability to identify isolated sallies and actions of forlorn hopes to take the said breech, can through further analysis, combining shot impact analysis on surrounding walls, coupled with isolated small unit identification from selected finds, start to be honed in upon.[1] However, small-scale breaching becomes far more analytical by looking at the level of mining throughout Britain. On a stratigraphic level, very little is likely to be represented, soil context and stratigraphical analysis becoming completely indiscernible, with little character or relatable features, a factor commonly identified through First World War battlefields, particularly Messines Ridge.[2] Equally ephemeral in representation, the occasional use of mines, particularly in the transferred nature of religious war transplanted from Eastern Europe to Ireland, makes our case study at this level become even less discernible.

When looking for such features, our first port of call should be highlighting preventative measures, such as trees, waterlogged ground and pools of water in a discernible alignment, vibrations beneath the earth providing a ripple/rustle effect, such features positioning along a particular alignment representing the likely spread of said countermine.[3] Equally, looking for sections of often discernible trench, mimicking openings at the bases of walls should be considered in this light.[4] Isolated resistivity tests should highlight likely trench presence through increased groundwater waterlogging increasing the localised soil electrical current, meaning likely presence will provide clear geophysical linear anomalies. However, trenches of this nature should be considered in their minority, the ability to actively highlight their presence stratigraphically at sites such as Pontefract and Limerick merely highlighted by their extensive size and relatively good condition of surviving roof props. With an eastwest alignment, an accumulation of 300 props at Limerick presents the most extensive undermining activity yet identified

---

1 *Archaeology of the English Civil War*, Worcestershire County Council, p.10; Barratt, *Sieges*, p.161; Courtney, 'Early-modern siege', p.56.
2 Robertshaw, Andrew, and Kenyon, David, *Digging the Trenches: The Archaeology of the Western Front* (Barnsley: Pen and Sword Publishing, 2008) p.64; Osgood, Richard, and Brown, Martin, *Digging Up Plugstreet: The Archaeology of a Great War Battlefield* (Yeovil: J H Haynes and Co., 2009) p.84.
3 Lawrence, *The Complete Soldier*, p.345.
4 Barratt, *Sieges*, p.83; Harrington, Peter, 'Siegefields: An Archaeological Assessment of "Small" Sieges of the English Civil Wars', in Pollard, Tony, and Banks, Iain (eds), *Journal of Conflict Archaeology* vol. 1 (Glasgow: Centre for Battlefield Archaeology, 2005) p.101; Wiggins, *Limerick, 1642*, pp.36, 119.

DESTRUCTION

within an archaeological context.[5] However, in order to gain the most probable analysis possible, a comparison of the historiographical resource is required to provide chronology and sequencing over the site's five-week siege. Further archaeological survey of the chalky clay strata of the present Norman motte reveals the actual substrate of the castle is peppered to the north and south-east with a further two mining attempts and three successful countermines, although levels of dateable timber remains scant. It may well be the underlying chalk, acting as a lye for the overlaying chalk bond in the walls that proved so successful in preventing the defence's overall collapse, as revealed by little break in the stone bond over sites of major mining activity.[6] However, the silty clays surrounding said fortifications may also explain why further outside mining may have failed, collapsing in on themselves.[7]

---

5 Wiggins, *Limerick, 1642*, p.3.
6 ibid, pp.16, 36.
7 ibid, pp.79, 119.

23

Theoretical Modelling

While we can create an ideal that sieges can be accurately modelled on, unlike their static battlefield neighbours, the level of variables and differences possible within an urban context mean that a fully successful model is always going to prove problematic. Therefore, this is merely a study focusing upon limited defensive sections and structures that are mathematically provable. What we ultimately see being enacted is the standardisation of British defensive engineering,[1] a factor that ultimately peaks about 1590, but does not develop beyond this, merely coming into line in the late 17th century with European Trace Italienne fortress types becoming prominent, rather than in other military pursuits creating a distinctly 'British' model. The subjectification of further defensive sites during the Commonwealth ultimately stunts any possibility of a 'military revolution' being realised and thus defensive networks from the 17th century onwards need to be looked at in a pan-European focus, rather than an isolated developmental hub.

Fortifications cannot be modelled via trends because every town is different. However, recent work by Foard, regarding mapping musket ball scatters at Grafton Regis, if mapped nationally with localised angles of fire and action correlation on the same surface – e.g. overlaying as shots fired at the same wall – a means of applying manual analysis might become applicable. A theoretical analysis might be applied through the simple application of a landscape levels survey, using theodolite, map and aerial-based evidence combined. For this we need an area of level ground unlikely to have had its height altered in the past 400 years acting as a measurement benchmark – a town square would act as a suitable point with a measurement for argument's sake of 2.14m. We then take the model created within the manual for a particular set of earthworks and set a series of points of significant angular change that can be plotted upon an urban landscape, e.g.:

- bastion 5, angles same for bulwark, 110°x 80°x90°;
- sconce 20, 80° x170°/90°x70°;
- redoubt 12, 80°x90° all way round;
- ravelin/hornwork, 3 pts;
- line circumvallation, 7 pts, 110°$_2$.

To this base level of measurements we shall also add a further 10 measurements for actively modelling similarities between drill book and real life earthworks landscape in the intervening 400 years has a tendency to change, with the installation of urban amenities/storm drains/sleeping policemen, often built over each other, thus drastically changing a preserved 17th century landscape. As such, these points act as our controlled anomaly for those features interrupting reconstructed landscapes. By undertaking a combined levels and GPS survey, possible modelable material might be overlaid to see levels of similarity between them. It might be now that we can apply surveys to buildings and their destruction. Should the

---

[1] Foard, Glenn, 'The Civil War Siege of Grafton Regis', in Fitzroy, Charles, and Harry, Keith (ed.), *Grafton Regis: The History of a Northamptonshire Village* (Cardiff: Merton Priory Press, 2000) pp.49-63.

THEORETICAL MODELLING

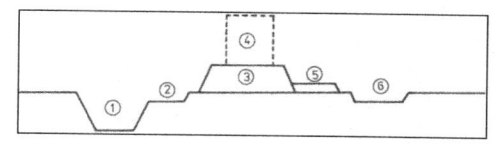

Figure 38: Typographical defensive features that can be modelled. 1. Ditch; 2. Berm; 3. Ramparts; 4. Walls; 5. Firing steps; 6. Inner magazine. (Matousek, 2005, Fig.5, p.122)

current rental/tithe plots still apply to present town planning systems, the ability to see whether clear overlapping of defence survey might be undertaken. Should they overlap perfectly, we can understand the nature to which we can lower the scale of investigation due to destruction associated with the storming and subsequent slighting of said fortifications. Referring to previous archaeological work done in the face of urban development, the possibility of highlighting possible battlefield deposits as identified through manual trends can thus be applied, as well as a possible route of advance through the town. However, should they lie outside the remit of the survey, the ability to identify further archaeological deposits might be approached, associating approximate angles of destroyed property to the walls of the fortifications to a width of 100m, the range that besieging gun batteries were likely to be set.

24

Experimental Archaeology

While it might not be possible to actively map and model these fortifications at present, the ability to replicate the conditions and site formation processes at creation are. During our brief survey above, Harrington in particular highlighted the nature of slump lines, siltation and middening processes occurring prior to the finished defensive fortification being erected; anything lying above this material is considered to be slighting material, representing a *terminus post quem* context for environmental propagation to take place on site, suggesting overall a level of abandonment or continuing upgrades over a period of time, as suggested by a number of examples from above for clear ditch recutting to retain the fortification's integrity. As such, while archaeology provides us with the preconception that fortifications either took a long time to erect or maintain, contextually we are leaving ourselves open to obvious preconceptions from a modern standpoint further analysis of localised strata has the evidence to prove such actions could have happed subsequently to the main structure being taken, and as a result merely represents slighting evidence.

To put these site formation processes to rest, a team from Charles University, Prague, investigated the site of the 1647 siege camp around Trebel Castle, flanked at Thein by a series of interconnected trenches, redoubts and gun emplacements stretching for 1km.[1] The majority of the ditches adhere to Dutch models as highlighted above, taking makeshift processes of soil settling to fulfil the earthworks' intentions rather than continued redevelopment, the area it occupied measuring south-west to west 60m2x60m2, repeated across seven differing earthworks, its makeup highlighted through alternating strata bands of sands and peaty clay, representing the use of easily available materials in accordance with our understanding of their construction.[2] By taking direct models from Naronowicz-Naronski of 1659, similarities between models and those being surveyed can be compared to varying levels of accuracy. Thus with the top of the surveyed rampart tapering from 1.7-2.5m, to the base 0.5-0.8m, with an outside ditch/rampart depth of 1-1.1m on the north and south sides, compared with the southern and east sides at 1.2x0.6m-3x1.1m, the west side being demolished and open to interpretation, presents the mathematical accuracy available to reconstruction.[3] By modelling in 1:1 scale, discrepancies to drill book norms can be evaluated, any changes present highlighted as Swedish remodelling on capturing said positions.[4]

---

1 Matousek, Vaclav, 'Building a model of a field fortification of the Thirty Years' War near Olbramov (Czech Republic)', in Pollard, Tony, and Banks, Iain (eds), *Journal of Conflict Archaeology* vol. 1 (Glasgow: Centre for Battlefield Archaeology, 2005) p.118.
2 ibid, pp.119-20.
3 ibid, pp.120-21.
4 ibid, pp.122-28.

Day	Number of workers	Result
1	8	E Bank 15mx4090cm
2	22	NW bank 17m
3	22	W 6m
4	26	Finish rest of redoubt
5	14	Turfing

    By presenting such models in histogram form as above, in summary our drill book analysis must also incorporate the level of space and time such structures take to construct surely it is more practicality than drill book adherence that needs to be considered, such as differing environmental factors, rain and enemy fire decreasing rate of work from 23 hours for mere excavation, to 68 hours for formation.[5]

---

[5] ibid, p.129.

25

Basing House

However, in many cases, it was not distinguishable military fortresses that were targeted. In the religious and social circle inhabited during the War of the Three Kingdoms, many manor houses became focuses for retribution due to their proximity to major roads or the capital, but equally for the ephemeral feature as acting as an example towards the holding and abuse of high office.[1] Such an instance can be seen at Basing House. Rivalling Hampton Court in its heyday, it was the home of the Marquesses of Winchester, a major Catholic family. While strategically holding a commanding position over the main road to London from the West Country, it also acted as a restaging point for local Royalist forces between the garrisons of Alton, Farnham and Winchester.[2] Invested four times between 1642–45, it proved a major nut to crack. While situated atop a Norman motte, the site was dilapidated until the need for defence arose, thus requiring the Royalists to equally defend a barn on the other side of the road to the main house, using this as an outwork, while burning down all local buildings, a factor represented through the fact that no houses within the village date to before 1645.[3] Within the house, further consolidation was undertaken through the creation of an h-shaped glacis, a bank designed for the deflection of cannon shot, but equally acting as a firing step for potential defenders behind the position of the garrison gate. All other gates were packed with mounds of turf and timber, a sure defence against breaching attempts, a factor that played increasingly to the garrison's favour.[4] Evidence is seen equally for the packing of surviving towers with clay in order to support light cannon, while a set of horn works have been discovered on the far side of the house where remaining walls are lowest, the intention being to provide a steady fire on the Parliamentarian lines of circumvallation.[5] The house was provided with a ready water supply, although its relatively open position, coupled with its proximity to the cess pit, meant that there was constant susceptibility to typhus throughout the garrison.[6]

Combatting this, the Parliamentarian besiegers created a series of lines of circumvallation across Cowdery's Down, previously used for the site of a Saxon burh, only being recently realised through a current geophysical survey. The defences were made easy through a low-lying chalk bedrock, although their extent is unknown due to the building of the Basingstoke Canal in the 1880s, but the ability of the garrison to sally out to local villages to restock supplies and food, possibly suggests they were to little avail.[7] The equal use of the local church, with its raised position enhanced for a rampier gun platform, and the reuse of a set of local Iron Age earthworks known as 'Oliver's Battery' (a factor also seen at

---

1   Harrington, *Fortifications 1642-51*, p.38.
2   ibid, p.60.
3   Allen and Anderson, *Basing House*, pp.14-17; Harrington, *Fortifications 1642-51*, p.70.
4   Allen and Anderson, *Basing House*, pp.51, 58.
5   ibid, p.23.
6   Emberton, Wilfred, *Love Loyalty: The Close and Perilous Siege of Basing House 1643-5* (Basingstoke: W.J. Emberton, 1972).
7   ibid, pp.13.

Maumsbury Rings), enhanced through a large scoop taken out of the middle, possibly for the positioning of an artillery magazine, shows the level to which such a site could be enhanced in a relatively short amount of time.[8] Thus, while in the long-term not effective, it is a site that incorporates the full plethora of military theory and localised terrain and exploits them to the maximum extent. It contradicts the idea of defensive landscapes being terrain-orientated, but rather manufactured in the face of strategic necessity.

---

[8] Allen and Anderson, *Basing House*, p.113; Harrington, *Fortifications 1642-51*, p.31.

26

Alton

When looking at the battlefield landscape fought over at Alton, two boundary rings have to be drawn in the form of the main battle zone and outlying defences surrounding the town. The houses within the main church precinct remain intact, now as a modern Quaker meeting hall. Birch, in his account of the battle, tells how the Royalist garrison of the town decided to find cover behind the graveyard wall surrounding the church, the present line of the wall possibly proving original, older unrendered stone-clad foundations being reused to hold a concrete upper wall, unsuspectingly retaining the original fabric of this barricade.[1]

However, Elias Archer, in his account, clearly points out that the Royalist forces surrounding the church had ensconced themselves in a series of horn works, which the Parliamentarian forlorn hope had difficulty removing them from.[2] While Archer may well have been a gentleman lieutenant in the London Trained Bands, he was not a military engineer and therefore he could quite easily have mistaken the form these particular earthworks took. Antiquarians since the 1890s have been discussing the approximate site of these defences, but to little avail. However, by looking at the 1666 town map, on the northern edge a wedge-shaped enclosure is depicted surrounding the church, in the same manner as a Dutch ravelin for deflecting artillery fire (Fig. 39).[3] It is quite possible that the defences had been slighted to a less than satisfactory level, meaning that the present graveyard was allowed to retain the original form of the defence, its present preservation doubtful due to urban development cutting away the back half, the graveyard falling out of use during the 19th century. Further evidence of defences was revealed during excavations in 1982–83 at Amery Cottage, 230m west of the church, in the form of a ditch cut measuring 3mx0.7m, its fill containing 17th century ceramics and clay pipe, and its extent from the church suggesting further lines of circumvallation running out from the main church.[4]

Despite the relative lack of evidence for the conflict surviving within the town, we need to look at the battlefield landscape in a wider strategic context. Recently at Bentley, two miles outside Alton, a series of possible earthworks relating to the battle have been identified (Fig. 40).[5] We know that Lord Crawford, in apprehension of an assault occurring, built a series of defences surrounding the town.[6] The first at Isington, Bentley, is cut into malmstone, with a north-facing escarpment in the style of another Dutch-style horn work, curving to the east.[7] Arguably, for such a feature to work effectively, a series of

---

1 Morris, Richard, *The Storming of Alton and Arundel 1643* (Bristol: Stuart Press, 1993) p.8.
2 Humphries, Julian, *Clash of Arms: Twelve English Battles* (Swindon: English Heritage, 2006) p.157; Adair, *Sir William Waller*, p.142.
3 Humphries, *English Battles*, p.155.
4 Archaeological Survey Church Precinct, Alton <http://historicenvironment.hants.gov.uk/ahbresults.aspx> (accessed 16/03/2014).
5 Lyne, Malcolm, 'Civil War earthworks East of Alton', *Proceedings of the Hampshire Field Club and Archaeological Society* vol. 46 (March 1991) pp.181-87.
6 Cansfield, Peter, *The Battle of Alton: An account of the famous battle in 1643 during England's Civil War* (Alton: Peter Cansfield's Associate's Literati, 1999) pp.19-20.
7 Lyne, 'Civil War earthworks', p.181.

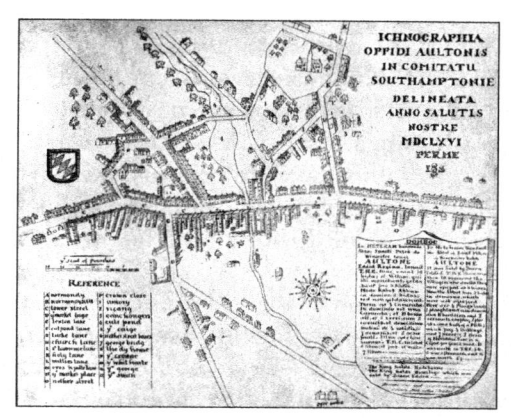

Figure 39: 1666 Map of Alton. Take note of the arrowhead form of the church precinct in the top of the image, possibly the remains of close defences around the Royalist headquarters in the form of a redan.. Could this possibly mean that established defences from 1643-4 were merely incorporated into the built landscape of the town?

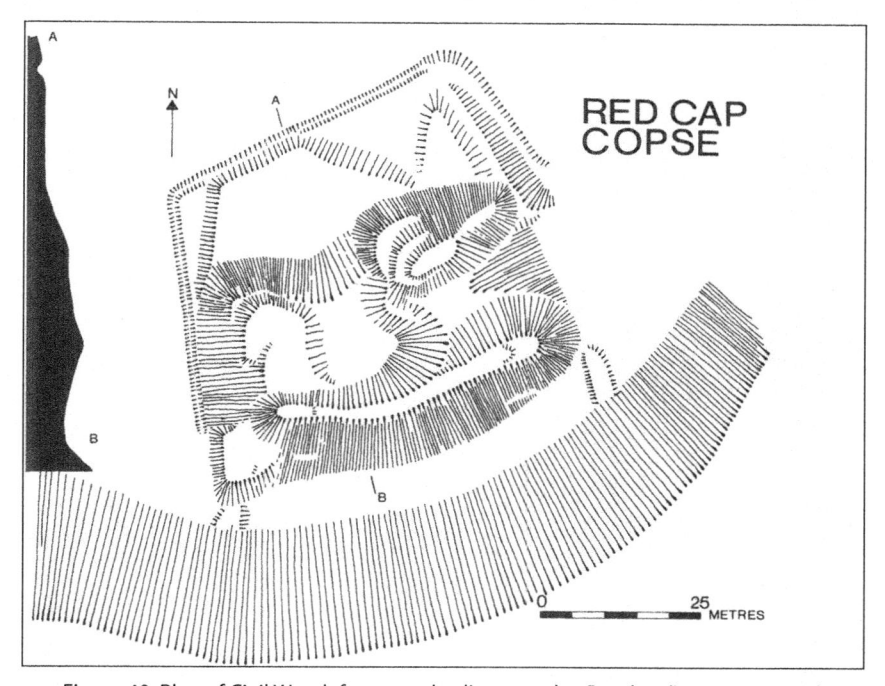

Figure 40: Plan of Civil War defence works discovered at Bentley. (Lyne, 1991, 183)

outposts of a similar nature would have to be erected on hilltops across the Binsted plateau.[8] Measuring 62.5mx37.5m, with a maximum elevation of 4.5m, its centre is represented through a hollow, possibly acting as a magazine.[9] The north side of this defence is reinforced with a further rampier.[10] If such a mound was able to carry a saker, a 6 pdr field gun at a 10o angle, the ball would travel 2,170 yards, cutting off any possible travel along the Farnham-Alton road, localised woodland suggesting such a feature was concealed.[11] This possibly represents initial fortification during the garrisoning of the town by Bolles,

---
8   ibid.
9   ibid.
10 ibid.
11 ibid.

THE ARTE MILITAIRE

a second phase undertaken by Crawford, represented through an overlapping, unfinished 6ha ravelin, butting onto the south-west corner of the original defences, any possible undulation showing the nature of the defences preserved through a later landscape garden.[12] This has further been expanded to the west through LIDAR scanning revealing a north–east-facing sconce, the remains shown through the modern footings to field boundaries.[13] This therefore presents a view of Alton's defences as extensive, using the latest theories on military engineering, but constantly having to be upgraded due to gradual abandonment of sections of the town, coupled with growth and truncation of the garrison due to the strategic situation.

A factor wholly supporting the inclusion of the Winchester to Basing area as a heritage landscape study can be seen through the further discovery of another battery site midway down the Wey valley at Court Gardens, Long Sutton, a mile away from Hopton's headquarters at Odiham, suggesting the building of outlying manned fortlets throughout this stretch of the Hampshire countryside to act as stop lines preventing an unopposed advance into Berkshire and Oxfordshire by Waller.[14] Therefore, from a landscape analysis perspective, Alton has a huge level of potential for a fully inclusive military heritage analysis, interpretation and conservation.

---

12   ibid.
13   ibid.
14   ibid, p.184.

27
Conclusion

A study such as this cannot hope to cover or broach every piece of information that the military manual and its use could reveal. Ordering and collating every single aspect of the soldiers' life and existence, it provides a valuable insight into life on the battlefield and, if exploited correctly, can reveal a huge amount more about what these actions left behind. Through integration with programmes like GIS, of available maps, metal detectors, landscape regression and presumed distribution and extent of battle lines according to written accounts and historical interpretation, with developmental movement and extent of unit movement according to military practice of the time accounted for, the boundary rationale for historic battlefields might be improved. Rather than creating a static landscape filled with ruins and graves, it can become a place where the ebb and flow of history is clearly discernible and forces the clear portrayal of the landscape as we see it today. Such actions can further break down parts of the battlefield to include zones of influence relating to differing characterisation of actions, thus allowing different preservation rationale to be implemented to further preserve their remains, but also extend the frequency of low-level investigation to allow wider interpretation on these sites. This method of battlefield investigation has the scope to move interpretation of the typical battlefield from the blank field to a space where a number of ephemeral actions take place, in essence bringing these actions into contemporary consciousness.

Appendices: Author's Note

A lot of military manual-based drill is uniform in nature and thus leaves very little archaeological residue. While to the beholder, firing by extraduction vs. firing by rank or volley, doubling front to the left, right and centre, might prove and appear very different in performance, a lot of what they leave is merely repeating the same rule, or indeed under present archaeological rationale, not likely to be traced. Therefore, what is represented here are extracts from the most important, or indeed less studied military manuals, combined to hopefully provide an appearance of what would appear in the ideal manual. Like original manuals, and certainly replicated in archive copies by the likes of Sir John Gell and Richard Barnstone of Gamul's Regiment, dotted amongst these sample chapters will be annotations and notes highlighted, explaining likely advances towards representing such information on an archaeological landscape, queries regarding possible means of exploring key trends, measurements of likely bodies of study and actual evidence that suggests such practices' prevalence. While certainly not exhaustive, it should hopefully stimulate and question the frequency of investigation under which future archaeological and material culture study might be undertaken.

Throughout the following works you will see represented in the appendices, I have attempted to present an active commentary on their archaeological value and how this might be applied to research rationale. This has been represented by comments rendered within square brackets. Where illustrations have also been highlighted, this represents the presence of resources within the original text unable to be reproduced within this publication, but should act as a guide for finding original resources within the reader's own research.

Appendix I

Extracts from *Observations upon military & political affairs written by the Most Honourable George, Duke of Albemarle, &c.* by George Monck, Duke of Albemarle (1608-70) (London: Printed by A.C. for Henry Mortlocke ... and James Collins, 1671).

Pages 42-3

CHAP. XIII. **What strength Divisions of Horse ought to be from four thousand to ten thousand, when they are to March in an Army, and when they are to Fight a Battle; or if Foot be to Fight on the Flanks of each Division of Horse, or when they come to be Embattled to Fight on the Flanks of an Army. That small Divisions both of Horse and Foot are much better than great Divisions for Service either in Campaign, or within Enclosures; because they are not so apt to fall into Disorder, and are much more ready to be commanded upon all occasions.**

An Army which is embattled in small Divisions of Horse and Foot, is not so easily routed as that Army which is embattled in great Divisions. And small Divisions are much more ready than great Divisions: for besides seconding one another, and wheeling upon all occasions, they will likewise out-front an Army which is embattled in great Divisions: The which is one of the greatest advantages that can be taken in the embattling of an Army. Also small Divisions of Horse and Foot are much readier for Service, where you cannot embattle them according to the rules of Art, by the nature of the place, or within enclosures, or where the brevity of the time will not give you leave. To conclude, an Army that is embattled in small Divisions is much more troublesome for an Enemy to deal withal, than an Army that is embattled in great Divisions.

[At battlefields such as Dunbar, Newburn and Nantwich, as there is a high profile representation of general actions, we can actively plot the spread of deployment, and thus our metal detecting survey merely needs to overlay this.]

It is most convenient, and ready to have your Divisions of Horse and Foot, to March at the same strength, or some ten or twelve men more in a Division, than you intend to fight them in a Battle: by this means your Army will be much readier, and sooner embattled upon all occasions. If you fight your Horse in a day of Battle on the Flanks of your Body of Foot (which is the usual way of placing the Horse) and if you intend to Skirmish in the day of Battle with a small Division of Foot on each flank of each Division of Horse (which I hold to be the best and strongest way of embattling your wings of Horse) provide always that your Musketeers in each Division of Foot, that are to Skirmish on the flanks of each Division of

THE ARTE MILITAIRE

Horse in a Day of Battle, be so ordered that they may be sheltered by Pikes from the Force of the Enemies Horse. And in what order the two Divisions of Foot shall fight in a Day of Battle on the flanks of each Division of Horse, so as to have the Musketeers sheltered by the Pikes from the force of the Enemies Horse, shall be demonstrated unto you in the following figures.

[Suggest one single battle plan can be applied to all Monck's actions? How much of a role does time and landscape play on effective deployment?]

Pages 44-5

If your strength of Horse be four thousand, and if they be to fight on the flanks of a Body of Foot, and each division of Horse to have a division of Foot fighting on each flank, then each Division of Horse ought to be forty in front, and three deep; and so the strength of each Division of Horse will be an hundred and twenty. If your strength of Horse be five thousand, then each Division of Horse ought to be an hundred and fifty strong, fifty in front, and three deep. If your strength of Horse be six thousand, or ten thousand, then ought you to have an hundred and eighty in a Division, sixty in front, and three deep. And of this strength (as is aforesaid) ought your Divisions of Horse to be.

[Therefore can always assume, using Ward's model of spacing, Monck's bodies of horse cover area of battlefield of 120180ftx18ft.]

If you intend to fight Foot on the flanks of each Division of Horse in a Battle, the Divisions of Foot that shall fight on each flank of each Division of Horse, shall be in strength twelve files of Pikes, and twelve files of Musketeers, which in all make a Body, or a Division of an hundred and forty four men. And on the flanks of each Division of Horse, when you come to embattle them to fight, you must place a Division of Foot of an hundred and forty four men, half Pikes and half Musketeers. The order how the Divisions of Horse and Foot shall march together when they come near an Enemy, and how they shall embattle, and skirmish, shall be demonstrated in the following Figures. The Divisions of Foot before spoken of, will serve to fight on the flanks of any Division of Horse of what strength you please to have them.

[For foot, model close order 24ft/order 36ft/open order 72ft x close order 12ft/order 18ft/open order 36ft. Also suggest diminishing role of pike not apparent at end of Civil War through ratio of pike to shot equalling at 1:1.]

In the first place, for your better understanding of this new way of Discipline (the which I am well assured you will find very serviceable and advantageous against an Enemy, if you make use of it) I will demonstrate unto you in the following Figure, in what order a Division of Horse, and two Divisions of Foot shall stand ready to march, to be embattled when occasion shall serve. The which order must be observed by all the rest of the Divisions. By this means you may understand how all the rest of the Divisions of Horse and Foot that are to fight on the flanks of an Army in a day of Battle may be ordered for a march, and to be in readiness to be embattled, when an Army cometh near the Enemy.

[Description of battalia order = possible emergence of English Model?]

These Figures following lettered with *A B C D E F G*, shew you the order of the Divisions of Horse and Foot (I mean those Divisions of Horse and Foot that are to be embattled together in a day of Battle on the flanks of the Body of Foot) to be ready to march when occasion shall serve, or to be embattled. And this order which shall be here set down for this one Division of Horse figured with the Letter *A* in the following Figure, and the two Divisions of Foot figured with the Letters *B C D E F G*, the same order ought to be observed after the same manner for a march when you come near an Enemy. By this means your Army will be much the sooner embattled upon any occasion, and always in a readiness to receive your Enemy: if so be your Divisions of Horse and Foot, when they march, be of the same strength as you

APPENDIX I

desire to have them when they are embattled to fight, and that you march your Divisions of Horse and Foot by Brigades as you do intend to fight them.

Pages 46-50

[An illustration was provided in this section of the original manuscript.]
The Figure before, figured with the letter A, stands for a Division of Horse; the order that they are in, in rank and file, is their order. The figures figured with B C D E F G, are small Divisions of Foot, the which shall be at large demonstrated in this following observation: the order that they stand at in rank and file, is their order, *viz.* three foot in file, and six in rank. The distance of ground between the Divisions of Musketeers D F and the Division of Horse A, is thirty paces, three feet to the pace. And this distance of ground of thirty paces between the two Divisions of Musketeers D F, and the Division of Horse marked with the letter A ought to be when the Divisions of Horse and Foot are embattled to fight. The distance of ground between the Division of Musketeers, and the Divisions of Pikes is twelve Footmen. Which are Pikes, and which are Musketeers this following demonstration will declare unto you. The figure before, figured with the letter A, is a Division of Horse of threescore in front, and three deep; and in the strength of the Division is an hundred and eighty Horse. The figure with six files, and six ranks of small pricks figured with the letter C, is a Division of Musketeers, in strength six and thirty, each small prick standing for a Musketeer. The figure figured with the Letter B with cross strokes, is a Division of Pikes of twelve files and six deep. The strength of the Division is seventy two Pikemen, and each stroke standing in way of a rank stands for a rank of Pikes being twelve in rank; and each stroke standing in way of a file is to be accounted for a File six deep. The figure figured with the letter D is a Division of Musketeers of the same strength that the figure C is. The figures figured with the Letters E F G, are the same that B C D, and the little small strokes in the Front, Rear, and Flanks of the Divisions of Horse and Foot stand for Officers.

[Model Battalia frontage: 354ft close order, 378ft order and 400ft open order.]
When these two Divisions of Foot, and one of Horse are to march away by small subdivisions, as the way will give leave; then the right-hand division of Foot figured with B C D is first to march away: next, the Division of Horse signified by the Letter A, then the left-hand Division of Foot figured with the Letters E F G is to follow the Division of Horse figured with the Letter A. You are to appoint to every Division of Horse two Divisions of Foot, like as you see in this former figure of A B C D E F G, if your Foot will hold out to do it. If you have not so many as to do it, you ought not to fail to flank each Division of Horse in the Vanguard of your Army with two Divisions of Foot, as is set down in the former figure. And each Musketeer of those Divisions of Foot which are to be embattled on the flanks of each Division of Horse ought to have, when they come to encounter with the Enemy, two pair of Bandoliers, or a pair of Bandoliers, and a dozen of Charges in each Musketeers Pocket. Likewise each Musketeer ought to have twelve spare Bottles besides his Bandoliers furnished with Powder and Bullet: and each two Divisions of Foot ought to have a Powder-Bag full of Powder carried along with them. All the Divisions of Horse and Foot that are to be embattled together on the flanks of your Army in a day of Battle, for the Wings of your Battle being divided into Brigades, are to march after this order as is here set down for the marching of this one Division of Horse, and two of Foot when you are near an Enemy and marching towards him. This way of fighting Foot amongst Horse is much the stronger way of embattling an Army in my judgment than any other that I have either seen or read of: and hereafter in a fit place I shall shew sufficient reason for to prove it so to be.

The following figure marked with the Letters H I J K L M N O, shall shew you in what manner the Musketeers in the two Divisions of Foot that are embattled on the flanks of each Division of Horse, as you see them in the foregoing figure marked with the letters A B C D E F G, how, I say, the aforesaid Musketeers shall be drawn into a fit Order to give fire on the Enemies Horse or Foot upon any occasion.

95

THE ARTE MILITAIRE

The words of Command that you are to give the Musketeers to bring them into the Order of the following Figures *K L N O*, from the Order of the foregoing figures *C D F G*, are these words of Command which follow. Command the two first Ranks of the two Divisions of Musketeers marked with the Letters *C* and *D* to march forwards till the two last ranks of the aforesaid two ranks of both the Divisions be twelve foot beyond the front of the Pikes, then command them to stand; then command the two ranks of Musketeers that belong to the Division of Musketeers marked with the letter *C*, to turn to their left hands, and the two ranks of Musketeers marked with the letter *D*, to turn to their right hands: then command these four ranks of Musketeers, the which are now files, to march forwards till they meet. Then command those Musketeers which before did turn to their right hands, to turn to their left hands, and those Musketeers which did turn to their left hands, to turn to their right hands, and file even with the Pikes. Then command the two last ranks of Musketeers of the two Divisions of Musketeers marked with the letters *C D*, to turn to their right hands about, and march forward, till the two rear ranks of both the Divisions be twelve feet beyond the rear rank of Pikes in the Division of Pikes marked with the letter *B*.

[Model Battalia depth with advanced shot: 36ft close order/42ft order/60ft open order.]
Then command the four ranks of Musketeers to stand, commanding the two ranks of Musketeers that belong to the Division of Musketeers marked with the letter *C*, to turn to their right hands, and the two ranks of Musketeers marked with the letter *D*, to turn to their left hands. Then command the four ranks of Musketeers, which are now files, to march forwards, and meet in the rear of the Pikes. Then command those Musketeers which did before turn to their right hands, to turn to their right hands again, and those Musketeers which did turn to their left hands, to turn to their left hands again, and file even with the Pikes. Then command the two middlemost ranks of Musketeers, which are left of both the Divisions of Musketeers marked with the letters *C* and *D* to march forward, and front even with the Musketeers in the front of the Pikes. Then command the Division of Horse marked with the letter *H* to close their ranks and files to their close Order: and the Division of Pikes marked with the letter *B*, and the two ranks of Musketeers, which are now in the rear of the Pikes, to close their ranks and files to their close order.

The same words of Command and Order must be observed by the two Divisions of Musketeers marked with the letters *G F*, as is here set down, and observed by the two Divisions of Musketeers *C* and *D*. And these words of Command which are here set down will bring the former figure marked with the letters *A B C D E F G*, into the form and order of this following figure marked with the letters *H I J K L M N O P Q R S*.

Pages 51-63

[An illustration was provided in this section of the original manuscript.]
By the words of Command which are before set down, the Musketeers in the former figure marked with the letters *A B C D E F G* are brought into this order and form, as you see them in the figure marked with the letters *H I J K L M N O P Q R S*. Now what order this figure marked with the foregoing letters is in, I will here declare unto you.

The Division of Horse marked with the letter *H* is threescore in front, and three deep, who are now at their close order in rank and file, the which is a foot and half in file, and six in rank. Likewise the two Divisions of Pikes marked with the letters *I* and *O* on the flanks, and the four ranks of Musketeers in the rear of the Pikes marked with the letters *L* and *Q* are at their close order in rank and file, the which is one foot and an half in file, and three in rank. Also the three ranks of Musketeers marked with the letters *M K N R P S* are at their order in rank and file; the which is three foot in file, and six in rank. These twelve ranks of Musqueteers, which are in the front stand ready to advance with the rest of the Horse and Foot against an Enemy, and to be commanded to make ready, and give fire on the Enemies Horse or Foot, as occasion shall serve, as you see them in the figures marked with the letters *M K N R P S*.

APPENDIX I

When these twelve ranks of Musketeers which are in the front, are commanded to give fire upon the Enemy, you must command them to do it in this manner: Command the twelve ranks of Musketeers marked with the letters *M K N R P S* to make ready: being ready, command them to present, the which you must command them to do after this manner. Let the first six ranks of Musketeers before spoken of present, kneeling upon their right knees; then let the six last ranks of the former twelve ranks of Musketeers move up close to the first six ranks of Musketeers which are presenting and kneeling on their right knees. Then command all the Musketeers in the six last ranks to step forward with their right legs within the in-side of their Leaders right legs, and step forward with their left legs close up to their Leaders left legs without-side of their Leaders left legs, presenting their Musket over their Leaders heads in the first ranks.

[Turn in body orientation mirrored in linear orientation of musket shot towards left incline?]
The twelve ranks of Musketeers marked with the letters *M K N R P S* being thus presented as is here set down, command them to give fire together; and when they have given fire, command them to advance easily with the rest of the Foot and Horse, and make ready again, and give fire after the same manner again, as is before spoken of, and so often as you please. The four ranks of Musketeers, which are in the rear of the two Divisions of Pikes marked with the letters *L* and *Q* will serve, if any of your Musketeers in the front shall be hurt or slain.

[Were all arms of service required to learn each other's drill in order to work in synergy? The ability for horse to become entangled with deployment of shot is quite clear.]
Now I have shewed you how the Musketeers in the Divisions of Foot, which are to fight on the flanks of each Division of Horse in a day of Battle, are to give fire on the Enemies Horse. I will now shew you in the next figure marked with the figures of 1 2 3 4 5 6 7 8 9 10 11 12, how the Musketeers shall be sheltered by the Pikes from the Enemies Horse, when they shall charge the Divisions of Foot, which are on the flanks of each Division of Horse. But first I will set down the way how you shall bring the Musketeers in the former figure marked with the letters *M N R S* to the order as you shall see them in this following figure marked with the figures 1 2 3 4 5 6 7 8 9 10 11 12. You must command the two ranks of Musketeers, six in front, and two deep on the right hand Division of Foot marked with the letter *M*, to turn to their left hands, and command an Officer to lead them down on the right hand flank of the Division of Pikes marked with the letter *I*, keeping one foot and an half distance from the right hand file of the aforesaid Division of Pikes, until he bring the two men that were the left hand men of the two ranks of Musketeers marked with the letter *M*, even with the bringers up of the right hand file of the Division of Pikes marked with the Letter *I*. Then command them to turn to their right hands about, and close their ranks and files to their close order. After that, command the two ranks of Musketeers six in front, and two deep on the left hand of the aforesaid Division of Pikes marked with the letter *N*, command, I say, those two ranks of Musketeers to turn to their right hands, and command an Officer to lead them down on the left hand, on the left hand flank of the Division of Pikes marked with the letter *I*, keeping one foot and an half distance from the left hand file of the Division of Pikes marked with the letter *I*, until he brings the two men that were the right hand men of the two ranks of Musketeers marked with the letter *N* even with the bringers up of the left hand file of the Division of Pikes marked with the letter *I*. Then command the two files of Musketeers (the which were before ranks) which you have drawn down on the left hand flank of the Division of Pikes marked with the letter *I*, to turn to their right hands about: then command them to close their ranks and files to their close order. The same order must be observed with the four ranks of Musketeers, six in front and two deep, marked with the letters *R* and *S* on the right and left hand of the left hand Division of Pikes marked with the letter *O*, as is here before set down for the four ranks of Musketeers marked with the letters *M* and *N*. Then command the four ranks of Musketeers marked with the letters *K* and *P* to close their ranks and files to their close order. And these words of Command before

THE ARTE MILITAIRE

set down will bring the former figure marked with the letters *I J K L M N O P Q R S* to the order of this figure marked with the figures of 1 2 3 4 5 6 7 8 9 10 11 12.

[An illustration was provided in this section of the original manuscript.]
By these words of Command before set down, you see the Musketeers marked with the letters *M N R S P K* in the figure before this former figure, are now brought into this order, as you see them in this figure before marked with the figures of 5 6 11 12 9 3 under shelter of the Pikes: The Musketeers and Pikes being at their close order standing in a readiness to receive a charge from Horse, and the Pikes to shelter the Musketeers every way upon occasion from the force of the Horse. The figure marked with the figure 1, is a Division of Horse, threescore in front and three deep, being at their close order. The way how the Musketeers shall be sheltered by the Pikes from Horse, I will here declare unto you: Command the two right hand files, and the two left hand files of the Division of Pikes marked with the figure 2 (the which Division of Pikes is twelve files of Pikes, and six deep) to charge to their right, and left hands: the two right hand files to the right hand, and the two left hand files of Pikes to the left hand over the shoulders of the Musketeers on the right and left hand marked with the figures 5 and 6: commanding these four files of Musketeers marked with the aforesaid two figures to turn to their right and left hands. When the two right hand files, and the two left hand files of Pikes of the figure marked with the figure 2, are commanded to charge to the right and left hands, then command the other eight files of Pikes of the figure 2, which have not as yet charged their Pikes, I say, command the three first ranks of those eight files to charge their Pikes to the front over the shoulders of the Musketeers marked with the figure 3. Then command the three last ranks of Pikes of the eight files of Pikes to charge to the rear over the shoulders of the two ranks of Musketeers marked with the figure 4. And these two ranks of Musketeers in the rear marked with the figure 4 must observe to turn to their right hands about, when the Pikes are commanded to charge to the rear.

[Area occupied by regiment of foot prepared for cavalry: 48ftx24ft.]
The same Order and words of Command, the which are here set down for the right hand Division of Foot, marked with the figures 2 3 4 5 6 7 must be observed by the Officers of the left hand Division of Foot, marked with the figures 7 8 9 10 11 12. The Musketeers which are placed without-side of the Pikes marked with the figures 3 4 5 6 9 10 11 12 must stand ready with their Matches, Cocks, and Pans guarded, and ready to give fire either by one rank at a time, or two ranks, as the Officers shall see occasion to command them, which must be done after this manner: If you command only the outermost ranks to give fire, then must you command them to present kneeling on their right knees, and command them to level so low, that they shoot at the Horse legs, and by that means they will shoot clear under the tops of your Pikes being charged. If you please to command two ranks of Musketeers to give fire at one time, the Musketeers being ready to present command your Pikemen to port their Pikes: then command all your Musketeers to present, the first rank of Musketeers kneeling on their right knees, the second rank of Musketeers must move up close to the first rank of Musketeers, every Musketeer in the second rank stepping forward with his right leg within the inside of their Leaders right legs, and step forwards with their left legs close up by their Leaders left legs without-side of their Leaders left legs, and so present their Muskets over their Leaders heads. After the Musketeers in the first rank have thus presented, command them to give fire; then may you, if occasion serve, command your Pikemen to charge their Pikes again, and your Musketeers to make ready again.

But here some may object, that if any one of these two Divisions of Foot marked with the figures 2 3 4 5 6 7 8 9 10 11 12 should be charged by Horse several ways at once, then the four corners of the Division of Foot will be ill defended, by reason that the two outermost files of Pikes to the right and left hand are charging to their right and left hands; so by this means they conceive the four corners of the Division of Foot will be left naked for want of Pikes to defend them. To prevent this objection, the

APPENDIX I

Captains, Lieutenants, and Sergeants ought to be placed on the four corners of a Division of Foot with the Musketeers, as you see them in this foregoing figure, marked with the figure 7. For you must understand that each little long stroke at the corners of the Division of Foot stands for an Officer. Now all the Captains that command the Foot on the flanks of each Division of Horse in a day of Battle ought to have Pikes, and the Lieutenants and Sergeants ought to have Partizans and Halberds of eleven foot in length.

[Was there set drill for reforming after the unit was disordered/shaken, and how much more difficult from close order vs. order? If halberds as long as described here, the circle of archaeological influence around the square formation is 180ftx5659ft. If that is the case, a modelable artefact collection area for an engagement between two bodies of pike = a 24ftx3542ft area needing to be covered for just one body.] In this Service against the Horse, are two chief things that the Commanders of the Foot who command any Foot amongst the Horse in a day of Battle ought to give their Soldiers a strict charge to observe: the first is that the Musketeers when they are to give fire should always take aim at the Horses legs. The second observation is that your Pikemen charge their Pikes against the Horses, and not against the Horsemen, when the Foot are charged by Horse, and that your Pikemen charge not their Pikes, until the Enemies Horses are come within forty paces of your Foot.

If you fight Foot among your Horse on the flank of your Army, as you see them placed in these two figures before marked with the letters *H I K L M N O P Q R S*, and the figures 1 2 3 4 5 6 7 8 9 10 11 12. Then you must observe when your Enemies Horse come to charge your Horse, or the Foot on the flanks of your Division of Horse, that your Divisions of Horse move not from the two Divisions of Foot on their flanks (unless your Enemies Horse be put to the retreat) but to keep an even front, with the two Divisions of Foot on their flanks, and receive their Enemies Charge, keeping the aforesaid order. But in case your Enemies Horse rout any one of the Divisions of Foot on the flanks of any one Division of Horse, then the Commander of the Division of Horse, that is to march between two Divisions of Foot, must be in a readiness to Charge the Enemies Horse that hath routed his Foot, either with part of his Division of Horse, or the whole, as he sees occasion, or as he may with convenience.

That your intention of fighting Foot amongst the Horse may not be discovered by your Enemy, who hath not been used to the like Discipline; or at least that he may not know the way and order that you intend to fight your Foot in, let your Divisions of Foot, which are to fight on the flanks of your Horse in a day of Battle, as you see them in the two former figures: let, I say, the two Divisions of Foot which belong to each Division of Horse, march in the rear of the Divisions of Horse, as you see them in the foregoing figure, till they come within Musket-shot of their Enemies Horse: then draw up the two Divisions of Foot, the one on the one flank of a Division of Horse, and the other on the other flank of the same Division of Horse in the same order as you see them in this foregoing figure.

CHAP. XIV. What Strength each Division of Horse ought to be from three thousand to ten thousand, to fight on the flanks of a Body of Foot in a day of Battle, if you will have no Foot to fight amongst the Horse.

IF your strength of Horse be three thousand, and if they be to fight on the flanks of a Body of Foot in a day of Battle without Foot to fight amongst them, then each Division of Horse ought to be thirty in front, three deep, and ninety in a Division. If your strength of Horse be four thousand, then the strength of each Division of Horse ought to be an hundred and twenty, forty in front, and three deep. If your strength of Horse be five thousand, then each Division of Horse ought to be an hundred and fifty strong, fifty in front, and three deep. If your strength of Horse be six thousand, or seven thousand, then they ought to be an hundred and eighty in a Division, sixty in front, and three deep. If your strength of Horse be eight thousand, nine thousand, or ten thousand, then ought each Division of Horse to be an hundred in front, and three deep, and three hundred in a Division.

THE ARTE MILITAIRE

[Regimental frontage area 90ft180ft.]
Your Divisions of Horse from ninety to an hundred and eighty (if you have no Foot to fight amongst your Horse) ought to charge their Enemies Horse after this manner. Each Division of Horse from ninety to an hundred and eighty in strength ought to be sub-divided into three subdivisions, as is here set down, and shall be declared unto you by this following figure, marked with the letters *A B C*.

[An illustration was provided in this section of the original manuscript.]
The three subdivisions of Horse marked with the letters *A B C* are a Division of Horse of ninety, sub-divided into three equal sub-divisions, being thirty in a Division, ten in front, and three deep. The distance of ground between the subdivision marked with the letter *A,* and the subdivision marked with the letter *B,* is twenty paces, three feet to the pace. The like distance of ground is between the subdivisions of Horse marked with the letters *B* and *C*: the little strokes that stand in the fronts, flanks, and rear of the three subdivisions, stand for Officers.

Now when the Vanguard of your Horse comes within fifty paces of the Enemies Horse, let the two subdivisions of Horse marked with the letters *A* and *C* advance towards their Enemies Division of Horse upon an easy trot: and the Officers of the two Divisions of Horse must be careful that they Charge all together the Division of the Enemies Horse which they meet with. And when the two subdivisions on the right and left hand marked with the letters *A* and *C* do advance towards their Enemy to charge them, and then let the middle subdivision of Horse marked with the letter *B* follow after easily upon a walking pace. And when the Officer in chief that commands the middle subdivision of Horse marked with the Letter *D,* sees the other two subdivisions of Horses marked with the letters *A* and *C* to be mingled with the Enemy; then let him command his subdivision of Horse to advance upon a round trot, and charge his Enemy. The same order must be observed by all the Divisions of Horses that are but ninety in strength, when they come to charge an Enemy. And the Divisions of Horse from ninety to an hundred and eighty in strength must observe the same order in charging their Enemy, as is here set down in this Division of Horse of ninety, marked with the letters *A B C,* if no Divisions of Foot be to fight amongst the Horse.

If you be eight thousand, nine thousand, or ten thousand strong in Horse, then each Division of Horse, when you come to fight in Battle, ought to be three hundred in strength: and each Division of Horse ought to be sub-divided into five equal subdivisions, as you see them in this following figure marked with the letters *D E F G H*.

[An illustration was provided in this section of the original manuscript.]
In these five subdivisions of Horse marked with the letters *D E F G H*, there are sixty Horses in each subdivision, twenty in front, and three deep. So that the five subdivisions marked with the letters *D E F G H* are a Division of Horse of three hundred in strength, sub-divided into five equal parts, and being at their close order in rank and file: And the little small strokes that you see in the flank, rear, and front, stand for Officers. The distance of ground that is left between the subdivisions marked with the letters *D* and *E* is twenty paces, three feet to the pace. And the distance of ground between the subdivisions of Horse marked with the letters *E* and *F* is twenty paces. The same distance of ground is between the subdivisions of Horse marked with the letters *F* and *G,* and *G* and *H*.

[As Monck has presented previously his unit schematics at a company level, how much of the above material is actually workable?]

Pages 64-5

If you intend to have your Divisions of Horse to be three hundred in strength, my opinion is, that each Division of Horse ought to be sub-divided into five equal parts, as you see them in this figure marked with the letters *D E F G H*. For these reasons a Division of Horse for three hundred in strength being divided into five equal parts, as you see them in this foregoing figure, will take up much more ground in front, than a Division of Horse that is but three hundred in strength, and not sub-divided. Now it is one of the chief advantages that can be taken in a day of Battle, by your Divisions of Horse to out front your Enemies Divisions of Horse.

Besides, a Division of Horse of three hundred in strength being sub-divided, as is before set down, will be better commanded, and not so subject to fall into a disorder upon any occasion, as a Division of Horse of three hundred in strength, all in a body.

Moreover, you may charge an Enemy three several ways with a Division of Horse of three hundred in strength, being sub-divided as you see them in this foregoing figure; whereas you can charge an Enemy but one way with a Division of Horse of three hundred in strength, being all in one body.

The first of the three ways to charge your Enemy with a Division of Horse of three hundred in strength, and sub-divided, is in this manner; when a Division of Horse thus sub-divided into five equal parts cometh within forty paces of your Enemies Division of Horse which they are to charge; then let the two subdivisions of Horse marked with the letters *D* and *H* advance, and charge their Enemies Division of Horse on the flanks; and then let the other three subdivisions of Horse marked with the letters *E F G* advance, and charge their Enemy in the front of their Division at the same time.

The second way is this, when you come within forty paces of your Enemies Division of Horse, then command the three subdivisions of Horse marked with the letters *D H*, to advance upon a trot, and charge their Enemy: then command the other two subdivisions marked with the letters *E* and *G* to follow upon an easy pace, until they see that the three sub divisions marked with the letters *D F H* be mingled with their Enemy. Then let the two sub divisions marked with the letters *E* and *G* have order to advance upon a good round trot, and charge their Enemy.

[540ftx76ft diameter area of influence cavalry engagement.]

The third way of charging your Enemy is, to command the five subdivisions of Horse marked the letters *D E F G H* to charge the Enemy together in an even front. And I account any of these three ways better to charge a Division of the Enemies Horse to rout them, than to charge a Division of the Enemies Horse with a Division of three hundred Horses in one Body together, without being sub-divided.

Pages 66-7

CHAP. XV. By the following Figures are declared what Strength each Division of Foot ought to be to Fight a Battle, and Encounter with Foot: and the order that must be observed for doing the same; and how they shall easily, and readily be in order to defend themselves against the charge of any Horse.

For Field-Service you must observe to have as many Pikes as Musketeers amongst your Foot; and each Division of Foot ought to be two hundred eighty eight in strength, half Pikemen, and half Musketeers; and you must rank your men but six deep: so that in the Division of two hundred eighty eight men, there will be four and twenty files of Pikes, and four and twenty files of Musketeers, six deep. The order that they must be drawn into, to be in readiness to fight with Foot, and to defend themselves against Horse, shall be declared unto you by the following figures.

But in the first place I will shew you the order that these four and twenty files of Pikes, and four and twenty files of Musketeers must be drawn into. The first order that the aforesaid two hundred eighty eight men must be drawn into, is, as you shall see them in this following figure, marked with the figures 1 2 3; and the distance that they are at in rank and file is their Order.

[An illustration was provided in this section of the original manuscript.]

THE ARTE MILITAIRE

The figure marked with the figure 1 is a Division of Pikes of four and twenty files, six deep. The six ranks of small pricks marked with the figure 2 are a Division of Musketeers consisting of twelve files, six deep: And the like are six ranks of pricks on the left hand of the Division of Pikes figured with the figure 3.

Now the way that you must observe to bring these four and twenty files of Pikes, and four and twenty files of Musketeers into the order, as you see them in the following figure marked with the letters *A B C*, is by these words of Command.

Page 68

Command the three first ranks of Musketeers of the two Divisions of Musketeers marked with the figures 2 and 3 to march forward, till the last ranks of Musketeers of both the Divisions of Musketeers have marched twelve feet beyond the first ranks of Pikes. Then command them to stand, and cause the three ranks of Musketeers at the left hand to turn to their right hands, and the three ranks of Musketeers on the right hand to turn to their left hands. Then command them to march forward, and join together before the Division marked with the letter *A*. Then command the Musketeers, which before you commanded to turn to their left hands, now to turn to their right hands; and those Musketeers that you commanded before to turn to their right hands, command them to turn to their left hands. Then file the Musketeers that you have brought before the front of the Pikes, even with the files of Pikes. Then command the other six ranks of Musketeers on the right and left hand of the Division of Pikes to advance forwards, and front with the Musketeers, which are in the front of the Pikes, leaving eighteen foot distance between the Divisions of Musketeers, marked with the letters *C* and *B*, and *B* and *D*, as you see them in this following figure, marked with the letters *A B C D*; and the distance that they are at in rank and file is their Order.

[Firing by Horne battaille creates a 66ft frontage to the regiment.]

Pages 69-73

[An illustration was provided in this section of the original manuscript.]
The figure marked with the letter *A* is a Division of Pikes consisting of four and twenty files, six deep. The three ranks of small pricks marked with the letter *B* are four and twenty files of Musketeers, three deep. The three ranks of small pricks marked with the letter *C*, are twelve files of Musketeers, three deep: the like are the three ranks of Musketeers marked with the letter *D*. And the Musketeers standing in this order as you see them in this foregoing figure, marked with the letters *B C D* are now in a readiness to give fire on an Enemy. Now the way that the Musketeers must observe in firing on their Enemy is thus: Command both your Pikemen and Musketeers to shoulder their Arms, and march together in the same order as you see them in the foregoing figure, marked with the letters *A B C D*, commanding the three Divisions of Musketeers, marked with the letters *B C D* to make ready; and when the Musketeers are all ready, command the two first ranks of Musketeers in the aforesaid three Divisions of Musketeers to present. The three first ranks of the three Divisions of Musketeers marked with the letters *B C D* must present kneeling upon their right knees. The second ranks of the aforesaid Divisions of Musketeers must march up close to the three first ranks of Musketeers which are presenting on their right knees; every Musketeer in the second rank stepping forwards with their right legs within the inside of their Leaders right legs, and then step forwards with their left legs close up to their Leaders left legs, without-side of their legs, and present their Muskets over their Leaders heads in their first ranks. And after the two first ranks of Musketeers of the three Divisions of Musketeers marked with the letters *B C D* have thus presented, command them to give fire together And when these Musketeers before spoken of have fired, let the three first ranks of the three Divisions of Musketeers marked with the letters *B C D* remain kneeling on their right knees. Then command the second ranks of the three Divisions of Musketeers to kneel upon their right knees,

APPENDIX I

as close to their Leaders right knees as they can. Then command the last ranks of the three Divisions of Musketeers marked with the letters *B C D* to march up to their Leaders, stepping with their right legs within side of their Leaders right knees, and step forwards with their left legs without side their Leaders left legs, and present their Muskets over their Leaders heads, and then command them to give fire.

[Lead shot evidence for the first two ranks kneeling is possibly represented by a higher proportion of flattened balls, with less opportunity to fire high? Where advancing fire is clear by definable linear shot accumulations, there is a possibility of the percentage of flattened shot increasing as opposing accumulations occur closer together?]

After the last rank of the three Divisions of Musketeers marked with the letters *B C D* have fired, command the two first ranks of Musketeers of the aforesaid three Divisions of Musketeers which are kneeling, to stand up; commanding your Division of Musketeers marked with the letter *A*, and the three Divisions of Musketeers marked with the letters *B C D* to march on easily, and make ready again, and when they are ready, let them give fire in the same order as they did before. This order of marching and giving fire must be observed by all the other Divisions of Foot, that are to fight in the Body of an Army.

Or if you approve not of the way of Musketeers firing, as is here set down, you may subdivide them after the old manner, and so command them to give fire.

The order that this Division of foot marked with the letters *A B C D* must observe to defend themselves, against Horse is after this manner, as you shall see them placed in the next figure, marked with the figures 1 2 3 4 5 6 7. And the way to bring the three Divisions of Musketeers, and one of Pikes marked with the letters *A B C D* to the order of the figure following, marked with the figures 1 2 3 4 5 6 7 is done after this manner.

You must command the last rank of Musketeers, of the Division of Musketeers marked with the letter *B*, to turn to their right hands; then command an Officer to draw them away on one side of the right hand file of the Pikes, and draw them in between the third and fourth ranks of Pikes marked with the letter *A*. Then command your Pikemen to advance their Pikes, and close their files, and ranks to their close order. Then command the Division of Pikes to advance forward, till they come within three feet of the last rank of Musketeers which are in the front of the Pikes. Then command the two last ranks of the Division of Musketeers marked with the letter *C*, to turn to their left hands. Then command the two last ranks of the Divisions of Musketeers marked with the letter *D* to turn to their right hands. Then command two Officers to lead these four files of Musketeers (which were before four ranks) into the rear of the Pikes marked with the letter *A*; the which four files are there to meet and join together in the rear of the Pikes. Then command those Musketeers which did before turn to their left hands, to turn to their right hands; and those Musketeers which before turned to their right hands, to turn to their left hands. Then command the first rank of Musketeers, which is only left of the Division of Musketeers marked with the letter *C*, to turn to their left hands. Then command an Officer to lead them down close on the out-side of the right hand file of the Pikes; and when the Officer hath brought the Leader of the file of Musketeers right against the bringer up of the right hand file of Pikes, command the file of Musketeers to stand. Then command the half file of that file of Musketeers to double his front to the left hand. Then command those two files of Musketeers to turn to their right hands about. Then command the first rank which is left of the Division of Musketeers marked with the letter *D*, to turn to their right hands, commanding an Officer to lead them down close on the out-side of the left hand file of the Pikes: and when the Officer hath brought the Leader of the file of Musketeers right against the bringer up of the left hand file of the Pikes, command the file of Musketeers to stand. Then command the half file of that file of Musketeers to double his front to the right hand. Then command those two files of Musketeers to turn to their right hands about. Then command the Musketeers which have not as yet closed their ranks and files, to close their ranks and files to their close order, and file and rank even with the Pikes.

This which is here set down is the readiest, and easiest way to bring the former figure marked with

THE ARTE MILITAIRE

the letters *A B C D* unto the order of this figure following, marked with the figures 1 2 3 4 5 6 7. And this Division of Foot is now in a readiness to withstand the charge of any Horse.

Pages 74-77

[An illustration was provided in this section of the original manuscript.]
The figure marked with the figure 1, is a Division of Pikes, consisting of four and twenty files, and three deep. The figure marked with the figure 2, is a Division of Pikes of the like number that the figure 1 is. The two ranks of small pricks in the front of the Pikes, figured with the figure 3, are two ranks of Musketeers, having four and twenty in a rank. The two ranks of small pricks in the rear of the Pikes marked with the figure 4, are two ranks of Musketeers, having four and twenty in a rank. The two files of pricks on the right hand of the Division of Pikes, marked with the figure 5, are two files of Musketeers, six deep: and the like are the two files of pricks on the left hand of the Division of Pikes, marked with the figure 6. The little strokes at the corner of the Division of Foot, marked with the figure 7, stand for Officers. And the rank of small pricks between the two Divisions of Pikes marked with the figures 1 and 2, are one rank of Musketeers consisting of four and twenty Musketeers in number.

You see in this figure marked with the figures 1 2 3 4 5 6 7, the Musketeers standing under the shelter of the Pikes, the Pikes and the Musketeers being all at their close order, and in a readiness to receive a charge from Horse; and the Pikes sheltering the Musketeers every way upon occasion from the force of the Horse.

Now the way how these Musketeers and Pikemen shall defend themselves against Horse, I will here declare unto you. If you perceive your Enemies Horse to divide themselves into four parts to charge any one Division of Foot which is placed in this manner as you see them in this foregoing figure: then command the two right hand files of Pikes, and the two left hand files of Pikes of the six ranks of Pikes marked with the figures 1 and 2, to charge to their right and left hands over the shoulders of the Musketeers on the right and left hand, marked with the figures 5 and 6. Command also the four files of Musketeers, marked with the aforesaid two figures, to turn to their right and left hands. When the two right hand files of Pikes are commanded to charge to their right and left hands, then command the other twenty files of Pikes in the first three ranks of Pikes, marked with the figure 1, to charge to the front over the shoulders of the Musketeers, marked with the figure 3. Then command the twenty files of Pikes marked with the figure 2 to charge to the rear over the shoulders of the two ranks of Musketeers in the rear marked with the figure 4. And the aforesaid Musketeers must observe to turn to their right hands about, when the Pikes are commanded to charge to the rear.

The Musketeers which are placed without-side of the Pikes, marked with the figures 3 4 5 and 6, must stand ready with their Matches, Cock, and Pans guarded, and to be ready to give fire either by one rank at a time, or two ranks, as the Officers shall see occasion to command them; the which must be done after this manner. If you command only the outermost ranks of Musketeers to give fire, then must you command them to present kneeling on their right knees, and command them to level so low with their Muskets, that they may shoot at the horses legs; by that means they will shoot clear under the tops of your Pikes being charged. If you please to command two ranks of Musketeers to give fire at one time, then as soon as the Musketeers are ready to present, command your Pikemen to port their Pikes: then command all the Musketeers beside of the Pikes to present, where the first ranks of Musketeers are to kneel on their right knees; then the second ranks of Musketeers must move up close to the first ranks of Musketeers, every Musketeer in the second ranks stepping forwards with their right legs within the in-side of their Leaders right legs; then they must step forwards with their left legs close up by their Leaders left legs, without-side of their Leaders legs, and present their Muskets over their Leaders heads in the first rank. When the Musketeers have thus presented, command them to give fire. And if Horse charge a Division of Foot which stand in the same order that this Division of Horse doth, marked with the figures 1 2 3 4 5

APPENDIX I

6 7, you must command your Pikemen to charge again, and be careful to place the Captains, Lieutenants, and Sergeants of the Division on the four corners of the Division, as you see them in the foregoing figure marked with the figure 7.

Pages 84, 93-96

CHAP. XVIII. Some certain Observations to be kept in the fighting of Battles, and some Directions for the Embattling of an Army.

WE may observe two especial ends which the great Commanders of the World have ever striven to achieve, Victory, and Over mastering their Enemies. The latter by cunning, and wisely carrying of a matter before it come to trial by blows: the former by forcible means, and fighting a Battle: the one proceeding from Wisdom, and the better faculties of the soul; the other depending upon the strength and abilities of the body. The latter end is principally to be embraced, as the safest course in these uncertain and casual events. For that which rests upon corporal strength, and make execution the way to a conclusion, is full of hazard, and little certainty. And yet of all the actions of War, the most glorious and most important is to know how to give Battle: For the art of embattling an Army hath always been esteemed the chief point of skill in a General (for skill and practice do more towards the Victory than multitude) seeing the gaining of one or two Battles acquire, or subvert whole Empires, Kingdoms, or Countrys: And therefore a General of an Army ought to know all the advantages which may be taken in a day of Battle; and how to prepare against disadvantages which may happen. Concerning both which I will here give you my opinion.

Advantages bring hope of Victory, and hope conceives such spirits as usually follow when the thing which is hoped for is effected; whereby the courage becomes hardy, and resolute in Victory; and where the Soldiers fear no overthrow, they are more than half Conquerors. So on the other side, disadvantages and danger breed fear, and fear so checks valour, and controls the spirits, that Virtue and Honour give place to distrust, and yield up their interest to such directors as can afford nothing but diffidence and irresolutions.

It is most necessary for a General in the first place to approve his Cause, and settle an opinion of right in the minds of his Officers and Soldiers: the which can be no way better done, than by the Chaplains of an Army. Also a General ought to speak to the Colonels of his Army to encourage their Officers with a desire to fight with the Enemy; and all the Officers to do the like to their Soldiers. And the better to raise the common Soldiers spirits, let their Officers tell them that their General doth promise them, if they will fight courageously with their Enemy, and do get the day, that they shall have, besides the Pillage of the Field, twelve-pence apiece to drink, to refresh their spirits when the business is done. The which I am confident will make the common men fight better, than the best Oration in the world.

It is very fit a General should use his best endeavour to understand the strength of his Enemies Horse and Foot, and how they are armed both with Offensive and Defensive Arms, and what proportion of Pikes they have to their Musketeers. Also he must endeavour to know by name and place the Chief Officers of his Enemies Army, and their abilities in Martial Affairs; by the which means he may guess where the Chief Commanders do command in a day of Battle: So he may easily know how to place his Army best for his own advantage. This if carefully observed will be of very great use.

You ought to know that novelties, and unexpected adventures are very successful in Battles, and in all Martial designs.

A General must be careful never to hazard a Battle with his Enemy, when he finds him embattled in a ground of advantage, although he do out-number him much with men: The safest way then will be to fight with him by Famine: For although a Generals Fortune should be generally subject to his will, yet by his wisdom he should rather follow Reason than Fortune in such cases.

THE ARTE MILITAIRE

A General ought to be careful when an Enemy approaches near him, to send out some two or three knowing Officers with a good strong party of Horse and Dragoons to make good the Horsemen's retreat upon occasion whereby to discover the Enemies strength, and order of his March: and that they take notice of what advantages may be taken of the ground which lies between them. And the party that is sent ought to have order, if it be possible to take some stragglers, that the General may the better understand the strength, and condition of his Enemies Army.

If you intend to give Battle, you must have regard to these principal things that follow: You must never suffer yourself to be forced to fight against your will; and never to fight your Soldiers when their spirits are either dismayed, or cast down. If you resolve to fight with your Enemy, then you ought to choose a place for the Battle fit for the quality, and number of your Soldiers. For if you fear to be enclosed by a great number, you ought to shelter your flanks, or at least one of them, by the nature of the place, as by a River, Wood, or some other thing equivalent: If you be weak in your Cavalry, you must avoid the Plains, or fight with Foot amongst your Horse, as is showed in the three next Battles: If you be strong in Horse, you must avoid strait passages, or enclosed places.

You ought to know that directions are the life of Action, and the sinews and strength of Martial Discipline; and therefore you must give punctual orders to your Marshal of the Field, and your Major-Generals, and Colonels of the Brigades both of Horse and Foot before they begin to fight: And your Orders ought to be written, if you have time: for after the Battle is once begun, is impossible for a General to give Orders, more than in that part where he is present at the same time.

That you may know how to place your Divisions of Horse and Foot at their true distances, you ought to allow unto every Horseman in the Front of the Divisions of the Van-guard, and Battle six foot of ground in breadth; and to every Foot Soldier in the Divisions in the Van-guard, and Battle you ought to allow five Foot. Also you must observe, that between every two Divisions of Horse and Foot in the Van-guard of your Army to allow an hundred paces of ground in breadth, three feet to the pace: besides what you allow for the Division in the Battle, which is for the reserve. You ought likewise to allow between the Vanguard of your Horse-Troops an hundred paces; and between the Van-guard of your Foot an hundred and fifty paces, three feet to the pace. This order must be observed both in placing the Divisions of Horse and Foot, and the Van-guards, Battle, and Rear-guard of your Army; that the foremost Troops being put to recoil, may not fall upon those which should come up to relieve them, nor the Battle upon the Rear.

[750ft frontage +720ft largest possible brigade frontage = 1,470ft largest possible army frontage x 1,440ft.] You must always be careful to place the best Regiments either of Horse or Foot on the Wings of your Army.

Appendix II

Extracts from *The first part of the principles of the art military practiced in the wars of the United Netherlands, under the command of His Highness the Prince of Orange our Captain General, for as much as concerns the duties of a soldier, and the officers of a company of foot, as also of a troupe of horse, and the exercising of them through their several motions: represented by figure, the word of command and demonstration / composed by Captain Henry Hexham, Quartermaster to the Honourable Colonel Goring* by Henry Hexham (1642).

Page 5

NEXT Follows the Postures of the Pike, and Musket, represented by figure, having the word of command under every of them, with brief observations on the first page, answering to the number of every figure.

The postures of the Pike may be done, either standing or marching. In marching (as well as in standing) a pike-man may advance, shoulder, or charge his Pike, either to the Front; to the Rear, to the right, or left flank, according to the term of direction given him by his officer.

The postures likewise of a musketeer are also done, either marching, or standing, by himself, or in his squadron, company, or division.

[Accumulations of associated musket furniture identified within the immediate country surrounding a battlefield should be highlighted in relation to the known approach of varying forces to the battlefield. More musket furniture is likely to be lost in passing and as such should be represented as e.g. remnants of bandoliers, small change, occasional musket ball, hobnails, possibility of sword chape, buttons etc. lost on march.]

A good musketeer that is ready, and well made by his officer, will fall naturally and gracefully to the doing of his postures, and will take delight in handling of his Musket, avoiding antique, and dancing postures, which heretofore have been taught by some officers, but now is grown ridiculous, not beseeming and becoming the grave comportment, and carriage of a Soldier.

A Captain then, having a commission given him to raise a company, ought to make choice of the taller, and abler men for his pikes, and of the shorter, stronger, and well set with good legs, for his musketeers: yea, such as may be able to endure both hardship, and labour. And thus much as a short preamble by the way, before we come to shew the figures of the postures themselves.

THE ARTE MILITAIRE

Page 6

Brief observations upon the postures of the Pike, answering to the number of every figure following.

1. Set the butt end of your Pike near your right foot on the outside, holding it right up in your right hand, about the height of your eye, and your arm a little bending, and your right foot forward.
2. With the right hand alone bring your Pike just before your body, bearing it directly right up, raising the butt end from the ground, then take the Pike with your left hand about the height of your girdle.
3. Forsake the Pike with your right hand, and with the left hand alone raise up the Pike, that the But end be about the height of your thigh, then take the But end in your right hand, without stooping to it.
4. Forsake the pike with the left hand, and with your right hand alone carry the pike right up locking the pike between your shoulder and arm, your right hand holding the butt end of the pike, about the height of your hip.
5. Sink your right hand a little, and with your left hand take the pike, as high as well you can reach, and bring the pike just before your body.
6. Forsake the pike with your right hand, and bring down the pike in your left hand, that the butt end be near unto the ground, then with your right hand take the pike about the height of your head.
7. Forsake the pike with your left hand, and with the right hand only set the butt end on the ground, on the outside of your right foot, as in the third posture.
8. Bring the pike just before your body, & raise the butt end from the ground, bearing it forward, then take it with your left hand a little beneath your right.
9. Bring forward the pike with your left hand, and take it in your right, reaching backward as far as well you may.
10. Forsake your pike with your left hand, & with the right only lay it upon your right shoulder, bearing the butt end about a foot from the ground, holding your thumb under the pike, the better to govern it, carrying the pike forward.

[Although clearly unlikely, defences and buildings associated with military activity may well act as a focal point for analysis of pike drill specifically shouldering one's pike, the low overhang of masonry coupled with the quality of pike heads possibly resulting in a number being knocked clean from their staves, although the likelihood such objects would be reused or picked up limits this formation process validity.]

11. Bear your right hand with the pike backward, as far as well you can, with your left hand take the pike forward, and with the right bear the pike upwards.
12. Forsaking the pike with the right hand, cast the point forward, that the butt end may conveniently be taken in the right hand.
13. Take the butt end of the pike in your right hand, holding it about your hip, and raising the pike with your left hand about the height of your breast, carry the pike directly before you, your left foot toward.
14. Raise the right hand and stretch it backward, your left hand being at your breast, your left elbow against your hip.
15. Bear down the butt end of the pike with your right hand, and raise the pike with the left, and so advance, as in the sixth figure.
16. Sink your right hand, and with your left take the pike as high as well you may reach, bringing the pike just before your body.

APPENDIX II

[Again highly unlikely, the ability to identify instances whereby port and charge your pike are represented archaeologically, might be seen through identifying the peripheries of a zone of influence associated with a push of pike or a regiment charging for horse, pike heads likely to be cut from their stave by circling cavalry, or broken away during hand-to-hand combat. This also could prove a focal point for discovering broken or fragments of armour or conducting localised soil compaction analysis through section analysis.]

Unnumbered pages

[An illustration was provided in this section of the original manuscript.]

17 Forsake the butt end with your right hand, bearing forward your Pike in the left hand, and take the pike backward in the right hand, as far as well you may reach.
18 Forsake the Pike with your left hand, and with your right only lay it upon your shoulder, or as in the twelfth figure.
19 Bear the pike with your right hand backward, take it forward in your left hand as you may conveniently reach, bearing the pike with your right hand upward.
20 Forsaking the pike with your right hand, bear it over your head, and at the same instant turn your body to the left hand, that you may conveniently take the butt end of the pike in your right hand.
21 Having the butt end of your pike in your right hand, stretch your right arm backward, and set your left hand at your breast, &c, as in the sixteenth figure.
22 Slip your left hand forward as far as well you may, and lift the pike upwards to your head, and with the right hand bear the butt end somewhat downward.
23 Forsaking the butt end of the Pike with your right hand, bear up the pike over your head with your left hand only, at that instant turn your face to the right hand, and be ready with your right hand to take the Pike more backward.
24 Having the pike in the right hand, forsake it with your left, and with the right hand only lay it upon your shoulder, as in the 12 and 20 figure.
25 This is to be done in three motions, as the contrary is shown in the ninth, tenth and eleventh figures. Bear the pike with the right hand backward, with your left take it forward, bearing the butt end downward, then slip down your right hand a little above your left, and set the butt end on the ground, as in the ninth figure.
26 This is to be done by several palming postures, with the right hand bear the butt end of the pike backward, as far as you can, and continue palming till you come to the head of your pike.
27 With your left hand hold the pike a little below the head, your right hand more backward, as far as the cheeks, or arming reach, set your right hand upon your hip, your elbow stretch forth, and your left hand more forward before your breast.
28 Remove your right hand to your left, & in your right hand only carry your pike, your hand being upon your hip.
29 This is to be done by several palming postures backward, bringing forward your right hand as far as well you can, and with the left hand gripe the pike backward as far as you can.
30 Forsake the pike with your right hand, bring forward the pike with the left, & take it backward with the right, and so continue palming, until you have the butt end of the pike in your right hand.
31 Stretch your right arm backward with the pike in your hand, your left hand at your breast, and your elbow upon your hip, as in the sixteenth figure.
32 This is to be done in three motions, first bearing the pike right up before the body, and so forward as from the advance in the 6, 7 and 8 figures, only you must observe to set the butt end of the pike at the inside of the right foot, which is your close order.

THE ARTE MILITAIRE

33 The butt end of the pike resting against your right foot, take it in your left hand, about the height of your girdle, and step forward with your left foot, the knee bent, lay your left arm, upon your knee couching down low, and draw your sword over your left arm.

34 Raise your body right up, set your pike against your right shoulder with the left hand, the butt end being still upon the ground, then put up your sword.

Page 9

[An illustration was provided in this section of the original manuscript.]

Page 10

Brief observations upon the postures of the Musket, answering to the number of every figure on the other page.

1 This figure shows a musketeer marching with his musket on his left shoulder aslope holding the butt end of it with his left hand, and his match between the two lesser fingers, with his rest in his right hand, and his right leg before.

2 How he carries his musket shouldered with the rest crossed, close to the inside of his musket his match between his two fingers, holding his thumb upward to the fork of the rest, and his right leg before.

3 Draw the right leg to your left, and withal sink your musket, and then slip your rest, griping it with your right hand between the breach and the thumb-hole.

4 Hold the musket upright, in your right hand, and on your side, raise your left hand to the fork of your musket, and set your thumb against the Fork.

5 Sink your right hand, and gripe the musket fast in your left hand, with your rest on the outside, holding your thumb hard against the care of your Fork, to lock the rest fast to your musket in your left hand, that you may have the use of your right hand, to do the postures following.

6 Take your match from between your little finger, with your thumb, and the second finger of your right hand, being turned with the palm from you.

7 Bring the right hand with the match backward, and your left hand with the musket and rest forward, turning your face a little backward, and blow of your match with a good blast.

8 Holding your match between your thumb and second finger, then bring it to the cock, & press it into the cock with your thumb.

[Possibility of dislodging incorrectly tensioned serpentine/pan cover.]

9 Your thumb and finger being upon the cock, and your second and third finger under the cock, pull the cock down to the pan, and with your thumb and middle finger, either raise or sink it, that it may fall right into the pan.

10 Lay the two fore fingers of your right hand upon your pan, the thumb behind the escutcheon of the pan, the easier to lift up the musket, and so bringing up the musket with both hands toward your mouth and yet not stooping, blow again your coal.

11 Open your pan with your two fingers, and withal bring back your right hand to the thumb-hole of your musket, your second finger to the trigger, and with your left hand fix the fork of the rest to your musket, your thumb against the fork, and set the pick end of the rest upon the ground.

12 Lye on, and lift up your right elbow, bringing the butt end of your musket within your shoulder, near your breast, winding your shoulder to it, holding it fast from recoiling, presenting a faire body, the small end appearing a little above your shoulder, having the left leg before, bending a

APPENDIX II

little with the knee, and resting stiff upon your right leg, take your mark breast high.
13 First, sink the butt end of your musket, and with the rest bring it to your right side: then step forward with your right leg, and carrying your musket in your left hand, fall away.

[Rather than acting as some observations upon best practice and means using armament, this breaks the drill down into constituent parts so that even a recruit can practice and gain a high level of proficiency outside of drill ground practice. It is a systematic explanation.]

14 Take the match out of the cock with the thumb, and second finger of your right hand, holding the musket and rest in the left hand only.
15 Return the match between the two lesser fingers of your left hand, from whence you had it.
16 Bring up the musket with the left hand only towards your mouth, and withal, blow your pan stiffly, not stooping with your head, in the meantime take your touch box in your right hand, as this figure shows.

Unnumbered pages

[An illustration was provided in this section of the original manuscript.]

17 Hold your touch-box between the thumb, and fore-finger of the right hand only and so prime as shows the figure.

[Possibility of losing incorrectly attached powder horn cover. Alternatively, if kept in bad condition, there is a need to analyse working parts to understand unidentified finds in relation to musketry. Possible loss of pan pricker at this stage?]

18 Lay the right thumb over the barrel near the pan, and with your two fore-most fingers shut the pan.
19 Hold your musket fast with the right hand at the breech, the left as before, turning the pan downwards, that the loose powder may fall off.
20 Hold your musket in both hands as before, heave it up towards your mouth, not stooping blow off the loose dust, or corns.
21 Hold your musket in both hands as before, bear it upright towards your left side, and with all step forward with your left leg, then holding the musket only in the right hand at the breech forsaken your rest.
22 Having forsaken your rest, take the musket into your left hand, about the middle of the barrel, so as the butt end touch not the ground, trailing your rest between your musket, and your body.
23 Take your charge in your right hand, with the thumb, band fore finger thereof, thrust of the cover.

[Possibility of loss of lead/copper cartridge holders at this stage.]

24 Draw back your left hand with the musket, as far as conveniently you can, and with your right hand put powder in to the bore of the barrel, holding the charge between your thumb & fore-finger only, as this figure shows.
25 Take your bullet forth of your bag, or out of your mouth, and then put it into the muzzle of your musket.
[At this stage, look for adherence to drill book manuals/intuitive thought through isolated evidence for chewing/deformation, evidence of large calibre ball not fitting barrel. It is possible at this stage

THE ARTE MILITAIRE

to also find evidence for scrap lead held and lost from ball pouch, and stray sprue from individuals fashioning their own ammunition.]

26 With your right hand turning the palm from you, draw forth your scouring stick, bearing your body, and your left hand with your musket, so far back as you can.
27 Having drawn forth your scouring-stick, set the rammer head against your breast, and slip your hand close to your rammer, that you may the easier put it into the muzzle of your musket.

[Evidence for hard ramming is represented through irregular circular deformations on one side of ball. Also look for alternations from normally shot e.g. no wad=striations from escaped gas on sides of ball, wad and missed ball=completely circular shot, double shotted=one flattened side to ball, triple shotted=double flattened ball, accompanied by local one side flattened shot, slug shot=elongated rhomboid shaped shot. At this point it is also likely that a metal scouring stick ends up lost, also representing a firing position. At this stage you need to remember, only round shot with no deformation is likely to represent a firing position, where clear linear accumulations of shot, actual firing position is likely to be 50 yards behind the orientation of shot.]

28 After your bullet, least it should fall out again, either in skirmishing, or upon a sloping trench, put in some Harts hair, or some other stopping, and then with your scouring-stick ram home your powder, bullet, and stopping twice or thrice.
29 With your right hand turned, draw your scouring stick out of your musket, as before.
30 Your scouring stick being drawn forth of your barrel, turn it, and bring the scouring-stick end to your breast, and so slip your hand within a handful of the end.
31 Return the scouring stick into its socket; from whence you had it.
32 Bring forward your musket with your left hand, and bear it right up, take it into the right hand at the breech, and so hold it in your right hand only, either to shoulder it or to lock it to your rest and so much for your marching postures.

[An illustration was provided in this section of the original manuscript.]

Page 14

Brief observations for a Musketeer.
When a Musketeer is to be exercised in his squadron, Company, or division, all postures both marching, and standing are readily done, and reduced to these three words of command, to wit.
- Make ready.
- Present.
- Give Fire.

For first a good Musketeer, which hath all his postures perfectly, hearing his officer give the first term of direction make ready, will quickly run them over, even from unshouldering of his Musket, to the guarding of his pan, which is the sixth posture standing, and the eleventh marching before he comes to present.

Secondly, in presenting he will be sure to blow his match well, open his pan, and fall back with his right hand to the thumb-hole of his musket, & having his fore-finger upon the trigger, setting forward his left leg, will attend the next word of direction.

Thirdly, lying on before he comes to give fire, bending his left knee, will fall back with his right leg, bringing the butt end of his musket, close between his breast and shoulder, raising his musket fast, and hard to his shoulder will keep it fast from recoiling, & resting firm upon his right leg will give fire.

APPENDIX II

[Assuming a correlation between musket shot assemblage, representing characteristic flattening, over firing and characterised deformation, with fallen personal items e.g. scouring stick ends, powder-horn lids, sword chapes, loose change, buttons etc. it is hoped that gauging level and scale of lost accumulated items, a clear idea of firing posture might be assumed, e.g. kneeling=tumbled typology, firing from rest=flattened balls, firing full height/bastard musket (usually a shorter version of the typical issue musket in use at the time, typically either sawn off from previous examples or an entirely new issue of musket)=firing too high/rounded shot.]

Having given fire, he takes up his musket, and rest gracefully, and bringing up his right leg again, falls away in his rank, returns his match, clears his pan, prims his pan, & doth quickly all his postures standing, or marching, as hath been taught, and which shall be shown more at large by figure, when we come to the exercising of musketeers in gross.

Page 17

Practised in the wars of the united Netherlands.

Now follows the true form of exercising of a Foot Company of 40 pikes and 40 musketeers besides officers, represented by figure, the words of Command and demonstration: but before we come to the particular motions, it is necessary for a young soldier to know first what a File and a Ranke is.

[An illustration was provided in this section of the original manuscript.]

Files

- number
  - 1 The leader of the right hand file.
  - 2 The leader of the left hand file.
  - 3 The middle file on the right hand.
  - 4 The middle file on the left hand.
  - 5 The second file next the right hand.
  - 6 The second file next the left hand.
  - 7 The third file from the right hand.
  - 8 The third file from the left hand.

The Demonstration. Ranks.

- Letter.
  - a The first Rank of Leaders.
  - b The last Rank of Bringers up.
  - c The Ranks of the Leaders of half files to the front.
  - d The Rank of the leaders of half files to the Revere.
  - e The second Rank next the front.
  - f The second Rank next the Revere.
  - g The fourth Rank from the front.
  - h The fourth Rank from the Revere.
  - i The third Rank from the front.
  - k The third Rank from the Revere.

THE ARTE MILITAIRE

Page 18

Thirdly, to understand well the three distances, namely, *Open order, order* & *close order.*

The Definition.
Open order then, or the first distance is, when the soldiers both in *Ranke,* and *File,* stand sixe foot removed one from another, as the *scale,* and this figure following shows.

[An illustration was provided in this section of the original manuscript.]

Observations.
Because the measure of these distances cannot be taken so exactly by the eye, we take the distance of six foot between *File* and *File,* by commanding the soldiers, as they stand, to stretch forth their arms, and stand so removed one from another that their hands may meet.

And for the *Ranks,* we make account we take the same distance of six foot, when the butt end of the pikes doe almost reach their heels, that march before them.

Page 19

The second distance, or your *Order* is, when your men stand three foot removed one from another both in *Ranke* and *File,* and this *order* is to be used when they are embattled, or march in the face of an Enemy, or when they come to stand, or when you will wheel, as this next figure represents.

[An illustration was provided in this section of the original manuscript.]

Observations.
We take the second *order,* or distance between *File* and *File,* by bidding the soldiers set their arms a *Kenbowe* [akimbo], and put themselves so close; that their elbows may meet. And we reckon we take the same distance between the *Ranks,* when they come up almost to the swords point.

Note, that when you march throw any country, you must observe three foot only from *File* to *File,* and six from *Ranke* to *Ranke.*

The third distance, or your *close order* is commanded by this word *Close* which is, when there is one foot and a half from *File* to *File,* and three from *Ranke* to *Ranke,* as this Figure demonstrates.

[Approximately 6 ranks by 6 files= Open Order= 36ftx36ft, Order=18ftx18ft, Close Order=9ftx9ft, only applicable to pike. Double your fronts, 12 files by 3 ranks Open Order=72ftx18ft, Order=36ftx9ft, Close Order=18ftx4.5ft.]

[An illustration was provided in this section of the original manuscript.]
Observe that though this figure stands but at a foot and a half distance: yet this is for the pikes only, and must never be used, but when you will stand firm to receive the charge of an Enemy. The musketeers must never be closer, then the second distance of three foot in square, because they are to have a free use of their Arms.

[Regiment in square's circle of influence=50ft2.]

Page 20

This figure represents the 40 pikes, and 40 musketeers, standing in their order because the page will not bear the first four motions in their open order.

[An illustration was provided in this section of the original manuscript.]
Here begins the words of Command.
- 1 Stand right in your Files.
- 2 Stand right in your Ranks.
- 3 Silence.

[An illustration was provided in this section of the original manuscript.]

Here begins the first motion. 5. To the right hand.
It is to be noted, when you are commanded to be *As you were,* you are ever to turn to the contrary hand from whence you came, as for example, if you did turn to the right hand, you are to return to the left hand, and so in the rest.
  As you were, that is, as you stand in your order in the figure above marked with the letter I.

Page 21

- 9. To the right hand about.
- 10. As you were.
- 11. To the left hand about.
- 12. As you were.

[An illustration was provided in this section of the original manuscript.]

An Observation.
These turnings to the right or left hand, or to either hand about serve for the given or receiving of a charge upon the right or left Flank, or in the Revere about.

Page 22

As you were.
Because there is now room enough this figure shows them standing in their open order of six foot distance one from another both in rank and file from which standing they are to do these motions following.

Page 23

13. Ranks to the right hand double. The Demonstration.
The 2, 6, 8 & 10 ranks from the front marked with the Letters b, d, f, h, & k moues all together and doubles into their order on the right hand of the files numbered 1, 2, 3, 4, 5, 6, 7, & 8. making 5 ranks at their double open order of 12 foot, & 16 men in each ranks as is seen in this figure above.

THE ARTE MILITAIRE

Pages 24-5

The Demonstration.
This motion differs not from the former, but only that the utmost man of the second Ranke, and subsequently all the other ranks which moved before comes now up together to their order on the left hand of the files numbered, 8, 7, 6, 5, 4, 3, 2, & 1.

Pages 26-34

17. Files to the right hand double. The Demonstration.
The 2 file (next the right hand) moves & falls back between the right hand file, the 4th file between the 3. The 6 between the 5 & the 8 (or left hand file) between the 7 file all to their order, making four files, 20 men deep, and 12 foot distance betwixt file and file, as in this figure.

[An illustration was provided in this section of the original manuscript.]

[An illustration was provided in this section of the original manuscript.]

The Demonstration.
The files which moved before stand now still and the 2 file next the left hand file falls back between the left hand file, the 5 file between the 6, the 3 between the 4 and the 1 (or right hand file) between the 2 file making 20 men deep, and 12 foot distance betwixt file and file as before.

[An illustration was provided in this section of the original manuscript.]

[An illustration was provided in this section of the original manuscript.]

18. Half files to the right hand double your front. The Demonstration.
The leader of the half file on the right hand, (noted f) steps to his order beyond the right hand file number 1. and also all the rest of the files stepping to their order on their right hand, comes up together between the files numbered, 1 & 2, 2 & 3, 3 & 4, 4 & 5, 5 & 6, 6 & 7, 7 and 8 into the Ranks marked a, b,. c, d, & e at their order of three foot distance in file, and 6 in rank, as this figure above shows.

[An illustration was provided in this section of the original manuscript.]

[An illustration was provided in this section of the original manuscript.]

19. Half files to the right hand double your front. The Demonstration.
This motion differs not from the other, but that the leader of the half-file on the left hand & consequently all the rest of the files, steps to their order on the left hand, & comes up together between the files numbered 8 & 7, 7 & 6, 6 & 5, 5 & 4, 4 & 3, 3 & 2, 2 & 1 into the ranks marked (as before) with the letters a, b, c, d, and e.

[An illustration was provided in this section of the original manuscript.]

Page 35

[An illustration was provided in this section of the original manuscript.]

APPENDIX II

The demonstration.
When you will Countermarch to the right hand, the first Ranke of Leaders numbered 1, 2, 3, 4, 5, 6, 7 and 8. only must advance one step forward with the right leg, and then turn, and all the other Ranks must march first up to the place, from whence the first Ranke did Countermarch, before they turn, where the Sariant [Sergeant] stands marked with a star. This figure shows that between the ranks a and d there are 8 ranks met at their order, and the Captain counter marching to the Revere, with the first Ranke of Leaders, to the 6 rank marked f and the Lieutenant, with the rank of bringers up noted K towards the front to the rank noted e which represents the Countermarch incomplete, as is seen in this figure above.

Pages 38-40

This figure shows the Countermarch complete, when the Captain (or Officer) is come with the first Ranke of Leaders to the place, where the bringers up, & the Lieutenant stood, and the Lieutenant with the bringers up to the Captains place, standing in their open order in rank and file, as this figure demonstrates.

[An illustration was provided in this section of the original manuscript.]

Observe likewise, if you will now Countermarch to the left hand, the first rank must step forwards one step with the left leg: and then turn, and all the other Ranks behind, must come up to that place before they turn, where the Sariant with his Halberd stands as before. *Ranks to the left hand Countermarch.*

[An illustration was provided in this section of the original manuscript.]

Note that this figure (as the first) shows the Countermarch incomplete as before.

[An illustration was provided in this section of the original manuscript.]

This figure shows, that the Captain is Countermarch up with the first rank of leaders into that place, where the front stood before, and every rank, and file in their open order.
The like Countermarch is performed, either on the right, or left flank by giving first this word of command, *To the right,* or *left hand,* omitting the naming, either of *Ranks* or *files,* in saying only, *To the right, or left hand Countermarch,* which you lift.

Page 41

Observations before yow wheel.
- First
    ◊ *Files to the right,* or *left hand,* or *to the middle.*
- Close to your Order.
    ◊ To 3 foot between File and File.

If you would close your files to the right hand, the outermost file on that hand stands still, and the next on the right hand, (numbered 2) moues first to their order, and then all the files ciphered, 3, 4, 5, 6, 7, & 8 the left hand file closes in all to their order. And if you would have them close to the left hand, the outermost file also on that hand stands still, and then the file next the left hand (numbered 7) moves first, and afterward all the other files, noted 6, 5, 4, 3, 2, & 1 (or the right hand file) close all to their order.

But if you desire to have your files close to the *middle,* then the two middle most files numbered 4 & 5 close first to their order of three foot, and having their distance, the other files numbered 2, 3 and 1 on the right hand, and the files, 8, 7 and 6 on the left hand closes both ways into their order.

THE ARTE MILITAIRE

- Secondly
    - *Ranks to your Order Close.*
- that is
    - To three foot between Ranke and Ranke.

Note, that in this motion also the *Ranks*, which stand in their open order on the other page, marked with the Letters, b c d e f g h i and k moving all together in an even front, comes up to their order, or distance of three foot, as this figure demonstrates, where both files & ranks stand in their order of 3 foot distance.

[An illustration was provided in this section of the original manuscript.]

Observe, that when you exercise a company single, you double your front before you wheel, in regard the body is small: but in a division, or a greater body, you close both your ranks and files to your order (as above) omitting the doubling, and then wheel: but being a single company when you wheel to the right hand, then double your front to the left hand: for so the leader of the right hand file will keep his place on that corner towards which you wheel.

[While obviously unintentional, the ability to wheel a body of troops as a unified body as it would be at order in line of battle is almost impossible. Assuming the optimal conditions and drill of the performing soldiers, the inside of the wheel is still required to perform a larger pace than the outside face. Therefore, assuming the outer section is at open order, with the inner at close order, this body should have a frontage of 22.5ftx18ftx4.5ft.]

[An illustration was provided in this section of the original manuscript.]

Pages 42-3

[An illustration was provided in this section of the original manuscript.]
Againe when you wheel to the left hand, double your front to the right hand, and then the two leaders on the left hand, doe but only turn their bodies like the point of a Compass, to that hand whereto they wheel, while the body comes about with a faster motion and an even front.

[An illustration was provided in this section of the original manuscript.]

Page 44

Note also, that after you have wheeled to which hand you list, and as often as you will, you give in a single company this word of command, *Half files as you were,* that is, as they stood in their order both in rank and file before; but in greater bodies where the doubling is omitted, you first open your ranks, by giving this term of direction. *Ranks backward to your open order,* and then likewise your files by commanding. *Files open* (both ways) *to your open order* of six foot as this figure both in rank, and file represents.

In opening of *Ranks* and *Files,* you must make all the *Files* or *Ranks,* saving the outermost on that hand from whence you mean to open (which must stand) to moue altogether, till the second *Ranke* or *File* from that which stands, have gotten its distance, and consequently all the rest.

Pages 45-7

Having performed the former Motions you may afterward exercise your company of Pikes, and

APPENDIX II

Musketeers together, or if you please each a part.

To begin then with the Pikes you may command them to do these motions standing, to wit.
- Advance your Pikes.
- Order your Pikes.
- Shoulder your Pikes.
- Charge your Pikes.
- Order your Pikes.
- Trail your Pikes.
- Check your Pikes.

But these Motions are to be performed, both standing, and marching, namely.
- Charge your Pikes.
- Shoulder your Pikes.
- To the right hand Charge.
- Shoulder your Pikes.
- To the left hand Charge.
- Shoulder your Pikes.
- To the Revere Charge.
- Shoulder your Pikes.
- Stand.
- Order your Pikes.

First, note that in charging half the Ranks only must charge their Pikes, the other hindermost half of the Ranks, doe but port their Pikes that is, they carry them so couched, over the Heads of the foremost as may give them no offence, either in charging, or retiring. Besides, this way the Pikes are not so subject, to be broken by the shot of the Enemy, as when they are advanced.

Secondly, they must likewise observe, when they charge standing, to fall back with the right leg, and marching to steppe forwards with the left.

Thirdly, the exercising of your Musketeers is likewise performed either or Marching.

That is, either by Ranks, or by Files after three manner of ways, to wit, first having an Enemy in your front. Secondly in your Revere, and thirdly upon your right, or left flank, as these figures following in exercising of 260 Pikes & Musketeers (besides Officers will demonstrate, whereof the first shows the manner of giving fire standing, upon an Enemy in your front, by commanding these three terms or direction) underneath.

[An illustration was provided in this section of the original manuscript.]

This figure above shows, that the first, and second rank of both the wings of Musketeers, having given fire are fallen away, and are a doing their postures, till they come in the vacant Ranks in the Revere noted, i & k, while the third and fourth Ranks (on both flanks) make ready, and advances up to the same ground where the first were: even with the front of the Pikes:

Note also, that the first Ranke falling back with their right legs, bending their left knee, lies on and gives fire (as hath bin taught) and the first Ranke falling away, the second Ranke in presenting, having their pans guarded, blows their matches, opens their pans, and steps forward with their left legs into the place of the first rank, lies on, gives fire, and fall away while the rest of the body of musketeers moves up to their place, and so two ranks at a time, making ready, you may give fire as often as you list.

You must observe likewise, that the musketeers in all these motions, do turn to the right hand, & so to have a singular care, to carry the mouths of their muskets aloft, as well when they are shouldered, as in priming, as also when they keep their pans guarded and come up to give fire. Moreover, if an Enemy should appear on either your right, or left flank, and that you resolve to maintain your ground, and would gall him from either flank: it is performed by giving first this word of command *To the right or left hand,*

THE ARTE MILITAIRE

which you please, and then making an interval of 6 foot distance between the two middlemost leaders of the half files, e &, for the half rank on the left hand, marked a b c d and e do fall away between the files to the Revere before the pikes and the half rank on the right hand k i g h & f, on the right flank likewise, you may give fire from either, or both flanks, as you list.

Again if an Enemy should shew himself in your Revere, the like is done by giving this term of direction, *To the right hand about,* and having given fire upon them, fall away to the place, where the front stood, even in the same manner as you did before.

The manner of giving fire marching and advancing towards an Enemy is performed, as this figure following represents.

[An illustration was provided in this section of the original manuscript.]
In advancing towards an Enemy, two Ranks must always make ready together, & advance ten paces forwards: before the bodies, at which distance, a Sergeant (or when the body is great some other Officer) must stand, to whom the Musketeers are to come up before present, and give fire. First, the first rank, and whilst the first Ranke gives fire, the second Ranke keeps their muskets close to their pans guarded: and as soon as the first are fallen away, the second presently presents give fire, and fall after them. Now, as soon as the two first ranks do moue from their places in the front, the two ranks next it must unshoulder their muskets, and make ready: so as they may advance forward ten paces, as before, as soon as ever the first two ranks are fallen away, and are to do in all points as the former. So all the other ranks through the whole company, or division must do the same by two one after another.

[Clear evidence of lines of 6+ depth is shot accumulation evidence of more undeformed shot, as a result of rushing to load weapon during rolling advance?]
A way how to give fire retreating from an enemy, which is performed after this sort as this figure following shows.

[An illustration was provided in this section of the original manuscript.]
As the troop marches, the hindermost rank of all, keeping still with the troupe *making ready:* and being ready the soldiers in that rank turn altogether to the right hand, and give fire, marching presently away a good round pace to the front & there place themselves in a Ranke together just before the front. As soon as the first Ranke turns to give fire, the Ranke next makes ready and doth as the former and so all the rest.

Last of all the troupe, or whole wing of Musketeers makes ready altogether standing and the first Ranke without advancing, gives fire in the place it stands in & speedily as may be yet orderly falls away the Ranks doing the same successively, one after another.

Page 48

A manner how to give fire, either from the right or left hand flank, as these 6 files of 60 Musketeers demonstrates.

[An illustration was provided in this section of the original manuscript.]
To the right hand, present, give fire, Captain, to the left hand, present, give fire.

The Demonstration.
The company or division marching, the outermost file next the enemy are commanded to make ready, keeping still along with the Body, till such time, as they be ready, & they turn all to the right, or left hand, according to the fight of their Enemy, either upon their right or left flank, and give fire all together: when they have discharged they stir not, but keep their ground, and charge their pieces again in the same place

they stand. Now as soon as the aforesaid file doth turn to give fire, the outmost next it makes ready, always keeping along with, the troupe, till the bringers up be past a little beyond the Leader of that file that gave fire last, and then the whole file must turn and give fire and doe in all points, as the first did, and so all the rest one after another. A Sergeant or (if the troupe be great) some better qualified Officer must stand at the head of the first file, and as soon as the second file hath given fire, and hath charged, he is to lead forwards the first file up to the second file, and so to the rest one after another till he hath gathered again the whole wing, and then he is to join them again in equal front with the pikes.

[To understand the full import of such drill, one cannot look at accumulation in isolation, but must understand the relation between different accumulations over a considerable distance in a landscape. By identifying particular processes for personal item deformation at one site, with possible orientation and accumulation of artefact deformation say at 50 yard distance from the other assemblage, a fuller, more relatable understanding of archaeological drill characterisation might be undertaken.]

Pages 6-8[1]

NEXT Follows the Postures of a Cuirassier, and a Harquebusier, with the words of Command, and the demonstration answering to the number of every figure, as they are set down by Captain Cruso in his 29 chapter, and represented by figure.

IT is to be supposed, that no *Cuirassier* or *Harquebusier*, will presume to mount on horseback, or repair to his Cornet, before his pistol, Harquebus, or Carabine be spanned, primed, and laden: and his Cases furnished with Cartouches, and all other Equipage belonging to himself, his horse, and arms made fixe and in a readiness.

[Many discovered spare pieces of armour (e.g. sections of tasset, gauntlet, powder-horn lids, wheel-lock spanners, spurs, sections of stirrup/tack) can be attributed to mounting a horse. Further experimental use-wear analysis of contemporary horse equipment needs to be undertaken to understand what is liable to be lost and indeed what morphology said artefact adopts.]

The first figure then shows a horseman how he is to mount on horseback, and takes both reins hanging in a loose position over the Horse neck, & upon the pummel of the Saddle, and first lays hold on the ends of the reins above the button in his right hand, and with the thumb, and the two first fingers of that hand, draws them to an even length. Then putting the little finger of his left hand, betwixt both reins under the button, with the other three fingers of the same hand on the further rein, and his thumb on the near side of the button to grasp both reins, that so (before he endeavour to mount) he may have his horse head in balance and at command: then grasping the pummel of the saddle with his left hand, and standing with his full body to the horse side, and just betwixt the bolster, and cantle of the saddle, always on the near side of the horse, with the help of his right hand, he shall putt his left foot into the left stirrup, & with his right hand taking fast hold on the highest part of the Cantle behind, he shall (with the help of both hands) gently (yet strongly, and in a right posture without inclining his body to either hand) raise himself until he may stand *Perpendicular* upon his left foot, and then putting over his right leg cast and place himself in the saddle.

  2. With the right-hand he is to turn down the Caps of the pistol cases.
  3. He is to draw the pistol out of the Case with the right hand, and always the left pistol first and to mount the muzzle of it, as in posture 15.
  4. He is to sink the pistol into his bridle-hand, and to remove his right-hand towards the muzzle, and

---

1 Author's note: When the original work was published in 1642, it was published as a three-part work – hence the page numbering reverts back to 6-8 according to changes in the arm of service (infantry to cavalry).

THE ARTE MILITAIRE

    there to rest the butt end upon his thigh.
5. He is to sink the pistol into his bridle-hand, and taking the key, or spanner into his right-hand, puts it into the Axletree, and winds about the wheel till it stick, and so to return the Spanner to its place, being usually fastened to the side of the case.
6. Holding the pistol in the bridle-hand (as before) he is to take his priming box into his right-hand, and pressing the spring with his fore finger, puts powder into the pan.

[Artefactual evidence powder-horn tops. As it is virtually impossible to load at the canter, any time we find powder caps in situ, it is highly likely we have an original loading position verified. Only comparative analysis of largely undeformed artefacts within the surrounding metres will actively verify this. This is also applicable to infantry.]

7. He is to press in the pan-pin with his right thumb, & so shuts the pan.

[The difficulty which loading from horseback permits should present a higher level of gun furniture represented, compared to infantry positions.]

8. With the bridle-hand he is to cast about his pistol, and to hold it on his left side, with the muzzle upwards.
9. With the right hand take forth your cartouche out of your pistol case: for now flasks are grown out of use amongst vs.

[This should be representable through musket ball morphology being represented through plug of sprue, acting as die for cartouche and powder measure to be turned around attached to the main ball.]

10. Put your cartouche into the bore of your pistol.
11. He is to draw his rammer out with his right-hand turned, and to hold it with the head downward.
12. Holding the rammer head in his right hand (as before) he is to take the bullet out of his mouth, or out of his bullet bag at the pistol case, with the thumb and fore finger, & put it into the muzzle of the pistol, and the Rammer immediately after it, & then rams it home.

[An illustration was provided in this section of the original manuscript.]

13. He is to draw forth his Rammer with the right hand turned, and to return it to its place.
14. With the bridle-hand he is to bring the pistol towards his right side, and placing the butt end upon his thigh, pulls down the Cock.
15. He is to take the Pistol into his right hand, mounting the muzzle upwards.
16. Having the Pistol in his right-hand (as in posture 15) with his forefinger upon the trigger, he is to incline the muzzle (with a fixed eye) towards his mark, not suddenly but by degrees (quicker or slower according to the pace he rides) and that not directly forward towards the horse head, but towards the right, turning his right hand so as the lock of the pistol may be upwards, and having gotten his mark he is to draw the trigger, and so give fire.

[From the author's own observation from re-enactment firearms, the ability to pull a trigger guard out of its normal morphology, coupled with the added impact of potentially loading a pistol wearing gauntlets, is likely to be represented through cavalry firing positions?]

17. He is to return his pistol into the Case, and then draws out his other pistol (as occasion may serve)

and doeth as before, and thus much for the postures of the fire lock pistol.

Now concerning the *Snaphance* pistol, or *Snaphance Carbine* (more usual in England then in these Countries) those postures, wherein they differ from the fire-lock pistol are these following, which begin with the 18 Figure.

18. Holding the pistol in the bridle-hand as before hath bin shewed in Figure 14, with the right-hand he is to bend the Cock.
19. With the right hand he is to pull down the back lock, and to secure the cock from going off.
20. With the right hand he is to draw down the hammer upon the pan.
21. With the right thumb he is to thrust back the back-lock, and so to give the Cock liberty. The 22. the 23. & the 24. figures shew the marching postures of a Harquebusier or a Carabine.

Pages 20, 47-8

THE EIGHTH CHAPTER. OF MINES.

AS a *Gallery* is an ancient invention, so likewise Mines, which we make at this day have been heretofore in use amongst the *Ancients* also: And this is the last thing wherewith the besieged are troubled.

A Mine then according to the definition of *Vegetius,* is a Cave by which one makes secret goings under the Earth, to come by night unawares to a Fortress, or by which one digs into the foundation, and bowels of a wall, or of a Bulwark, underpropping the earth with posts of wood, and laying under it dry wood, for when they would make a hole in the wall, they set fire on this wood, which being burnt with the props, the wall fell down, and the Besiegers being in a readiness attending the fall of the wall, ran presently up by that breach, to assault the Fortress; which is understood also of our modern Mines which we make in by blowing up the powder that is laid in them, whence it appears clearly, that this is also an ancient invention, being a little changed, and amended at this day.

This mining (or digging under the earth) is called in Latin *Cuniculus,* of which name ancient Writers, as *Julius Caesar, Livius,* and *Curtius* make often mention of in the description of this *Stratagem,* it signifies a Mole from whence the name is taken, because the Mines made under *Ramparts* and *Bulwarks,* resembles the holes and passages which Moles makes under the earth. There are others which derive this name from the Latin word *Cuneus,* because the Mines are made in the fashion of a *Wedge,* which is thick at the beginning, and diminishes little by little, even as the Mines which make a rupture in those places where they are made, may be compared to a wedge, which cleaves a piece of timber in sunder. Mines were of old called *Cuniculary.* He that is desirous to know more thereof, let him read *Vegetius* and *Vitruve,* who have written of Military inventions among the ancients.

We will here describe in a few words, how our *modern Mines* are made at this day.

The last means for the forcing of an Enemy besieged, to make him yield, is this making of a Cave or Mine under the earth, which is begun and finished (as is said) after you have brought your *Gallery* over to the *Berm,* or foot of a *Rampart* or Bulwark.

But before it is begun, you must have all things necessary, and in a readiness, for the effecting of this work, first of all ye must have Spades, Shovels, Pickaxes, and all kind of Masons tools, with all things requisite to pierce and break the Wall, wherewith the Rampart is made.

Afterward, one prepares props to support, and bear up the Mine from falling or sinking, being two, or two inches and a half thick, the length of them being not alike, because the entrance into the Mine is made higher then towards the end of it. One is furnished also with fire planks, for to line the Mine within, as above, that it may not sink and fall down, for it must be set with planks on all sides, as well as the foundation, especially if the earth be moulding and wet.

But before you begin to make your Mine, it will be necessary that you know the condition of the place, that is, whether the Bulwark be hollow and vaulted, or whether the foundation be laid with Branches,

THE ARTE MILITAIRE

Logs, or borne up with Piles: and whither water may not spoil your Mine, if you should mine too low. In case that the Rampart or the Bulwark into which you intend to mine, were laid with logs, or supported upon great Piles, which happens ordinarily in moorland and rotten places, upon which you must build your Bulwarks, and Ramparts; or when one can get no other Earth but sand: you must try and get out all these Piles with Cables or ropes by winding them out with an instrument ordained for this purpose. Now you must pierce and pull out these logs by such ways and means as is known unto Miners, for the making of a way and a chamber to lay your Gunpowder in. When you are assured that you can dig no deeper, but that shall come to water, then you must raise your Mine a little higher, to the end the powder may lie dire in it.

The Miners then beginning to break into the wall, do carry their Mine so close, and secret as possible may be, that the Besieged may not hear any noise, or gather any notice, where the mine is made, and how it runs: for if they do, without all question, they will make a *Counter-mine* to discover and spoil your Mine begun, so that you shall be driven to begin a new one in another place, as hath happened many times.

The height, and the breadth of the *Mine* must be made in such a manner, as you may only lay in the Barrels of powder, for it ought to be no higher, nor no broader, because your intention is, but only to chamber your powder in it, and therefore it must needs be so high as a man, and no higher, but that a man may only work in that upon his knees, and that he stoops lower, when he goes to lay the Powder into its chamber.

The height then must be but 4, or 4 foot and a half high at the most, and the breadth but 3 and a half or four foot, according to which measures, the props and the planks are framed, wherewith you are to underprop the Mine.

[A stratagraphical layer of 4.5ft×4ft×length of wall, 612ft thick, is laid at a 110° angle, according to Dutch/Germanic models used. Look for alternating species of wood at macrofossil level to gauge differentiation between construction and opposition siege action for gauging level of modelable material.]

When you begin to mine into a Rampart or Bulwark, you take out the earth, and carry it away in a vessel, or a pall of leather, which is light, in handing it one to another, till it be brought out of the hole, or entrance out of the Mine, and laid in the Gallery, to the end the Enemy may not see it, and guess where about your Mine is.

The *Master-miner*, which hath the conducting of the Mine, ought to be a man of great experience, how he ought to carry it, lest he be mistaken, and so make it in a place, where he ought not to make it. Therefore he must have knowledge of a *Compass*, and how the *needle* stands, that he may carry his Mine aright. He ought also to have skill in *Geometry*, to the end he may know of what height he must carry his Mine, according to the proportion of the Rampart.

The nearer he comes unto the place where he is to make his Chamber, the narrower ought the way of the mine to be, in such sort, that it must be no broader or higher at the entrance into the *Chamber*, but that a Barrel of powder may scarcely pass through the way for the straighter and the narrower the passage is into the Chamber, the easier the Mine is stopped.

The place where the Chamber is, ought to be so made, that the powder doth not break neither the one, nor the other side but that it may blow the earth upward. Nevertheless sometimes the Miners are commanded, to make their Mine so, as it may blow the earth into the Fortress, or else without which may be done, if they make that side, which is to be blown up, not so thick as the other: for the nature of powder is such, that it makes the greatest operation always towards the weakest place, and though it blows it up ordinarily: yet commonly it searches most often the place, where it may break out soonest in to the air, which appears both in your Canon and Muskets.

The bigness of the *Chamber* is divers, for it must be made according to the greatness and proportion of the wall or Rampart: nevertheless one must observe, that it be made as narrow as possible may be, and yet must have room enough to lay the Barrels of powder into it: the ordinary height is some six or seven foot, and the breadth four or five foot.

When the Chamber is ready, then you lay in your Barrels, the number whereof cannot be so precisely described. For one Rampart is greater than another, in so much, that a greater quantity of powder is requisite more for one place than another. The common opinion is, that a Barrel of powder will blow up a rod, or twelve foot of Earth. The Barrels are laid in such order, that in the twinkling of an Eye, they take fire all at one time, which causes a greater operation than if one Barrel should be blown up one after another. After that your powder is chambered, the with all expedition you must stop the entrance into the chamber, with thick and strong planks, and stop it hard, and ram it in with good Earth, and leave a little hole or train, to lay some powder in it, which train is carried to the very end of the mine, and stops up the passage of it with firkins of Earth, that the air may neither come in or out. For the stronger the Mine is stopped, it will take the greater effect. All things then being in a readiness, it is left so till one is commanded to give fire to it.

In the 163 figure is represented unto you a mine marked, *A B C D E*, is the way upon the Bulwark, *E* is the entrance into the chamber, *F G H* and *I*, is the chamber itself, wherein the powder is laid.

Here a question might be moved, whether mines ought to be carried with right lines, or crooked? The answer is, that mines, which are carried in a right line are sooner made, but because they take not so good effect, the other are to be preferred before them, which are made with oblique lines. For the windings and the turnings of them, adds strength unto them, that the powder hath not so much force to break the stopping. Now suppose that it should break the stopping *D, E,* the rest therefore is not broken, because the force of the powder is kept in by the Earth marked *D*, and driven back to blow upwards, or finding no vent to turn back again, where it was laid. But in a right line when the powder breaks the stopping, the effect thereof is hindered and diminished, for it is certain, that the stopping, which is made newly is not so firm as the old settled Earth, which hath lain a long time in it.

Pages 49-50

OF COUNTER-MINES THE NINTH CHAPTER.

Where there is an *Offensive* War, there is also a *Defensive,* as appears by mines: for the Besieged having discovered them, which one hath prepared for them, and that there is no hope left, but waiting for the Springing of an Enemies mine in their Rampart, and to give them an assault, then they are to stand upon their defence, and begin to make mines also, which they either doe to offend an Enemy, or to defend themselves by them. Therefore we must understand here, three kinds of mines to use, the works which are made to find out an Enemies mine, 2: The Countermines, which are made to spoil an Enemies mine, & 3 the cutting off of a Bulwark or a *Rampart* within, of the two former, we will treat in this Chapter.

For the first kind of Countermines, we understand those works, and mines, which are made to discover, and find out an Enemies *Mine,* and to kill the miners in it.

After one hath found it out, as also for the casting down of the same work, and the taking away of the powder chambered, the Enemy will find himself deceived, when he thinks to spring his Mine, attending the operation thereof in vain, because the powder is stolen out of it.

For to find out an Enemies mine, there are two manner of ways, the one which was used by the *Ancients,* and the other practised at this day.

Vitruvius in the said Chapter of his tenth book, describes the manner of the *Ancients,* and says that the City of *Apolonia,* being besieged, and the Besiegers having made some Mines under the earth to assault the Citizens, on a sudden within the walls; the Citizens being advertised thereof, were extremely affrighted thereat, and began to faint and lose their courage: because they knew no remedy to prevent it, and could by no means find out the place where the Mines were made. But *Trypho Alexandrin,* which lived in that age, the *Architector* of this City, caused to be made along under the walls a great many ditches, and withal some Mines under the walls continuing them beyond the Enemies, as far as one could

THE ARTE MILITAIRE

throw a stone. He caused to be hanged in these ditches vessels of Copper, under those places, where the Enemy wrought, which made a noise, by reason of the moving of the earth, whereupon he found out the Enemies Mines, and filled Cauldrons of brass full of boiling water, and melted pitch, to pore it down through those holes upon the heads of his Enemies mines. He cast down also men's dung, which was mixed with hot sand and gravel, which he did by night into the Enemies Mines, into which he had made diverse holes, and by this means slew a great many of them.

Herodotus in his *Melpomina* makes mention of a *Tinker,* which dwelt in the City of *Barca,* besieged by the *Persians,* who discovered the Enemies Mines by the means of a Buckler of Brass, which he hung in diverse places against the wall, and so found out at last the place under which the Enemy mined.

But at this day to find out an Enemies Mine, they use to make counter-ditches, as hath been said, and before a Mine is begun it is necessary to be informed, after the manner of the Ancients of the place, which may be undermined by an Enemy. But Mines are searched out after divers other ways.

Some are of the opinion, that round about the walls, and Bulwarks of a Town or a Fortress, (when the fortification is first begun) one should make hidden caves, and passages under the earth, by which one might discover, and find out an Enemies mine. But this me thinks is not good, because the walls and Bulwarks are made thereby slender & weak, and these caves & being made with posts, and planks, vaults in tract of time are subject to rot, and the Mines afterward falling down, all that labour is lost. Also it is dangerous to make vaults in Ramparts, and Bulwarks, seeing it is to be feared, that such a work is not durable, for it must bear up so great and ponderous a weight, besides it will cost excessive expenses. And though these Counter-mines should be thus made and ordained: yet it is not certain, but that an Enemy in mining may meet just with one of these Mines, and so take his way and advantage, either over or under it, and so let this Counter-mine alone.

A second opinion is this, & some finds it good, that one should hang trees, and other bushes in them, which are found often in the Ramparts of the *Cimbri,* which being stirred with the least motion, gives a sound, whereby one may find out the place where the mine is. But this is a thing uncertain, because the least gale of wind, will easily shake these bushes, and branches of trees. And if they do so this must be done in a still and a calm weather, when there is no wind stirring. And therefore I answer, one ought to search out an Enemies mine at all times, for it were an absurd thing, for one to stay from finding an Enemies mine out & till a calm time comes, who will advance (as much as possible may be) his work, without staying for still or faire weather. Therefore this way serves but for little use.

[Provide heritage meaning/modelable features to reinclude in fortress site interpretation as natural landscape.]

A third and a better way, and which is the ordinary way, is to set a drum in the place suspected, with some Dice, peas, or beans upon the head of it, which upon any stirring, will leap upon the drum, when it stands over the place where one works. Nevertheless you must not let it stand in one place only, but remove it now and then from one place to another, yea so often, till you are assured of the place, which is shaken by the work which is made under it. Some make use of a Basin of litany filled with water, and imagines, that the mine is there, where the water moves, but that is uncertain as that of the *Cimbri* is, spoken of before, but that of a drum is held to be the best and surest way. Notwithstanding one may make good use of Basins, when they are set upon a *Rampart,* as a drum with peas or other things. For by such a means one may know the place, which is undermined. The use of Basins without all question, took its Original from the Invention of a Kettle, whereof we have spoken even now.

A fourth opinion besides these which is in use also; is a great long iron Borer, to bore into the Earth, wherewith those which searched the Earth, bores a hole with it into the *Rampart,* & laying his ear to the hole to listen well if he can hear any noise, which is practised in suspected places. Many other Inventions are invented by necessity the mother of practise.

APPENDIX II

To resist then the mines of an Enemies, one makes use of this practise following. After you have curiously searched out the Enemies mines, and that you are assured of the place under which they are hid then you may find them out without all question, & nothing remains then, but to make a *Counter-mine* against them, which is made in the same manner as we have described in the former chapter, treating of mines, to wit, by underpropping the Earth with posts and laying planks between them, that the Earth may not tumble down. Now because one is not assured to meet just with the Enemies mine which may be made either too high, or too low, therefore you must make many, till by one of them you have found it out, & are come to the *Chamber* to take away the powder.

When an Enemies mine is carried so secret, and hidden, that one cannot find it out, then the besieged must of necessity resolve to quit that part of the *Rampart* or Bulwark under which they suspect there is a mine, and so cut it off inwardly. But for their advantage they make ready also their *Countermine* made in that place, & chambers their powder attending the effect of the Enemies mine, and when he springs his mine, then they retire themselves into their new work cut off, and the Enemy being lodged in that piece of the Bulwark or Rampart, which they have quitted, then they blow up their *Countermine,* and slay all those, which they find in it.

The like also is done in outworks, and Counterscarps, when one is driven to quit them, and that one cannot keep them any longer.

Appendix III

Extracts from *Military discipline: or, the yong artillery man Wherein is discoursed and showne the postures both of musket and pike: the exactest way, &c. Together with the motions which are to be used, in the excercising of a foot-company. With divers and severall formes and figures of battell; with their reducements; very necessary for all such as are studious in the art military* by William Bariffe (1635).

Pages 1-11

CHAP. I.

Concerning Postures and handling Armes.
THE first rudiments for the Discipline of Infantry ought to be an Instruction, for the well mannaging of their Armes; whereby they may be brought, to use them with ease and delight: whereas to the contrary (without exercise) both sorts of Armes, wil become a troublesom burden, unto the unskilfull Bearers. No man is borne a Souldier, neither can any attain, to be kilfull in the Art Military without practice. But by practice is gained knowledge, knowledge begets courage and confidence; few or none being fearefull to execute what by frequent practice they have throughly learned.

    Wherefore it is necessary for every one that intends any proficiency in this part of the Art military, to be instructed in the Postures and well handling of their Armes; a thing much to be desired in our Trained Bands, though small hope of amendment. Seeing the Souldiers are scarce called forth to exercise either Posture, or Motion once in foure or five yeares. Whose the fault is I know not, only I pray God that it may be amēded, lest shame and infamy be the least of euils which our carelesse security may bring upon us: Yet pardon this digression, for my zeale to my Countries good had almost transported mee beyond the bounds of my intent, but of this no more. I will now come to the postures of the Musket and Pike: which, I conceive, are fittest to begin from the taking up of their Armes, and arming the Souldiers concluding them with the laying down of their Armes, or disarming them. But before I begin the Postures: Mee thinks I heare some already inquiring what is a Posture. Wherefore that I may satisfie them, and not be troublesome to others. In briefe thus.

    Posture in a Souldier is the garbe or figure, that he useth in the handling of his Armes, consisting of severall Motions for atchieving of each Posture. The Motion being the working part, the Posture the alteration or act, either in circumstance or matter. As to rest your Musket being one Posture, to shoulder your Musket another, so likewise for the rest, howbeit some perchance will object, (as formerly hath bin

APPENDIX III

to one of *Athens*, making a long Oration in the praise of *Hercules* his valour) who ever doubted of it. So to me who ever questioned these for Postures: yet I have known them not only questioned, but written against, peremptorily concluding that there are but three Postures to be used for the Musket, whose errours I shal easily confute. But more of this after the Postures of the Musket. Wherefore for the more orderly proceeding conceive their Armes to lie before them on the ground, and then the first command will be, to stand to their Armes.

The Postures of the Musket.
    Take up your Bandeliers.
    Put on your Bandeliers.
    Take up your Match.
    Place your Match.
    Take up your Musket and Rest.
    Rest your Musket.
    Now if you please you may perform your saluting Posture.
    Poyse your Musket.
    Shoulder your Musket.
    Take your Rest into your right hand, and you are armed ready to March.
    Now to begin to make ready, which may be done either standing or marching.
    Take your Match between the fingers of your right hand.
    Put your Rest string about your left Wrist, and carry your Rest in your left hand.
    Return your Match between the fingers of your left hand.
    Unshoulder your Musket and Poyse.
    Ioyn your Rest to the outside of your Musket.

Open	your Pan.
Cleer	
Prime	
Shut	

    Cast off your loose Corns.
    Blow off your loose Corns, and bring about your Musket to the left side.
    Treile your Rest, & ballance your Musket in your left hand.
- Charge with
  - Powder.
  - Bullet.

Draw forth	your scowring stick.
Shorten	

    Put your scowring stick into your Musket.
    Ram home your Charge.

Withdraw	your scowring stick.
Shorten	
Return	

    Bring forward your Musket and Rest.
    Poyse your Musket and recover your Rest.

THE ARTE MILITAIRE

Ioyn your Rest to the outside of your Musket.
Draw forth your Match.
Blow your Coale.

[Blow off your coals When lowscale excavation areas correlate with accumulations of musket shot, one needs to soil sample to understand whether higher density charcoal inclusion in excavated material present represents material fall/powder residue from large-scale volleys? One needs to look to ephemeral soil sciences for further analysis of unconsidered areas of drill leaving little material remains.]

| Cock | your Match. |
| Fit | |

Guard your Pan.

[Experimental archaeology, providing differing artefact formation processes (e.g. incorrectly torsioned serpentine, broken naturally, impact trauma) needs to be undertaken to characterise and understand the morphology of drill, where particular artefactual trends can be perceived.]

Blow the Ash from your Coale.
Open your Pan.
Present upon your Rest.
Give fire brest high.
Dismount your Musket, joyning your Rest to the outside of your Musket.
Uncock and return your Match.

| Cleer | your Pan |
| Shut | |

| Poise | your Musket. |
| Shoulder | |

Take your Match between the fingers of the right hand.
Take your Rest into your right hand, cleering your string from your wrist.
Return your Rest into the left hand, the string loose.
Return your Match into your left hand.
Unshoulder your Musket and Poyse.
Rest your Musket.
Set the But-end of your Musket on the ground.
- Lay down your
  ◊ Musket and Rest.
  ◊ Match.

| Take off | your Bandeliers. |
| Lay down | |

March from your Armes.

There is likewise the Sentinell Posture, which is, The Muskettier having his Musket charged with Bullet, his Match cockt, his Pan guarded, stands with his Musket rested to perform such duty as shall be commanded or given him in charge. Some have likewise taught to make ready on, or from the Sentinell

APPENDIX III

Posture: But note that as none comes to stand Sentinell but comes ready charged: So if any occasion happen that he must give fire in the time of his standing Sentinel, it causeth a generall Alarme. So that he will have no fit time to make ready upon his Rest: Wherefore, I conceive it superfluous; but will ever conforme to better judgement.

We have also the Funerall Posture, which from the Rest is to be performed at 3. Motions, which cannot so well be exprest in writing, as it will expresse it selfe in Action. Wherefore seeing that it is rather an Ornament to Obsequies, than truly necessary for Armies I will not spend more time about it, but come to the Postures of the Pike. Yet before I passe upon them, give me leave to answer some, which out of a Criticall humour will always be carping at others, condemning these Postures, saying, There are more by halfe, then are either good or usefull; and that there are no more Postures to be used, but Make ready, Present, Give fire. The which we will not deny that in Service there are any other usefull: notwithstanding I would have them to know, that Make ready is no Posture, but a word of Command, including all Postures, from the first Arming of the Souldier to the present: or if the Muskettier be charged, shouldered or both, then the word (Make ready) commands the prosecution of the rest of your Postures which are between the Posture you then immediatly are at, when the word is given, and the other Posture, Present for which reason when we teach Muskettiers at first it is most necessary to instruct them punctually, from Posture to Posture: Which being once attained, he manageth his Armes more surely more comely, with more celerity, and with better execution: and at the first may as easily be taught the best way. But if he have got an habit of doing ill there wil be as much or more pains spent in reclayming his errours, as at first to teach him the best, safest, and readiest way.

CHAP. II.

Of the Postures of the Pike.

THAT which followeth next of course is the Posture of the Pike. Wherefore that we may observe order in our proceeding; we will likewise conceive their Pikes to lie in like manner before them on the ground. And then, as before, the first Command will be, To stand to their Armes.

Handle	your Pikes.
Order	

To your	open	Order.
close		

Charge with the But-end of your Pike at the inside of your right Foot, your Pike in the left hand, drawing your Sword over the left Arme.
- Charge to the
  - Right,
  - Left,
  - Reere.

Order your Pikes, and put up your Swords.

Note that these Charges at the Foot are to receive a desperate Enemy on Horse, upon a stand in some strait, or other place of advantage the Muskettiers to give fire over the Pikemens heads, or else-where, at the discretion of the Commander.

Port	your Pikes.
Comport	
Cheeke	

THE ARTE MILITAIRE

Treile	
Order	

Charge to the	Front	Order as you were.
Right		
Left		
Reere		

	Shoulder your Pikes	
Advance	your Pikes.	
Port		
Comport		
Cheeke		

Treile your Pikes		Advance as you were.
Charge to the	Front	
Right		
Left		
Reere		

Shoulder	your Pikes.	
Port		
Comport		
Cheeke		
Treile		

Shoulder your Pikes		Shoulder as you were.
Charge to the	Front	
Right		
Left		
Reere		

From Comport, Cheeke, or Treile, the Pikeman may at the discretion of the Commander charge either to the Front, Reere, or both Flanks, as shall be necessary or thought expedient. Wherefore we shall not need to do it but once over, for the Charges will be all alike, whether you Comport from Order, from Advance, or Shoulder. And so likewise for Cheek and Treile, &c.

From Comport Charge to the	Front	Comport as you were.
Right		
Left		
Reere		

Cheek your Pikes.		
From the Cheek Charge to the	Front	Cheek as you were.

APPENDIX III

Right		
Left		
Reere		

Treile your Pikes.		
From the Treile Charge to the	Front	Treile as you were.
Right		
Left		
Reere		

Order	your Pikes.
Lay down	

I shall undergo the censure of some, for that they will finde more Postures of the Pike here then formerly they knew of, and so by their conclusion more then there is any need of; for now-a-dayes there are such that will limit discipline, to the verge of their owne knowledge, and whatsoever else they shall see either acted or written by others that is without the lists of their kenning, they will peremptorily conclude for superfluous and improper, howsoever I shall always referre my selfe to the judgment of the more judicious.

The charges of the Pike are twofold either for defense or offence. Charges underhand or overhand but divers and different they are from their severall wayes and Postures from which they are or may be done, although they are not all always usefull, yet at sometimes they may be usefull, and therefore very requisite to be known to all such as either are, or at lest would be accounted for good Souldiers.

[Likewise for musket furniture, where evidence of push of pike is prevalent (e.g. pike blades), measure the angle of supposed break of socket to stave a much higher angle of break representing a charge overhand, a much shallower break underhand.]

As I have set down the Postures themselves both of Musket and Pike, so it were not much amisse, if that the Motions of Posture were likewise here exprest. But because they will take up too much time, & fill too much paper, and the Subject it selfe not pleasing unto many; I will spare my labour, and my booke the lines, rather suffering the censure of curtail'd brevity, then tedious prolixity.

Pages 13-5

CHAP. IV.

Of Rankes and Files, their places and dignities.
NOW that our Souldiers are somewhat skilfull in managing of their armes, and no lesse capable of the severall beats of the Drum, it is high time for them to know the difference between a Ranke, and a File. Wherefore* know that a Ranke is a row of men, sometimes more, sometimes fewer, standing, moving, or marching even a breast, or (as some write) pouldron to pouldron, or shoulder to shoulder. A File* is a sequence of men, standing one behinde another, backe to belly in a straight line from Front to Reere, consisting sometimes of 6, 8 or 10 Men, on some occasions the *Spaniards* make them 12 deepe. But when any one would shew much variety of exercise, then 8 will be the more pliant and dividual number, yet for service in the field, where men are not altogether so expert (as I could wish our Country-men were) 10 men is the fittest number, not onely for the cause aforesaid, but also because that 10 is the square root of a 100 and is a better number to draw Companies into grosser bodies.

THE ARTE MILITAIRE

[Therefore applying Monck's rules of spacing, Continental depths of regiments at file accumulations of 8, 10 and 12 are: close order 16ft/20ft/24ft; order 24ft/30ft/36ft; open order 48ft/60ft/72ft x close order 24ft/20ft/16ft; order 36ft/30ft/24ft; open order 72ft/60ft/ 72ft; doubled front, close order 48ft/40ft/32ft; order 72ft/60ft/48ft; open order 144ft/120ft/96ft x close order 8ft/10ft/12ft; order 12ft/15ft/18ft; open order 24ft/30ft/36ft.]

And now I thinke it would not be much amisse if I should here insert the severall places of digninity and precedency in Ranke, as also in File.

Wherefore because that Files are first to be drawn forth, and that by adding or joyning of Files together, Rankes are made; we will begin first with Files. Wherefore conceive their honour according to the figures or numbers hereunder placed, first in File, then of Rank, lastly of both cojoyned.

[An illustration was provided in this section of the original manuscript.]

It will not be of it selfe sufficient that I have both marked and figured the places and dignities to each particular man in his File and Ranke, but it will be looked for of some, that I should backe my opinions either with sound and good reasons of mine owne, or at the least with the opinions of some others: as for such as have employed themselves upon this subject, they have been as divers in their judgements, as their number, each man having a fancie to his owne way. And if it were much materiall, I might have here demonstrated unto you the severall opinions of *Leo, Robertellus, Count Mansfield,* Sir *Thomas Kellie,* and many others: whose workes being extant, I will spare the labour. But above all the rest that ever I read, Captaine *Iohn Bingham* hath in my judgement best delivered himselfe in this particular: which although he have exprest by way of Tetarchies and Mirrarchies, yet the same may be understood as well by Rankes and Files. His words are these:* Every Tetarch is over foure Files, in all which the Commander that hath the right, hath the first place; he that hath the point of the left, the second place; he that standeth on the right hand next to him, the third place. The last place is his that standeth next to the Commander of the right point on the left hand: He demonstrates it by way of figure thus.

[An illustration was provided in this section of the original manuscript.]

Pages 19, 31-4

Of Facing square, and how to performe it, the usefulnesse of facings, and the severall parts thereof.
WHEN we instruct our Souldiers how to face square (if the Body be but 8 deepe) command, the two first ranks stand fast, the two last Ranks face about, the rest of the Body face to the right and left. If the Body be deeper we command more Ranks to the Front, and so likewise to the Reere. It is very necessary for young Souldiers to move 10 or 12 paces upon every motion of facings, whether they are entire, or divisionall. Now I will pricke two severall figures of facing, which will be sufficient to demonstrate all the rest.

Face square and march.

[An illustration was provided in this section of the original manuscript.]

The words of Command, commonly used to produce this figure, are these as followeth.
  The two first ranks stand.
  The two last ranks face about.
  The rest of the body face to the right and left, (then) march all.
  To reduce them to their first order.
  Face all about to the right, march and close your divisions.

APPENDIX III

Face all to your Leader (who then stands at his front proper.)
Facing square another way, & marching upon it.

[An illustration was provided in this section of the original manuscript.]

The words of command customarily used to produce this figure are these as followeth,
Muskettiers face to the right and left.
Halfe files of Pikes face about to the right (then) march all.
To reduce them to their former order,
Face all about to the right, march and close your divisions.
Face all to your Leader.

Facings are so usefull and necessary, that you may as well dispense with any one of the grounds of Discipline, as with them; for they are usefull almost upon all occasions, and not onely sooner executed than any other of the motions, but may be needfull when Wheelings and Countermarches cannot be used, as in a strait. There are no more then foure facings intire, besides Angular; as for Divisionall, there be divers, and indeed very necessary many of them be, as occasion may offer it selfe for their severall uses; howsoever peremptorily to say, there be so many and no more, I conceive, hath beene concluded by none; but it still rests at the discretion of the Commander, to exercise more or fewer of them, as he best liketh, and the necessity requireth either for action or exercise.

Intire facings are so called when the aspect of the whole Company are directed one way.

Divisionall facings are so called, when the aspect of the Souldiers is at one & the same time directed divers and severall waies: as to the front and reere, the right and left, or to all foure at once, &c.

Angular Facings are so called, when the aspect of the Company is directed to the right corner man, which is the right Angle, or to the left corner man, which is the left Angle; or to the foure corner men, which are the foure Angles.

Angular facings were of great use among the ancients, for their figures called the Diamond, the wedge, the Sheeres, the Saw, and such like, when they made use of such formes of battell. But for the use of them in our moderne Discipline, I conceive there is little or none, onely thus, we honour the memory of the Ancients in their use. And some say they are very fit for exercise; for that by their use the souldier is made more apt and perfect in the other. Therefore let this suffice to be spoken concerning facings, and now be pleased to turne your aspect, and take a view how our young souldiers will behave themselves, in the performance of the doublings.

[Area comprised of square with 8/10/12 multiples at the close order.]

CHAP. LXXIII.

Of the Horne-battell; how to make it: and to reduce it by firing.

THE *Horn-battell* may be for the same occasion and use, as the *firing* by two *ranks* ten *paces advancing* before the *front:* and is by some held more serviceable, because that the *muskettiers* do their *execution* more roundly, without any intermission of time: and keepe themselues without stragling from their *bodies*. Besides, the *wings* of *Muskettiers* being so *advanced,* are more apt for *over-fronting,* and more easily to be wheeled; whereby to *charge* the *enemy* in *flanke;* each of these *wings,* or *divisions,* are to be *led up* by a *Serjeant* (or some other *superiour Officer*) unto the *place* appointed by the *Chiefe*. But because that it may be performed in time of *exercise,* by the intelligible *Souldier,* observe the *Command* which produceth this following *figure*.

135

THE ARTE MILITAIRE

Pages 196-204

Pikes, stand; Muskettiers, march; untill the Bringers up, ranke with the front of Pikes.

The Horne-battell.
[An illustration was provided in this section of the original manuscript.]
The *figure* being perfect, the *firstranke* of *Muskettiers, present* and *give fire wheeling off,* either all to the *right;* or to the *right* and *left* (according as they shall have direction) and placing themselues, orderly, in the *Reere* of their owne *files.* The *next ranke* (after the same manner) *firing* and *wheeling off,* and placing themselues *behinde* those, which were their *leaders.* Thus is every *rank,* successively to do the like: untill they have all *given fire.* If the *Commander* would still preserve, and continue the same *figure;* then let the *Muskettiers* still *move forwards,* into the *ground* (or place) of them that *fired* before them: and the *forme* will be still the same. And if by the *Chiefetain* it be found necessary, that after once or twice *firing over,* the *shot* should *flanke* their *pikes;* then the *Muskettiers,* must not *advance* into their *leaders ground;* but, to the contrary, every *ranke* is to *present* and *fire* on the same *ground* they *stand:* and that so soone as they are *cleere* of their *leaders.* Or if need be, the *pikes* may *advance* and *march* up, to make their *front entire:* which being done, the *file-leaders* of *Muskettiers* being in *front,* they are *reduced.*

CHAP. LXXIIII.

Of the Demie-hearse Battell: The use of the figure; how to make it, and to reduce it by firing.
THE next *firing* in *Front* which I present unto you, is the *Demie Hearse:* which is a *figure* most *firme,* most *sollid,* and most *stable,* yea, and doth as much *execution,* as any of the former: and that with halfe the danger. For the *pikes* in the former *figure,* they either *ranke even* with the *front* of Muskets: or else, the *division* of *Muskettiers* being *open* they become liable to the danger of the enemies *shot:* themselues not being able to do any thing, either *offensive* or *defensive.* But, to the contrary, in this *figure,* they are securely covered by their owne *Muskettiers:* untill they approach nearer to the *enemy.* Whereby they may be able to do some *service;* either by sending their *showres* of *arrows* amongst them, for bringing their *array* out of *order,* or else, by *closing neerer,* come to the *shocke,* and so try the *fortune* of the *day.* But not to hold you longer in *circumstance,* take the *words* of *command:* which produce the *figure,* as followeth.

Pikes, stand, Muskettiers, advance before your Front of Pikes: and close your Divisions.

The Demi-hearse.
[An illustration was provided in this section of the original manuscript.]
For the *firings* on this *figure,* they may be divers; yet I shall content my selfe onely to shew two of them: The *first* is, that the *Muskettiers* may at the discretion of the *Commander, give fire* in *front:* and so *wheele off* by *division* (or all to the *right,* as shall best please him that *commands* in *Chiefe*) placing themselues in the *Reere* of their owne *divisions* and *files* of *shot,* which is just *before* the *front* of *pikes.*

The *next ranks* then *moving forwards* into their *leaders ground,* are to *present, fire, wheele off,* and place themselues after the same manner: the *rest* of the *ranks* of *Muskettiers,* doing the like, untill they have all *given fire:* which *firing,* doth nothing alter the *forme* or *figure* of *battell.* Having *fired* once or twice over this way, the *second firing* shall serue for *reducement:* which is indeed the *firing* intended to be exprest by this figure. And that I may by *words,* the more clearly explaine the *worke,* take these *directions* following.

The *first ranke* having *given fire,* are to *wheele* equally *off* by *division:* each part falling *file-wise downe,* close by their *flanks* of *Muskettiers:* untill the *leaders* of the *ranks* of *Muskets* come downe as low as the *first ranke* of *pikes;* which being performed, they are to *face outwards,* and to move so farre forth in a *strait line,* untill they have *ranked even* with the *first ranke* of *pikes.* But herewithall are they to observe, that they must leave an *Intervall* betweene the *innermost-musket* of each *flanke*; and the *outermost-file-leader* of the *pikes*. So soone as the *first ranke* hath *given fire* and *wheeled away*, the *second ranke* is to *give fire, wheeling off*, as before, and *passing downe* betweene the *Intervals* on the *flanks*: placing themselues after their leaders. The same is every *ranke* successively to do, untill all the *Muskettiers* are *drawne* from before the *front*, and placed on the *flanke* of their *pikes*. But when there are not above *two ranks of Muskettiers* to *give fire*, then the *pikes* may *port*; and when the *Muskettiers* have *fired*, and are *wheeled away*, they may *charge*. And lastly, the *pikes* being *re-advanced*, the *body stands reduced*, as at first.

CHAP. LXXV.

Of giving Fire, advancing, by way of Introduction: with the beneficiall use of the Bow and Pike.
I Shall next offer to your perusall, a *figure* of *Introduction*: which is a *passing through* or *betweene*: Being a *firing* by way of *advancing* against the *enemy*, and of *gaining ground*. I will not dispute how usefull it is; but sure I am, it is over-ballanced with danger. As for such whom I haue seene to *practise* it, they have rather used it for *varietie*, in a well experienced *Company*, then for any knowne *excellency* it hath in it selfe. But if these *lines* happen to be over-lookt by any, that preserues a better opinion of this *firing* by *introduction*, then I do: I shall be willing to leave them to their owne liking, while I in the meane time proceed to shew the manner of the *execution*, which is usually one of these two wayes. The first, when the *Motion is begun by the second ranke from the front*. The other, when *it is begun by the Bringers up*. Neverthelesse you must note that your *files* of *Muskettiers* must be *opened* to their *open order*; before the *firing* begin: that so, the *Muskettiers* may *passe* betweene the *Intervals* of each *file*, to *give fire* in the *front*. And therefore take the words of Command and Direction; which will produce this Figure following.

Muskettiers, make ready to give fire by introduction to the right.

Files of Muskettiers, open by Division to your open order.
[An illustration was provided in this section of the original manuscript.]
This *firing* by introduction may be thus performed. The Pikes being flankt with their Muskettiers, the first ranke of each flanke, *present* and *give fire*: having *fired*, they *stand* and *make ready* againe in the same place. The second ranke passing forwards before the first, doe there *fire* and *stand*: the third rank then passing forwards after the second, and standing even in ranke with them that first *fired*; that so soone as the second ranke hath *fired*, they may quickly step before them, and *fire* in like manner. In this *firing*, still the ranke which is next to *fire*, stands even in ranke with them which last *fired*; untill those which *stand presented*, have likewise *given fire*: after which they then passe before them; the Ranke which was their next followers, passing forwards and ranking with those which last *fired*: every man following his Leader successively, untill the *Bringers up* give *fire, & stand*, and then the Figure will become a *Horne battell*. All the while that this *firing* by Introduction, is continued, the Pikes may be shouldered (if there be no feare of *horse*) or otherwise at discretion. If you continue this *firing* twice over; the Muskettiers will have their *right places*: which being done, *march* up your Pikes, to ranke even with your Muskettiers in *front*, and they are *reduced*. For the other way of *firing by introduction*, the first ranke (or *file-leaders*) are to *give fire* as before, and to stand, the last ranke (or *bringers up*) in the interim of their *firing; marching up*, and *ranking even* with the second ranke: the rest following their *Bringers up*; as they do when *Bringers up* double their *front*. The first ranke having *fired*, the *Bringers up* step immediately before them; *present, and give fire*; the rest stil, successively, doing the like, untill every rank have *given fire* once over. Observe withal that the *file-leaders* are to *give fire* twice over: being the first & the last & then to *stand*, the Pikes marching *up*, even with their front of Muskettiers. And thus they are *reducd*, as at first. The Pikemen, all the time of this *firing*, doe no service: Notwithstanding, if one *halfe* of them had *bowes* fastened unto their Pikes (being able and well practised men) they might, whilest the Muskettiers are in *firing*, be dealing

THE ARTE MILITAIRE

of their doles about: and although their *arrowes* did not happen to wound mortally, yet the whisteling noyse, the terrour of the sight, and the severall hurts (which could not chuse but be many) would be a great abatement to the stoutest courages. And great pitty it is to see, the lusty *Pike-man* poorely to droppe downe by the *Musket-shot;* himselfe not being able to hurt his enemy at that distance, nor defend himselfe.

Page 212

CHAP. LXXVII.

Of the Convex Halfe Moone; The use of the Figure: and of severall wayes of firing upon it.
THE *Convex halfe-moone,* or *semicircular Battell,* is a *forme* both good and usefull; which the *time,* the *number,* and *place* (with other *circumstances*) may make either *beneficiall* or *prejudiciall.* Wise *Captains* and *Commanders* ever foreseeing with providence, what *formes* or *figures* may be most *profitable* and *available,* for the present *service.*

Pages 216-8

CHAP. LXXVIII.

Of Extraduction: the severall uses, firings, and Reducements.
THE next *Firing* which I shall take upon me to demonstrate, shall be by way of *Extraduction:* which is also a *firing in Front.* It may be to singular good use, in a *strait* or *passage* where your *Wings* and *Reere* may be *secured:* your enemy being supposed to be too powerfull for you, either in *Horse* or *Foot,* or both. Having gotten into some *strait,* there fill the *mouth* of the *passage* with your *Pikes*: and if the length of your *Company* be not sufficient to do it, then *double* your *ranks* (as in this following figure) and let your *pikes* either *order, advance, port,* or *charge:* according to the occasion; your *Muskettiers* being in the *Reere,* may *march up* into the *Front,* and *fire.* But before I shew the *firing,* observe these following *directions,* which produce the *Figure.*

Pikes stand, Muskettiers face to the Reere, and March untill you are cleere of your body of Pikes;

Then face inward, and close your division: that being done face to your Leader, and double your Rankes.

This being performed, the *Pikes* are all in *front*, the Muskettiers in *Reere*.

A firing by Extraduction.
[An illustration was provided in this section of the original manuscript.]
Having ordered your *batell* in this manner, let the first rank of Muskettiers (which are those that follow next after the Pikes) *face* to the *right,* and *march* forth (*file-wise*) *to close* by the *right flanke* of Pikes, untill he that is the *leader* of them, be come into the *front* of Pikes, then he is to *leade* them quite *crosse* the *front* of Pikes; untill he have attained the further part of the *front* to the *left;* which being done, they are all to *stand, present,* and *give fire.* You must note withall, in this *firing,* that he which was the *right hand man* of the Ranke, and was the *leader* of the *section,* now becomes the *left hand man,* when he *gives fire;* and that having *fired,* they are to *wheele off* to the *left,* close to the left flanke of Pikes, and so to fall in the *reere* of the Muskettiers. In the *interim,* whilest that the ranke which first *fired,* is *wheeling* away, the second rank is *marching* into their *places* to give *fire.* And in this manner they may maintaine their *Battaile,* so long as they please: the Pikes either *porting* or *charging* all the whiles. The Muskettiers in the time of their *crossing the front,* are to *crouch,* or *stoope under* their Pikes; that so they may be no impediment

APPENDIX III

to the Pikes in their *charge*. There is another way of *firing by Extraduction*, which is, *that the right hand leader of Muskettiers, placeth himselfe before the right file leader of Pikes*: the *rest all falling beyond him*: neverthelesse because I conceive it not to be so good a way as that already shewne, I will not trouble you with it: but come immediately to the *deducement* of this, which is as followeth. Command your Pikes to *stand*, and your Muskets to *double* their *front* by *division*: but if you want room to doe it, then first *double* your files the *contrary hand* of that, which you *doubled* your rankes; and so hauing *doubled* by *division*, as aforesaid, they will be *reduced*, as at first.

[How many items found dropped in association with musketry, without clear morphology, actually relate to firing positions and not simply the individual hurrying to retire to the rear by countermarching/ rank retiring to the rear? Thus, it requires artefact relation and sphere of influence to be shifted by 20ft to the left/right of said position.]

CHAP. LXXX.

Of dismarching, or firing in the Reere: the severall wayes, and how they ought to be performed.
HAVING so long maintained *Battaile* in the front, I will now *face* them *about*, and see how they will behave themselves upon their *firings* in the *reere*. Which kinde of *firings*, may be very *beneficiall* and *serviceable*, many wayes. For by keeping an orderly *march*, and *firing* in the *reere*, the eager *enemy*, (by a too hasty pursuit) may be *disordered*. Or if it so happen (as many times it doth) that you have a *disadvantagious* place to imbattell on; by this *firing* you may *march away*: still preserving your *order* and *array*, untill you have brought your adversary into some ambushment, or such like inconvenience. For the manner of comming of the *firing*, it must either be by *facing about, wheeling about*, or *countermarching*: the Pikes are to be shouldered. The figure followeth.

Pages 222, 227-9

CHAP. LXXXI.

Of firings in flanke, in generall; and more particularly, of the gathering firing.
THE Muskettiers being all on the *right flanke*, (as in the last Chapter is directed) it would be needlesse to make a Figure, whereby to demonstrate the *standing* of the *body* seeing that none can be so ignorant, but must needs know that all the Muskettiers being upon the *right*, the Pikes must be upon the *left*. Nevertheless, I shall endeavour to shew what is meant by *firing in flankes*. Which (for the generall) are of these two kindes. The *first* is, when the *enemy skirmsh with us in flanke as we march*: the other, when as by some *sudden attempt* or *ambushment*, the *whole body* is *engaged*, and so forced to *stand*, and to *face to the right*, or *left*; or both. By which *facings*, the *flanks* become *fronts accidentall*, and their *firings* wil be after the same manner of the *firings in front*. Wherefore seeing I have already spoken sufficiently of them, I will now shew *firings in flanke*, marching: the particulars whereof, are as followeth. The first is for the outmost file to give *fire*, and stand untill the next file have fired, which by some is called the *gathering firing*. Secondly, *firings* in *flanke*, and *leading* them up, between the Muskettiers and Pikes *firing*; in *flanke*, being *led off* by the *bringers up*: *firings* in *flanke*, *sleeving up* on the contrary *flanke* of Pikes: *firing in flanke*, and drawing them up betweene the *innermost files* of Pikes. All these *firings* in flanke, are to be performed upon a *march*, the Pikes are to be *shouldered*. Our first *firing* in *flanke*, followeth.

The Command is, **Muskettiers, give fire to the right: and gather up your files.**
[An illustration was provided in this section of the original manuscript.]
This kinde of *firing* on the flanke, I have seene and knowne used, by many good and able souldiers.

THE ARTE MILITAIRE

Neverthelesse, in my opinion, the men stand in a great deale of danger, when having *given fire,* they can doe no good; but stand like so many markes for their *enemies* shot. Notwithstanding, it may be that such whom I have frequently seene to use it in their practise, may be able to render good reasons for the *service*; though as yet I cannot conceive it. I will therefore surcease any further prosecution my opinions, and shew the manner of execution: which is to be performed as followeth. The Command being, to *give fire to the right,* presently the *outermost file* to the *right, faceth* outward, and *presents*: the rest of the *body,* still *marching* forwards. Then the *presented file, gives fire,* and *stands facing* againe to their first front. By that time, the *body* will be marched cleere of the *standing file,* then the next *outermost file, presents* and *fires*; in like manner: the *body marching* as before. Having fired, they in like manner *face* to their first front, and *stand*; a *Serjeant* leading up the file, that first fired on the *out side* of the file that last fired. Then they both *stand* together, untill the third file hath *given fire* after the same manner. And then the *Serjeant* leads up the two files, even with the third, which last fired. And after this manner, the files of Muskettiers *face* to the flanke: and give fire, successively: and stand, untill the *Serjeant* leads up the rest of the files which fired, *even* with the *front* of the file, which last fired. Thus having all fired over, they are to *march up* againe, *even* with the *front* of Pikes, and this *reduceth* them, as at first.

[In order to understand a battlefield as a series of systems, a level of accountability regarding contextual understanding between different archaeological collections, sections of landscape and findspots needs to be understood. Obviously with battlefields often taking up enormous sections of landscape, this is often not possible and thus a huge resource base is lost. However, for the sake of argument, let us presume we have a find spot of musket furniture and personal items and a completely different set of musket balls of varying morphology. By measuring the distance between them (e.g. 50 yards) and by undertaking artefactual analysis to ascertain the associated finds definitely relate to musketry, we provide a base for regimental analysis. By further measuring and GPS plotting, we can assume a clear corridor under which further metal detector survey can be undertaken clearly associated with this unit. However, by equally measuring the angle between the base assemblage and ordinance and thus providing individual orientation and therefore relevance, the ability to further understand drill book analysis can be ascertained (e.g. firing to flank). This further widens the field of investigation by taking our bare pair of parallel lines and adding limited investigation fields of deviation to further investigate.]

Pages 231-3

CHAP. LXXXIII.

A firing in Flanke, led off by the Bringers up.
THE next *firing in flanke,* which I propound to your perusall, will be nothing differing for *manner* of *execution,* from the *firings* in *Flanke*; formerly shewed. The onely *difference* arising betweene them, is, that the *other files* of *Muskettiers,* after that they had *given fire,* were *led off* by their *proper file-leaders*; and this, to the contrary, must be *led off* by their *Bringers-up.* And this, indeed, if the *body* be upon a *slow march,* is the *readiest* and *quickest* way: and doth more speedily *secure* the *Muskettiers,* after that they have *given fire.* The *words* of *Command* and direction, which produce the *firing,* are as followeth.

Muskettiers, give fire to the Right: wheeling off, after your Bringers up; and placing your selues betweene your Divisions.
[An illustration was provided in this section of the original manuscript.]
For the *manner* of *execution,* or way to performe this *firing,* it is as followeth. The *body* must be conceived to be *marching*; upon all these *firings in flanke*: and that with their *pikes shouldered.* This being presupposed, the *Command* being given, the *outmost-file presents* to the *right,* and *gives fire*: then *faceth* to the *right,*

APPENDIX III

after their *bringers up*; who *leadeth* them *off, crosse the reere of Muskettiers, marching them up* betweene the *divisions,* the *bringers up* supplying the *file-leaders* place; and *marching even* in *ranke* in the *front*, with the *file-leaders*; the *file-leader* of the same *file,* becomming the *bringer up* in the *Reere.* The *files* of *Muskettiers,* or *Pikes* (according as the *command* shall be given) are as they *march,* to *open*; thereby giving way to the *Muskettiers,* after they have *fired*; to *come up* betweene the *divisions,* and so soone as the *first file* that *fired,* is *cleare* from the *right flanke*; the *second file, presents* and *fires*: in like manner *wheeling off,* as before, and *marching up* betweene the *Pikes* and *Muskettiers*; every *file,* successively, *giving fire,* and *wheeling off* as aforesaid. This firing may be performed, *once, twice,* or *oftener over*: according to the discretion, of the *Commander.* Nevertheless, if it be *twice* performed, the men are *reduced* as at first; every man hauing his *right* place. If you *fire* them but *once,* or *thrice* (or any odde number of times) over, then you must *countermarch* your *files* of *Muskettiers* to *reduce* them. There is another way for the *bringers up* to *wheele off*: and each of them to *leade off* his *file*; untill he comes to the *Reere* of the *division* which is betweene the *Muskets* and the *Pikes*; and there he is to *stand,* and *ranke* with the *bringers up,* the rest that follow, *passing* on forwards, by way of *Introduction,* and every man *ranking* before him, that was his *leader* in the *wheeling off*; untill the *proper file-leader* be come into his place againe. And after this way, they may *give fire*; each *firing* being his owne *reducement.*

[While at present it is unclear when presented with metal detector surveys representing musket shot, how to break down individual groupings within the larger assemblage into actions and spheres of influence, it might be argued that certainly a difference in firing by rank and by extraduction would be highlighted by the individual frequency and spacing between shots, volley fire providing a regimented/uniform morphology, firing by extraduction often rushed forward being more ragged and thus providing an uneven shot frequency. Bodies of investigation would be chosen through micromanaging blocks of 6+ shot within the overall make-up of the larger assemblage.]

Pages 254-6

CHAP. XCI.

Captaine *Wallers* Triple firing to the Front.
THIS *Triple firing to the Front,* hath had the approbation of good and well experienced *Souldiers*: who have all acknowledged it to be both *sollid* and *serviceable. Bringing many hands to fight, in very good order: the pikes being securely covered by their Muskettiers, in front.* Neither need *they* be idle in time of *battell,* if they have any *Bowpike-men* amongst them: for that they may send their *whistling Archery* over their *Muskettiers heads,* without *offence* to their *friends*: though not without *dammage* to their *enemies.* If any carpe at the *depth* of the *Muskettiers* (either in this *figure,* or in any other in this *booke*) I shall request them to suspend their *censures,* and wisely to conceive by a little, what a great deale meaneth. My intent not being, to make my *booke monstrous,* by having *little leaves,* and *large figures.* Onely I desire with this *small number,* to shew the *nature* of severall *formes* and *figures* of *battell*; the *manner* of their *firings* and *wheelings off*; their *orderly placings,* and severall *wayes* of *reducement*: not having the least conceit, to induce any to beleeve, *that men are able long to continue battell, at foure deepe*; although at (sometimes, and for *stratagems*) they may be *reduced* into a *lesser number.* But lest by *digression,* I too farre trespasse upon your patience; I will returne to shew the *manner* of the *firing.* Onely first obserue, the *words* of *command* and direction; which produce the following *figure.*

Muskettiers of the Reere, double your front of Pikes, by Division.
[An illustration was provided in this section of the original manuscript.]
The *Command* being given, the *first ranke* of *Muskettiers* (both of *front* and *flanks*) *present* to the *front* and

give fire: *wheeling off* to the *right* and *left* by *division*. The *Muskettiers* of the *front-division* being *wheeled off* (as aforesaid) *close* by the *flanks* of their *owne Muskettiers*, passe directly downe betweene the *Intervals*: and place themselues *even* in *ranke* behinde the *Muskettiers* of the *reere division*, which are upon the flanks. This you may perceive by the *pricks*, that come downe *betweene the Intervals*: the *Muskettiers*, also, that *fired* at the same time on the *flanks*; *wheele* also *off*; (the *right flanke*, to the *right*; the *left flanke*, to the *left*) *marching* directly downe, *even* with the *reere ranke* of *pikes*; and there place themselues againe *even* in *ranke* with the *last ranke* of *pikes*. This done, the rest of the *ranks* (successively) *give fire*, and do the like: every *Ranke* taking his place, after the *ranke* which *fired* last before them; the other *ranks* moving one *ranke* forwarder. The *Muskettiers* having *given fire* once over; and *falling off* according to this direction, they will be *reduced* to the *flanks* againe, as they were at the first. The *firing* may be continued, or the *pikes* may *charge*, at discretion of the *Commander*.

[Much has been made of this and indeed similar firing systems introduced by the likes of SMG Henry Tillier, although their true application remains unclear. From the description of drill presented here, it is likely this refers to a number of battlefield situations, including continuous advancing volleys by extraduction by multiples of two ranks, the engagement of multiple units overlapping the firing frontage of said regiment, thus suggesting defensive mathematics and angles can be equally be referred to the field of battle for interlocking fields of fire; or indeed a more effective and supporting means of integrating Swedish style deployment at a regimental scale. The ability to ultimately see this incorporated into the archaeological records is by finding musketball assemblages associated with each other, divided at an illogical length, so that assemblage is larger than the other, representing the free movement of supporting pike within this formation. Oblique facings might be realised through taking an angle out of 90° of the associated assemblage, showing deferral from the 180° line.]

Bibliography

Primary Sources

Bariffe, William, *Military discipline, or The young artillery-man* (London: Andrew Kembe, 1657).
Bryon, John (1638), *The Rudiments of Militarie Discipline* (Amsterdam: Da Capo Press, 1969).
Cruso, John, *Militarie Instructions For The Cavall'rie* (Cambridge: University of Cambridge, 1632).
Hexham, Henry, *The first part of the principles of the art military practiced in the wars of the United Netherlands, under the command of His Highness the Prince of Orange our Captain General, for as much as concerns the duties of a soldier, and the officers of a company of foot, as also of a troupe of horse, and the exercising of them through their several motions : represented by figure, the word of command and demonstration / composed by Captain Henry Hexham, Quartermaster to the Honourable Colonel Goring* (Delft: 1642).
de Gheyn, Jacob (1607), and Blackmore, David J. (ed.), *The Renaissance Drill Book* (London: Greenhill Books, 2006).
Matthew, Christopher (ed.) *The Tactics of Aelian or On the Military Arrangements of the Greeks: A New Translation of the Manual that Influenced Warfare for Fifteen Centuries* (Barnsley: Pen & Sword Military, 2012).
Monck, George, *Observations upon military & political affairs written by the Most Honourable George, Duke of Albemarle, &c.* (London: A.C. for Henry Mortlocke and James Collins, 1671).
Ward, Robert, *Anima'dversions of warre; or, A militarie magazine of the truest rules, and ablest instructions, for the managing of warre* (London: John Dawson, 1639).

Secondary Sources

Archaeological Survey Church Precinct, Alton <http://historicenvironment.hants.gov.uk/ahbresults.aspx>, (accessed 16/03/2014).
Adair, John, *Cheriton 1644: The Campaign and the Battle* (Kineton: Roundwood Press, 1973).
Adair, John, *Roundhead General: The Campaigns of Sir William Waller* (Stroud: Sutton Publishing, 1997).
Allen, David, and Anderson, Sue, 'Basing House Excavations 1978-1991', *Hampshire Field Club Monograph* 10 (Bristol: Hampshire Field Club and Archaeology Society, 1999).
Allmand, Christopher, 'The Fifteenth-Century English Version of Vegetius' De Re Militari' in Strickland, Matthew (ed.), *Armies, Chivalry and Warfare in Medieval Britain and France: Proceedings of the 1995 Harlaxton Symposium*, Harlaxton Medieval Studies VII (Stamford: Paul Watkins, 1998), pp.30-45.
Atkin, Malcolm, and Howes, Russell, 'The use of archaeology and documentary sources in identifying the Civil War defences of Gloucester', *Post-Medieval Archaeology*, issue 27 (The Society for Post-Medieval Archaeology, 1993), pp.15-41.
Atkin, Malcolm, *Cromwell's Crowning Mercy: The Battle of Worcester 1651* (Stroud: Sutton Publishing, 1998).
Barbero, Allessandro, *The Battle: A New History of the Battle of Waterloo* (London: Atlantic Books, 2006).
Barratt, John, *Sieges of the English Civil Wars* (Barnsley: Pen and Sword Military, 2009).
Barratt, John, *Cavalier Capital: Oxford in the English Civil War 1642-6*, Century of the Soldier 1618-1721 No.3 (Solihull: Helion and Company Limited, 2015).

Battlefields Trust/English Heritage/National Monuments Record, *Cheriton* <http://www.battlefieldstrust.com/media/578.jpg,> <http://www.battlefieldstrust.com/media/579.jpg,> <http://www.battlefieldstrust.com/media/580.jpg> (accessed 14:55 p.m., 24/07/2014).

Blackmore, David, 'Counting the New Model Army', *Civil War Times*, No. 58, (Leigh-on-Sea: Partizan Press, 2003), p.3, <http://djblackmore.wordpress.com/articles-2/counting-the-new-model-army-2/> (accessed 23:45 p.m., 28/08/14).

Blake, Andrew, Re-creating the Drill of the 95th Rifles, http://www,95th-rifles.co.uk/research/drill/ (accessed 11:24 a.m., 02/04/2014).

Bonsall, James, 'The Study of Small Finds at the 1644 Battle of Cheriton,, *Journal of Conflict Archaeology*, vol.3, no.4, (Glasgow: Centre for Battlefield Archaeology, 2007), pp.29-52.

Bornstein, Diane, 'Military Manuals in Fifteenth-Century England', *Medieval Studies*, vol.37 (Toronto: Pontifical Institute of Mediaeval Studies, 1975), pp.469-78.

Bradbury, Jim, *The Medieval Archer* (New York: St Martin's Press, 1985).

Brzezinski, Richard, *Lützen 1632: Climax of the Thirty Years War*, Campaign 68 (Oxford: Osprey Publishing, 2001).

Burgess, Christopher, 'In to the bog: "silently and in good order. German fashion … "', in Rotherham, Ian D., and Handley, Christine (eds.), *War and Peat: Landscape Archaeology and Ecology*, vol. 10, (Sheffield: Wildtrack Publishing, 2013) pp.13-58.

Callen, Matthew, To what extent did Royalist infantry tactics develop during the First Civil War (1642-1646)? (unpublished BA dissertation, Bath Spa University 2013).

Cansfield, Peter, *The Battle of Alton: An account of the famous battle in 1643 during England's Civil War* (Alton: Peter Cansfield's Associate's Literati, 1999).

Carlton, Charles, *Going To The Wars: The Experience of the British Civil Wars 1638-51* (London: Routledge, 1992).

Carman, John, and Carman, Patricia, *Bloody Meadows: Investigating Landscapes of Battle* (Stroud: Sutton Publishing, 2006).

Clements, Richard R., and Hughes, Roger L., 'Mathematical modelling of a mediaeval battle; the Battle of Agincourt, 1415', *Mathematics and Computers in Simulation* (Elsevier: 64, 2004), pp.259-69.

Combes, Pamela, 'The Ordnance Recommended to Arm the Defensive Earthworks Proposed for the Sussex Coast in 1587', *Wealden Iron*, No.15 (Tonbridge: The Bulletin of the Wealden Iron Research Group, 1995), pp.48.

Courtney, Paul, 'The Archaeology of the early-modern siege', in Freeman, Peter W.M., and Pollard, Tony, *Fields of Conflict: Progress and Prospect in Battlefield Archaeology*, BAR International Series 958 (Oxford: Archaeopress, 2001), pp.105-15.

Ede-Borrett, Stephen, *Lostwithiel 1644: The Campaign and the Battles* (Farnham: The Pike and Shot Society, 2004).

Emberton, Wilfred, *Love Loyalty: The Close and Perilous Siege of Basing House 16435* (Basingstoke: W.J. Emberton, 1972).

Ferguson, Natasha, 'CSI Cornwall: Investigating a battlefield', *The Searcher* October 2009 (Guildford: Searcher Publications Limited, 2009), pp.279.

Ferguson, Natasha, *An assessment of the positive contribution and negative impact of hobbyist metal detecting to sites of conflict in the UK*, PhD Thesis (Glasgow: University of Glasgow, 2013).

Ferguson, Natasha, *Tywardreath Artefact & Distribution Analysis Report*, <http://archive.today/FDyB5> (accessed 13:01 p.m., 21/05/2014).

Fiorato, Veronica, Boylston, Anthea, and Knusel, Christopher (eds), *Blood Red Roses: The Archaeology of a Mass Grave from the Battle of Towton AD 1461* (Oxford: Oxbow Books, 2007).

Flintham, David, 'A Hollar's-eye View of 17th Century Fortifications', *Fort*, vol. 39 (Croydon: Fortress Study Group, 2011).

Foard, Glenn, 'The Civil War Siege of Grafton Regis', in Fitzroy, Charles, and Harry, Keith (eds), *Grafton Regis: The History of a Northamptonshire Village* (Cardiff: Merton Priory Press, 2000), pp.49-63.

Foard, Glenn, *Battlefield Archaeology of the English Civil War*, BAR British Series 570 (Oxford: Archaeopress, 2012).

BIBLIOGRAPHY

Foard, Glenn, 'English Battlefields 991-1685: A Review of Problems and Potentials', in Scott, Douglas, Babits, Lawrence, and Haecker, Charles (eds), *Fields of Conflict: Battlefield Archaeology from the Roman Empire to the Korean War* (Dulles: Potomac Books, 2009), pp.133-59.

Foard, Glenn, *Naseby: The Decisive Campaign* (Barnsley: Pen and Sword Military, 2004).

Foard, Glenn, 'The Archaeology of attack: battles and sieges of the English Civil War' in Freeman, Peter W.M., and Pollard, Tony, *Fields of Conflict: Progress and Prospect in Battlefield Archaeology*, BAR International Series 958 (Oxford: Archaeopress, 2001), pp.87-103.

Foard, Glenn, and Morris, Richard, *The Archaeology of English Battlefields: Conflict in the Pre-Industrial Landscape*, CBA Research Report 168 (York: Council for British Archaeology, 2012).

Freeman, Peter W.M., and Pollard, Tony, *Fields of Conflict: Progress and Prospect in Battlefield Archaeology*, BAR International Series 958 (Oxford: Archaeopress, 2001).

Griffith, Paddy, *Forward into battle: fighting tactics from Waterloo to the near future* (Novato California: Presidio, 1990).

Hackett, Martin, *Lost Battlefields of Britain* (Stroud: The History Press, 2005).

Hale, John Rigby, *The Art of War and Renaissance England* (Washington: The Folger Shakespeare Library, 1961).

Hale, John Rigby, *Renaissance War Studies* (London: The Hambledon Press, 1983).

Harding, David F., *Lead Shot of the English Civil Wars: A Radical Study* (Oxford: Oxbow Books, 2012).

Harrington, Peter, *English Civil War Archaeology* (London: B.T. Batsford, 2004).

Harrington, Peter, *English Civil War Fortifications 164251* (Oxford: Osprey Publishing, 2003).

Harrington, Peter, 'Siegefields: An Archaeological Assessment of "Small" Sieges of the English Civil Wars', in Pollard, Tony, and Banks, Iain (eds), *Journal of Conflict Archaeology*, vol. 1 (Glasgow: Centre for Battlefield Archaeology, 2005), pp.93-113.

Hill, Paul, and Wileman, Julie, *Landscapes of War: The Archaeology of Aggression and Defence* (Oxford: Tempus, 2002).

Homann, Arne, and Weise, Jochm, 'The Archaeological Investigation of Two Battles and an Engagement in North Germany from the 19th century: A summary of work carried out at Idstedt, Grossbeeren and Lauenburg', *Journal of Conflict Archaeology*, vol. 5 (Glasgow: Centre for Battlefield Archaeology, 2009), pp.27-56.

Humphries, Julian, *Enemies at the Gate: English Castles under siege from the 12th century to the Civil War* (Swindon: English Heritage, 2007).

Kleinschmidt, H., 'Using the Gun: Manual Drill and the Proliferation of Portable Firearms', *The Journal of Military History*, 63:3 (London: The Society of Military History, 1999), pp.60-130.

Lawrence, David R, *The Complete Soldier: Military Books and Military Culture in Early Stuart England 1603-45* (Danvers: BRILL, 2009).

Lawrence, David R, 'The Evolution of the English Drill Manual: Soldiers, Printers and Military Culture in Jacobean England', in Langman, Peter (ed.), *Negotiating the Jacobean Printed Book* (Farnham: Ashgate Publishing, 2011), pp.117-35.

Logue, Paul, and O'Neill, James, 'Excavations at Bishops Street Without: 17th Century Conflict Archaeology in Derry City', in Pollard, Tony, and Banks, Iain (eds), *Journal of Conflict Archaeology*, vol. 2 (Glasgow: Centre for Battlefield Archaeology, 2006), pp.49-76.

Lyne, Malcolm, 'Civil War earthworks East of Alton', *Proceedings of the Hampshire Field Club and Archaeological Society*, vol. 46 (March 1991), pp.181-7.

McNutt, Ryan K., *Finding Forgotten Fields: A Theoretical and Methodological Framework for Historic Landscape Reconstruction and Predictive Modelling of Battlefield Locations in Scotland 1296-1650*, unpublished PhD Thesis (Glasgow: University of Glasgow, 2014).

Marix-Evans, Martin, *Naseby 1645: The Triumph of the New Model Army*, Campaign 185 (Oxford: Osprey Publishing, 2007).

Matousek, Vaclav, 'Building a model of a field fortification of the Thirty Years' War near Olbramov (Czech Republic)', in Pollard, Tony, and Banks, Iain (eds), *Journal of Conflict Archaeology*, vol. 1 (Glasgow: Centre for

Battlefield Archaeology, 2005), pp.115-32.

Meller, H., Friederich, S., Schürger, Andre, Alt, Kurt W., and Nicklisch, Nicole, 'Lützen Ein Ort der Erinnerung',. *Archäologie in Deutschland*, vol. 4 (Stuttgart: Konrad Theiss Verlag, 2013), pp.813.

Morris, Richard, *The Storming of Alton and Arundel 1643* (Bristol: Stuart Press, 1993).

Naismith's Rule of Walking <http://www.bbc.co.uk/dna/place-london/plain/A29848558> (accessed 08:15 a.m., 25/08/2014).

Nolan, T.J., 'Geographic Informations Science as a Method of Integrating History and Archaeology For Battlefield Investigation', *Journal of Conflict Archaeology*, vol. 5 (Glasgow: Centre for Battlefield Archaeology, 2009), pp.81-104.

Osgood, Richard, and Brown, Martin, *Digging Up Plugstreet: The Archaeology of a Great War Battlefield* (Yeovil: J. H. Haynes and Co., 2009).

Pollard, Tony (ed.), 'Capturing the Moment: The Archaeology of Culloden Battlefield', *Culloden: The History and Archaeology of the Last Clan Battle* (Barnsley: Pen and Sword Military, 2009), pp.130-62.

Pollard, Tony, 'Mapping Mayhem: Scottish Battle Maps and their Role in Archaeological Research', *Scottish Geographical Journal*, 125:1 (Perth: Royal Scottish Geographical Society, 2009), pp.25-42.

Pollard, Tony, and Banks, Iain, *Culloden Battlefield: Report on the Archaeological Investigation Project 1981* (Glasgow: GUARD, 2006).

Pollard, Tony, and Oliver, Neil, *Two Men in a Trench: Battlefield Archaeology the key to unlocking the past* (London: Penguin, 2002).

Porter, Stephen, *Destruction in the English Civil Wars* (Stroud: Alan Sutton Publishing, 1994).

Raymond, James, *Henry VIII's Military Revolution: The Armies of Sixteenth-Century Britain and Europe* (London: Tauris Academic Studies, 2007).

Reid, Stuart, *All the King's Armies: A Military History of the English Civil War 1642-1651* (Chalford: Spellmount, 2nd ed., 2007).

Roberts, Keith, *First Newbury 1643: The turning point* (Oxford: Osprey Publishing, 2003).

Roberts, Keith, *Matchlock Musketeer 1588-1688* (Oxford: Osprey Publishing, 2002).

Roberts, Keith, *Pike and Shot Tactics 1590-1660* (Oxford: Osprey Publishing, 2010).

Roberts, Keith, and Tincey, John, *Edgehill 1642: First Battle of the English Civil War*, Campaign 82 (Oxford: Osprey Publishing, 2001).

Robertshaw, Andrew, and Kenyon, David, *Digging the Trenches: The Archaeology of the Western Front* (Barnsley: Pen and Sword Publishing, 2008).

Rubio-Campillo, Xavier, Cela, Jose Maria, and Cardona, Francesc Xavier Hernandez, 'Simulating archaeologists? Using agent based modelling to improve battlefield excavations', *Journal of Archaeological Science*, vol. 39 (Elsevier, 2012), pp.347-56.

Rubio-Campillo, Xavier, Cela, Jose Maria, and Cardona, Francesc Xavier Hernandez, 'The development of new infantry tactics during the early eighteenth century: a computer simulation approach to modern military history', *Journal of Simulation*, no. 7 (2013), pp.170-98.

Schürger, Andre, 'Die Schlacht von Lützen – Stumme Zeugen einer blutigen Schlacht', *Archäologie in Deutschland*, vol. 1 (Stuttgart: Konrad Theiss Verlag, 2009), pp.22-5.

Schürger, André, 'Schlachtfeldarchäologie Battlefield Archaeology', in Meller, Harald (ed.), *Tagungen der Landesmuseums für Vorgeschichte*, Halle Band 2, (Halle: Saale, 2009), pp.143-44, Abb. 8, 9.

Scott, Douglas D., Fox, Richard A., Connor, Melissa A., and Harnon, Richard, *Archaeological Perspectives of the Battle of the Little Bighorn* (Oklahoma: University of Oklahoma Press, 1989).

The Sealed Knot Society, 'Handy hints from the Infantrie Garden by Seed-drill No. 5 – Keeping Your Distance', *Orders of the Day*, December/January (Nottingham: 2002).

Shiels, Damian, 'Battle and Siege Maps of Elizabethan Ireland: Blueprints for Archaeologists', *Journal of Conflict Archaeology*, vol. 3 (Glasgow: Centre for Battlefield Archaeology, 2007), pp.217-32.

Singleton, Charles, *'Famous by My Sword': The Army of Montrose and the Military Revolution*, Century of the

BIBLIOGRAPHY

Soldier 1618-1721 (Solihull: Helion & Company, 2014).

Sivilich, D. M., 'What the Musket Ball Can Tell: Monmouth Battlefield State Park, New Jersey', in Scott, Douglas, Babits, Lawrence, and Haecker, Charles (eds), *Fields of Conflict: Battlefield Archaeology from the Roman Empire to the Korean War: Searching for War in the Ancient and Early Modern World*, vol. 1 (Westport: Praeger Security International, 2007), pp.84-101.

Smith, Victor, and Kelsey, Peter, 'The Lines of Communication: The Civil War Defences of London', in Porter, S., *London and the Civil War* (Basingstoke: Macmillan Press, 1996), pp.117-49.

Spring, Laurence, *The Battle of Cheriton 1644* (Bristol: Stuart Press, 1997).

Sturdy, David, 'The Civil War defences of London', *London Archaeologist* (London: 1973), pp.33-48.

Thordeman, Bengt, *Armour from the Battle of Wisby, 1361* (Milwaukee: Chivalry Bookshelf, 2001).

Tincey, John, *Marston Moor 1644: The beginning of the end* (Oxford: Osprey Publishing, 2003).

Walters, M.J., and Hunnisett, K., *The Civil War Battlefield at Montgomery, Powys: Archaeological Assessment* (Welshpool: CPAT Report No.142, The Clwyd-Powys Archaeological Trust, 1995).

Ward, Simon, *Excavations at Chester: The Civil War Siegeworks 1642-6* (Chester: Grosvenor Museum Archaeological Excavation and Survey Reports, Chester City Council, 1987).

Warner, Tim, *Newark: Civil War and Siegeworks* (Nottingham: Nottinghamshire County Council Leisure Services, 1992).

Whiting, J.R.S., *Gloucester Besieged: The Story of a Roundhead City 1640-1660* (Gloucester: The City Museum, 1984).

Wiggins, Kenneth, *Anatomy of A Siege: King John's Castle Limerick, 1642* (Martlesham: The Boydell Press, 2001).

Woosnam-Savage, Robert C., '"To Gather an Image Whole": Some Early Maps and Plans of the Battle of Culloden', in Pollard, Tony (ed.), *Culloden: The History and Archaeology of the Last Clan Battle* (Barnsley: Pen and Sword Military, 2009), pp.163-86.

Wright, Simon, *Militarie Disciplines For The Royalist Army of the Sealed Knot* (Southampton: The Sealed Knot, 2003).